"The lives we need to have written for us are of the people whom the world has not thought of, far less heard of, who are yet doing most of its work, and of whom we can best learn how it can be best done."

From Ruskin's preface to " The Story of Ida."

" Go forth my book,
  And be to other men
  What thou hast been to me—
  Communion, fellowship, and hope!

  Go forth, my book,
  And rest your heart
  Against some heart to me unknown,
  And cry: Hail brother! evermore to you,
  Glad fellowship, and kindly love,
  And pleasant journey home!"

      Altered from Marvin's lines in " The Open Court."

MY LIFE

As Farmer's Boy, Factory Lad, Teacher and Preacher

By
ADAM RUSHTON

MANCHESTER
S. Clarke, 41, Granby Row
1909

Dedicated

TO

ALL SINNERS, ALL SAINTS, ALL ANGELS
AND ALL GODS

[All rights reserved.

CONTENTS

                                                                                      Page

INTRODUCTION   9

    Cloud of Witnesses—Books—Pictures—Letters—Diaries—Memories—Farm—Factory—Commerce—Missions—Old Age.

CHAPTER I.—BIRTH—PARENTAGE—EARLY DAYS 13

    Cheshire Hills—Martha Cooper—George Rushton—Barnaby Fair—Hurdsfield—My Birth—Accidents—Dame School—Prayer Meeting Hall and Josephus—John Hooley—Prayer on the Cliff—Dodgemoor Well—Garden Work—Cradle—Sunday School—Pothooks and Ladles—Enchantment—Hymn Writing—"The Covenanter's Grave"—"The Pilgrim Fathers"—The Tree Sanctuary—A Great Loss—The Farm Left.

CHAPTER II.—IN FACTORY AND FIELD 28

    In the Mill at eight years of age—Escape—Work in the Clough—Thoreau—Robin Hood—Birds—Fishes—Animals—Buddhists *versus* Christians—Factory Dungeon again—Steward and Danter—"Daniel in Lion's Den"—Sensation—Critics—Barnaby Fair—Bloomfield's "Farmer's Boy"—Translation—Beulah—Tiger and Missionary.

CHAPTER III.—THE MYSTICS—SUNDAY SCHOOL 36

    Thomas à Kempis — Pythagoras — Essenes — Gnostics — Hindoos — Neo-Platonists—Paul—Archimedes—Mohammed and Gabriel—Abelard and Bernard—Socrates and Dæmon—Erasmus and Luther—Tauler—Spinosa—Descartes—Emerson—School Methods—Grammar Class—Walker's Dictionary — Phonography — Face Washing — Monitor's Stick — Professor Blackie's wit—Joanna Southcottian.

CHAPTER IV.—WAGES—BOOKS—RELIGION 48

    Income and Expenditure—David Clayton—Shakespeare—Encyclopædia—Priscilla and John Alden—School Library—Homer censured—Combe condemned—Pollock praised—Last Days of a Philosopher—Books in the Mill — Rollin — Paley—The Steward—Warehouse—Paine's "Age of Reason"—Revivals—Dr. Birchenall's Young Men's Class—My Membership—Experience Giving—Conversion Seeking—Rev. A. Strachan—His Fascination—Rationale of Conversion—Hervey's "Reflections"—Baxter's "Dying Thoughts"—The Fourteen Volumes of Wesley's Writings secured by severe privation.

CONTENTS.

	Page
CHAPTER V.—THE PEOPLE'S CHARTER	63

Conflict in Wales—Frost, Williams, and Jones—Eddisbury Hills—Chartist Drill Ground—Parsonage Green Demonstration—Feargus O'Connor—Rev. J. Rayner Stephens—John Richards of Rainow—Stoppage of all Mills in the Town—Joyous Freedom—Richard Cobden and John Bright in the Town—John West and Timothy Falvey, Silk Weavers and Rival Orators—Sir Robert Peel and Disraeli Stealing Clothes.

CHAPTER VI.—NIGHT SCHOOLS—BOOKS—TRAVELS	70

Mechanics' Institutions — "Penny Magazine"—Byron—Castle of Chillon — Nibelungen Lied — "Saturday Magazine" — Erasmus — Snowdon—First sight of the Sea and Welsh Mountains—Bed and Board at Carnarvon—10,000 Methodists in Camp Meeting—Beauties of Welsh Language—"Ward's Miscellany"—Literature—Science—Religion—"Cosmogony of Moses"—Job and the Stars—Professor Wallace—A Limited Universe—St. Basil—Origen—"Bible Chronology"—Egyptian Chronology—Alexander the Great—"A Scottish Sabbath"—Methods of Reading—"Thomson's Seasons"—"Paradise Lost"—Milton and Duke of York.

CHAPTER VII.—HEALTH—EMIGRATION—METHODIST MINISTERS	81

Long Working Days—Ill Health—Combe on "Digestion"—"Blithedale Romance"—Emigration—"Good-bye"—Loss of Paradise—School — Chapel — Mother — Hooley Hay Experience — Methodist Preachers—Rev. Charles Burton, the Musical—Pilter is Coming!—John Farrar—Painting Heaven and Hell—John Rattenbury, Persuasive and Threatening—Alexander Strachan and Literature—Criticism—Augustine and Monica.

CHAPTER VIII.—TEMPERANCE—THREE ANGELS—SCIENCE STUDENT	92

Teetotalism—Three Nights' Debate—Ecton Woods—Two Drunkards Converted and Reverted—Tea Party Speech—Battles on Beeston Hill—Shadows of Coming Events—Picture of Three Angels—Country Walks — Literature — Science — Novels — The End — Edward Davenport—Serious Accident.

CHAPTER IX.—PLAN OF MUTUAL STUDY—SEVEN TEXT-BOOKS	100

"Mason on Self-Knowledge"—A Solemn Vow—Dr. Watts on "The Improvement of the Mind"—Plumeo—Studentio—"The History of Greece" — Leonidas — Demosthenes — Socrates — Delphi — Parnassus—Troy—"The History of Rome"—Romulus and Remus—Elijah—Numa and Moses—Cæsar—Cleopatra—Antoninus—Aurelius—Pliny—Cato—Vestals—Priests—The Pantheon—"History of England" — Hume — Walpole — Boadicea — Caractacus — Arthur — Alfred—John — Magna Charta — Welsh Bards — Wallace — Stewarts—Charles I.—Cromwell—Milton.

CHAPTER X.—SIXTH SUBJECT: HISTORY OF CHRISTIANITY	111

Heresy—Arius—Athanasius—Homoiousian—James I. on the Ten Heresies of Wightman—Angles and Angels—Emperor at Canossa—Luther at Worms—Bible Popes—Wickliffe, and the Bulls—Calvin and Servetus—Bruno Burnt—Descartes—Emerson—Crusades—Pope Urban II.—Peter the Hermit—Richard Cœur de Lion and Blondin—Saladin—The Scotch Covenanters—Peden, the Prophet—Claver-

Contents.

house—John Brown's Death—Drowning of the Women—The Pilgrim Fathers—The "Mayflower"—Lord Bishop—Lord Brethren—Roger Williams—Quakers and Witches—Miles Standish—Priscilla—John Alden—Peter Waldo—Arnaud—Conde—Navarre—Coligny—Huguenots—Black Bartholomew's Day—Te Deum chanted at Rome—Westminster Assembly—Tread Mill Creeds—Philip Nye and Reason—John Selden and Greek Testament—Cromwell—Milton—George Fox—John Biddle—Baxter—"Dying Thoughts"—Wesley and Priestley.

CHAPTER XI.—SCIENCE ... 125

Joyce's "Scientific Dialogues"—Archimedes—Eureka!—Sir Isaac Newton—Gravitation—Light—Dalton—Atomic Theory—Herschel—Pleiades—Heaven—Franklin—Electric Kite—Priestley—Oxygen—Hours of Work—Edward's Death—Brother Samuel.

CHAPTER XII.—OWENISM—VESTIGES OF CREATION—RITUALISM ... 130

Robert Owen's Mission—"The New Moral World"—Great Public Debate—Dr. Brindley and Lloyd Jones—"Vestiges of Creation"—Condemnation of the Book—Newman and Rome—Tract 90—Keble.

CHAPTER XIII.—FAMILY EXPENSE—MOTHER'S DEATH—USEFUL KNOWLEDGE SOCIETY ... 135

Removal to Sunday School House—Means of Living—Mother's Death—Funeral at Jenkin Chapel—New Home Arrangements—Shawcross and Potts—Mormon Baptism—Origin of Useful Knowledge Society—Grammar Class—Gray's "Elegy"—Methods of Teaching—Stenography *versus* Phonography—William Pedley and Air Pump—John Brocklehurst, M.P., President—Annual Meetings—John Wright—Joseph Wright, Flowery Speaker—James Rathbone, Funny Speaker—Blackberry Spot—John May—Rector Stanley, Scientific Speaker—Rev. Dr. Burnett, the Enigmatic Speaker—Rev. C. Cruttenden—Rev. S. Bowen, the Sledgehammer Speaker—Rev. G. B. Kidd, the Puritan—His One Book—His Checkered Career—Quiet Retreat—Samuel Greg, the Eloquent Speaker.

CHAPTER XIV.—DEBATING SOCIETY ... 153

Rules of Discussion—The True Church—Roman Catholic—Peter, the Rock—Donative of Constantine—Decretals—Forgeries—Apostolic Succession—Chain—Rotten Links—Rev. Meade—Protestants—Ridley and Latimer—Nonsectarian—A Plague on Both Churches—Constantine and the Cross—Massacre of Innocents—The Cross of Jesus going on before—Waldenses—Huguenots—Calvin—Servetus—Heathen Missions—Reflections.

CHAPTER XV.—JOSEPH BARKER ... 158

Personal Sketch—Trial—Baptism—Lord's Supper—Publishing Books—Wesleyan Fly Sheet—Inquisition—Everet—Dunn—Griffiths—Barker and Cooke's Ten Nights' Debate—Exciting Scenes—Barker and Unitarianism—Barker, M.P.—In Prison—On Trial—Acquittal—In America—Public Debate—Farming—Home Sick—Return.

CONTENTS.

CHAPTER XVI.—MARTINEAU—PRIESTLEY ... 168

Mental Conflicts—"Endeavours after the Christian Life"—Wesley and Whitfield—Dial of Fate—The Ticking Clock—Colony of the Departed—Memories—Priestley—Calvinism—New Birth—Minister with Stipend of £30—Nantwich Pulpit—"Corruptions of Christianity"—Relics—Miracles—Indulgences—Pope Leo X.—Tetzel—Churches—Cash Basis—Inquisition—Endowments—Tithes—Poor Rates—Taxes—Taine—Christ on an Ass—Asses on Christ.

CHAPTER XVII.—UNITARIAN MINISTERS—METHODIST CLASS MEETING 178

Channing—Theodore Parker—Slavery—The Absolute Religion—Cardinal Newman—Unitarian Chapel—The Narrow Way—Dr. Vance Smith, the Learned—John Wright, the Practical—T. E. Poynting, the Flowery—Coulston, the Dramatic Reader—Class Meeting—"Life of Dr. Arnold"—Spiritual Husbandman—A Lady in the Case—Dr. Birchenall's Letters—My Replies.

CHAPTER XVIII.—DR. BIRCHENALL'S CLASS—SKETCHES ... 186

M. Moss, the Sincere—S. Moss, the Disputant—T., the Warmhearted—J. Birchenough, the Aspiring—F. Follows, the Earnest—G. Follows, the Gifted—Brocklehurst, the Boanerges—J. A., the Confident—G. S., the Fluctuating—J. B., the Unstable—J. N., the Well-wishing—George Cox, the Devout and Steadfast—Coloquy—Reflections.

CHAPTER XIX.—WESLEYAN MINISTERS I HAVE KNOWN ... 193

Barnard Slater, the Genial—Israel Holgate, the Smooth Spoken—George Greenwood, the Ardent—William Bird, the Queer—J. Sidney Smith, the Eloquent—John Lambert, the Memoriter Speaker—Joseph Roberts, Missionary — Robert Jackson, the Determined — Thomas Hardy, the Peculiar—Joseph Mood, the Repeater—Thomas Harris, the Disciplinarian—Jabez Bunting, the perpetual occupant of Moses' Seat—Robert Newton, the Majestic—Adam Clarke, Great Commentator—W. M. Punshon, the great Preacher and Lecturer—William (Billy) Dawson, the Eccentric—Peter McKenzie, the Successful Anti-Grammar Preacher—H. Price Hughes, the Audacious—Charles Garrett, the Melting Preacher—James Caughey, the Great Revivalist—Reflections.

CHAPTER XX.—MARRIAGE—TRADE—REFUGEE MISSION ... 207

The Three Angels Again—Marriage—Red Wharf Bay—The Curate—Calvinism—Water Cure—Quakers—Dialogue on Religion—Age 30 to 33—Dr. Bardsley—Rev. G. B. Kidd—"Festus"—Improved Health—Silk Business—First and Last Trade Bill—Change for a Sovereign—A Councillor Swears and Pays—A Tradesman Smiles and Cheats—A Manchester Agents' Ways—Buyers and Treats—Sunday School—Teachers Ordered to Quit—Scholars Quitted without Orders—Ecton Retreat—Parnassus—Delphi—Pantheon—Garret School—A Band of Brothers—Samuel Greg.

CHAPTER XXI.—UNITARIAN COLLEGE, MANCHESTER ... 223

Entrance Examination — Sermon Writing — A Scene — Committee—Many Questions—Students Rejected—Students Accepted—Theological Studies under Dr. Beard—Literary Studies—Rev. William Gaskell—Close of College Course—Annual Meeting in Town Hall—Mr. Ivie Mackie — My Speech — Amusement — Review — Deansgate Slums —Mission Tutors—Characteristics—Preaching Appointments—Ainsworth—Rochdale—Mossley—Lydgate—Sheffield.

CONTENTS.

CHAPTER XXII.—MINISTRY AT PADIHAM 236

Ordination—Revs. Dr. Beard and William Gaskell—Settlement—Pendle Hill—Gentry—Religious Preaching—Ethical and Illustrative—Classes—"Agnes of Sorrento"—Study of Greek—Daniel Berry—Student at College—Minister—Public Hall—Clergy in Battle Array—Defence—House Attack—My Pursuit—Street Amusement—Wesleyan Minister—Old John and Curate—Door Locked—Subscriptions—Bazaar—Land Purchase—Sunday Chapel Scene—Characterization—Revs. Dr. Beard and Charles Williams—Accrington Public Hall—Crowd—Debate—Excitement—Burnley Congregation.

CHAPTER XXIII.—LEAVING PADIHAM 252

Review—Manchester—Rusholme—Town Hall—Scene—Surprise—Dr. Beard Explains—Padiham Studies and Discourses—Macauley—William Penn—Froude—Oxford Essays and Reviews—Intangible Heresy—Theodore Parker—Lyell—Owen—The Herschells—George Eliot—Mrs. Gaskell—Dickens—Thackeray—Poets—Emerson—Carlyle.

CHAPTER XXIV.—MANCHESTER DISTRICT UNITARIAN MISSION... ... 261

Blackley Mission—A Member's Death at Sea—First Service—Welcome Meeting—Old Minister—Moon and Stars—Eckersley's—Bennett's—Johnson's—Whittaker's—Lamming's—Cooke's—Griffiths'—Mrs. Collenge and the Bible—Village Blacksmith—Mutual Improvement Class—Three Freethinkers—Colenso and Bishop Patrick—Bazaar clears £220 in aid of Cotton Famine Fund—Sewing Class in School—Another Bazaar clears £320 for Debt on Schools—Organ Subscription, £40.

CHAPTER XXV.—MIDDLETON—OTHER MISSIONS 269

Temperance Hall—Silk Weavers—Naturalists—Herbs—Insects—Workers—Wood—Brookes—Lawton—Clegg—Keene—Miss Greaves—Highwayman—Escape—Woodland way—Success of the Mission—**Miles Platting Mission**—Stable Room—New Chapel—Workers—Bibby—Coleman—Fielding—Barnes—Burgess—Old Quaint House—A Genius—**Salford Mission**—Departure of Rev. J. C. Street—New Sunday School—Ivie Mackie's Aid—Workers—Hough—Jackson—Milne—Bowes—Phillips and Yates' Families—Inter-Marriages—**Ardwick Mission**—A Mossley Offshoot—Crabtree—Heys—Lawton—A Successful Cause—The Secret—**Platt Mission**—Ancient Chapel—Reynolds' Family—Smith and Ruskin—Brittain—Naturalist—Broome—Unique Flowers—Mrs. Gordon—Misses Gordon—Gawthorpe—Whitelegge—**Failsworth Mission**—Old Chapel—Workers—Allen—Partington—Wild—Hibbert—Silk Weavers—Mill Workers—Ruskin—Retreat to Established Church—**Swinton Mission**—Old Cottage—New Chapel—Helpers—Leigh—Boardman—Jackson—Collier.

CHAPTER XXVI.—CLOSE OF MY MISSION 27

Review—Excellent Committee—Good Supporters—Experience—Business Men—Millionaires—Blackley My Sole Charge—Welcome Meeting Review of Five Years—New Parsonage—Bazaar—Subscription—Money Obtained—House Built—Not occupied by me—Departure thence—Hindley Visit—Engaged as Minister—Invited to Rochdale Road Chapel—Interview with Mr. Harding and Rev. Steinthal—Mr. Eckersley's Report of Hindley—Why did I go?

CONTENTS.

	Page
CHAPTER XXVII.—HINDLEY MINISTRY	284

New Chapel and School—Bazaar and Subscriptions—Studies—Martineau — Darwin — Clericals — Lawsuits — Rivington Chapel — Mr. Darbishire — Squire Crompton — Customs — Humour — Mrs. Rushton's Accident—Cripple—No Cure—Visit of Brother Samuel—His Sudden Death—My Illness—Close of Ministry of Twelve Years—Macclesfield—Sweet Home—Farewell Meeting—Illness—Recovery—Hammond Family—Pioneers—Expulsions—In America.

CHAPTER XXVIII.—RESUMED MINISTRY ... 295

Search for a Sanctuary—Parsonage Street Chapel—King Edward Street Chapel—Upper Room—Spiritualism—Paradise Street Free Church—Sunday School—Successful Studies—Opposition—Dams Mission—Rev. Ashcroft—Richard Weaver—Replies—Many Duties—Failure of Health—Ministry Closed.

CHAPTER XXIX.—MACCLESFIELD AMATEUR PARLIAMENT ... 302

Babel of Tongues—T. Savage, Tory Premier—Mr. McGloon, Liberal Premier—Characteristics—"Mistakes of Moses"—Attitudes—Gladstone — Pint of Order—A Quart!! Hem! Haw!—Curate's Thigs of Fistles—Parson's ng-ng-ng — Letters from Ladies' Gallery — Clara — Agnes — Paradise in the Dam(n)s—Messrs. May and Mair—Vote for Release—Utility of such Debates—Defect of Church and Chapel Debates—Young Men's Christian Associations found wanting.

CHAPTER XXX.—CONTROVERSY ON SPIRITUALISM ... 313

Cranks—Niggards—Collections—Buttons—Pompey—Brudder Slowfoot Ghost Stories — Scientists — Crookes — Wallace — Lodge — Radium — Satan—The Vicar—Church Creeds—The Bible—Rev. David Simpson—Pope—Ingersoll—Weaver—Greek Testament—Curate and Medium—Trinity and the Devil—Curate's flight—Devil's exit.

CHAPTER XXXI.—PREACHING THE GOSPEL—REV. R. J. CAMPBELL—CRITICISMS ... 324

King Edward—General Booth—Gospel—Success—Failure—Bishop Carlisle—Rev. J. E. Rattenbury—Marie Corelli—Stead—Church and devil—Loyola—Hebrew roots—Boots—Feather—College studies—Campbell—Bible—Song of Solomon—Abraham—Isaac—Jane Eyre—George Eliot—Confession—Four young men—Marcus Aurelius—Dr. Forsyth—Dr. Fairbairn—Pharisee—Rascal—Hypocrites.

CHAPTER XXXII.—UPTON TOWNSHIP—VISITORS' CONVERSATION ... 336

Inhabitants—Circumstances—Pursuits—The Hall—The Grange—The Priory—Scenes—Children—Lovers—Parsons—Poets—Memorial Fane—Pilgrims departed—Pilgrims living—Life—Death.

INTRODUCTION

"ENCOMPASSED about with so great a cloud of witnesses," I am impelled to write a brief account of my somewhat extended life.

Piles of old letters are beside me, bringing vividly to view the forms and aspects of the writers so pleasantly familiar in days of yore. Heaps of diaries crowded with sketches, narratives and experiences are also there. Facts and fancies, joys and sorrows, successes and failures, victories and defeats, find record in their pages. Accounts found there of chapels and churches, literary and scientific societies, farms, gardens, and workshops, all await revision and restatement; and also for judgment as to their influence on myself and others. The books ranged around me, again, how mighty and beneficent have been their influence on my life. Some of them were secured only by great privation, and others were obtained by the sacrifice of some of the necessities of life. But the wealth of mind and soul conferred by these blessed ministrants was beyond price. The pictures on the walls—not one of them costly—are all rich in association and suggestion. Portraits, landscapes, historic scenes, and poets' dreams have all had some special influence on my life. The times, places, and events connected with the advent of each picture into the charmed circle have some interesting lesson to give; some important message to convey. But my strongest impulse to write, I think, comes from the great cloud of witnesses which memory presents to view. Under memory's vivid light my life course spreads out before me like a map, with numerous pathways displayed, along which innumerable beings come and go. There, clearly marked, is the road I trod in childhood's days, leading to lonely woodlands where birds built their nests and sang their songs, and where rabbits fed and ran; and to farm fields where ploughing, sowing, and reaping went on regularly as the seasons came and went. There it was I passionately desired to live, and learn, and labour all my days. But from that happy pathway I was rudely torn, and thrust on to a rough and dismal road which broke my health and broke my heart. Along that rugged road, leading to a factory dungeon and to warehouse slavery, I tramped regularly from day to day during twenty years of my life. Sometimes I did, indeed, in almost delirious joy, rush away to other pathways leading to Sunday School, night school, lecture hall and chapel. There it was I eagerly gained knowledge and love, and a clear sense of duty, to guide me in the life that now is, and to aid me in securing a heavenly and immortal life beyond the grave.

Then came on commercial undertakings with many journeys to Manchester, when I became familiar with many of the pursuits and prominent objects of the great and marvellous city—with its large warehouses, where eager and ambitious men make haste to become rich in gold while often they become poor in soul—with its palatial Exchange, where throngs of excited men rush and push more wildly, gesticulate more frantically, and shout more loudly than the frenzied crowds in a Welsh Revival—with its numerous churches, where white-robed priests perform high ceremonials, intone ancient sermons, drone out old creeds, and often prove more expert in securing temporalities than in saving souls—and with its drink saloons alluring masses of men and women into their fatal dens, and then vomiting them out drunk into the midst of street orgies where sirens are singing, bacchanals dancing, gamblers victimising, and burglars, garrotters, murderers, and suicides are doing their diabolical deeds. Appalled by scenes of vice, by gambling modes of trade, by mammonish churches, and by street noises, I wished to flee from the city and never enter it more. Instinctively and impulsively I exclaimed:—

> "O for a lodge in some vast wilderness,
> Some boundless contiguity of shade,
> Where rumour of oppression and deceit,
> Might never reach me more!"

But just then and there came the imperative command, "Go forth into the highways and byways, back-street ways and slum-ways, and compel the straying and sinning ones to come into the Kingdom of God." Inspired by this pressing message, and aided by a few faithful souls, this noble work, in some humble way, was done. A veritable Kingdom of Heaven was built up to which gathered doubting souls and found a cheering faith—deeply repentant wanderers from the right, who were led into a higher life—despairing prodigals, who were welcomed home—outcasts from the churches, who found a holy shrine—and anxiously inquiring minds of all kinds, who found an open door to a true church of God. But the fear, the anxiety, the anguish experienced when success was doubtful; and the joy and peace and triumph felt when success was achieved—these things can not be told.

And so, engaged in these arduous but uplifting labours, a whole generation of years has passed away, while the eyesight has become dimmed, the hair has whitened on the head, the furrows deepened on the face, and infirmity and old age have come on. All along, the soul has sought to peer through the veil of the future to get glimpses of the eternal city whose builder and maker is God. And now, in this quiet retreat, I wait awhile, in hope and peace, on the brink of the mighty waters of eternity rolling evermore.

> "And may there be no moaning of the bar, when I put out to sea;
> And may there be no sadness of farewell, when I embark."

Should my already long span of life become a little longer still, these records might be extended also, and become sufficient to make a book. As to the utility of publishing such a book, either before or after my death, judgments might be diverse. The lives of great men only are needed, it might be said, to make the lives of other men sublime. That judgment would suit well enough the bold, crafty, and ambitious men who grasp the great prizes of the world. But it would not suit at all the great majority of mankind, who plod laboriously and honestly along the middle and lower walks of life. Such would be checked rather than aided by unattainable objects placed before them. Fame's proud temple shining from afar would not tempt them to climb the giddy heights on which it stands. Pursuing the even and noiseless tenor of their way, they need only the stimulus of instances and examples of a more lowly kind. To wayworn and weary pilgrims of this class this simple narrative may be of use. Seeing it and reading it, some downcast wanderers may take heart again, and with new vigour pursue their earthly and heavenly way.

CHAPTER I

BIRTH — PARENTAGE — EARLY DAYS

FROM my study window the eastern Cheshire hills are in full view, and may be seen, on fine summer days, radiant with sunrise splendour or sunset glow—on stormy days enveloped in black thunder-clouds with lightning flashes breaking through—on winter days covered over with a sheet of glittering snow—and on every day presenting some aspect of majesty, or beauty, or serenity, to observant eyes. But even more interesting than the ever-changing beauty of this mountain range are the rich associations connected with its various localities. In the centre of the range rises a huge, dark-looking eminence called Pym Chair, at the foot of which stands an old, small, boxlike building called Jenkin Chapel. A mile away to the south, many years ago, was situated the farmstead called Hooley Hay. There lived the Cooper family, who were farmers, weavers, musicians, Methodists, and, to a considerable extent, readers and students of valuable books.

Martha Cooper, afterwards my mother, was the youngest member of the family and lived at home all her maiden life. In various situations on these Cheshire hills lived, in his early days, my father, George Rushton. He was born in Leek, but removed, when a boy, to Barley Ford farm on the Cheshire hills. Here, his only leisure was on Sunday afternoon, when he wandered into the adjoining woodlands, making acquaintance with birds, squirrels, stoats, and other wild creatures, resting betimes on banks of ferns and flowers, and reading in a small Testament, as advised when leaving home. From thence he removed to the Marsh Farm, in Rainow. Attending the Macclesfield cattle fairs, he sometimes joined in the singing matches in the public inns. The songs were about battle scenes on sea and land, and about the exploits of Robin Hood and Little John. Happily, he avoided being overcome with drink both then and in his after life. Later on, he became manager of Blakelow Farm on the slope of Tegs Nose Hill, where he was, from his position, under the necessity of enrolling himself in the Cheshire Cavalry. The drillings and journeyings of his regiment he got much to like, and hence he was greatly disappointed when these exercises nearly ceased after the battle of Waterloo. But another and more important engagement was at hand. At the Barnaby Fair following Wellington's great victory, he met, for the first time, Martha Cooper, and went with her all the way to Hooley Hay, from whence he had to return six or seven miles along rough mountain roads on a very dark night. But neither the length of the journey nor the roughness of the road, nor yet the goblin forms that roamed the region around—

> "So withered and so wild in their attire;
> That looked not like the inhabitants o' the earth,
> And yet are on't,"

affected the ardour of his suit. Not even the winged hounds which rushed with such an awful sound over those mountain heights prevented numerous visits to Hooley Hay. Love proved stronger than superstition, fear, and difficulties of all kinds, and so an ardent courtship went on during several years. Still, in this case, as in most others, true love did not always flow smoothly along. Misunderstandings would sometimes arise, and visits became few and far between. But Bible and hymn book, benedictions and prayers, always bridged over these chasms as they opened in the way. Love-letters from Hooley Hay were full of references to psalmists, prophets, evangelists, and Wesley's hymns. This method proved invincible. All difficulties vanished, and the two ardent lovers became husband and wife.

In the month of January of the year 1820 they settled in a house near the George and Dragon Inn, situated in Higher Hurdsfield. In that same house on the 21st day of February, 1821, I was born into the world.

The new life, thus started on its career came, in a few months, very nearly to a close. Making premature excursions on the hearth I fell down with my face on a heap of burning coal just raked from the fire-grate. Hearing a loud cry, my mother rushed into the house and snatched me from the burning mass and found a large red-hot brand fast on the nose. Plucking away the brand, the flesh came away with it, leaving a large hole from which the blood flowed in a torrent. Before the wound could be stanched I bled nearly to death. The scar of that nearly fatal wound I bear at this day. This event furnished my mother with the means of coupling my name with that of Wesley, who had a hairbreadth escape from a burning house. We were both brands plucked from the burning. This form of phraseology was very popular in Methodism, and was applied mostly to converted souls saved from the real fires of hell. It could not be applied to me, in this sense, as a child, but in later years this kind of phraseology was applied to me in full force. When I could neither be pursuaded nor coerced backward into irrational beliefs then, it was said, nothing remained for me but the lake that burneth with fire and brimstone. When I met these awful fulminations of my old religious friends with smiles and mild replies, they said such conduct would make my damnation the more hot and sure. Most, if not all, of those early religious friends will know better now, for they have passed the earthly veil beyond which celestial light breaks on such well-meaning benighted souls.

At three years of age I had another remarkable escape from death. Playing on the road in front of the house, a furious cow rushed at me and with its horns tossed me some yards high into the air. When lifted from the ground I was thought to be dead. After careful and continued treatment consciousness was restored, when I began to cry out that I had been " cob-a-balled by a cow." Many, various, and critical, have been my tossings since then, all of which I have, somehow, survived until the present hour. But the most critical and important uplifting of all is now at hand, for which I wait in resignation, hope, and peace. Poring over the question of memory in childhood I find the following testimonies of reliable persons. Sir Walter Scott says: "I remember when three years old lying on the floor of my grandfather's parlour wrapped up in a sheepskin warm from the body of a recently-killed sheep." Charles Dickens tells that he "remembered quite well a small front garden attached to the house at Portsea, from which he was taken when he was two years old." Jean Paul Richter says: "I am glad that I am able still to recall a dim faint recollection of the time when I was twelve, or at most, thirteen months old, like the first mental snowdrop out of the dark soil of childhood." In view of these statements I am safe, I think, in concluding that my own memory of the cow incident is clear and correct.

From the age of three to six years the faculties of observation and reason, as well as that of memory, were constantly and vigorously at work. At this period there was much cogitation by myself and other children about a newly-painted signboard containing a picture of St. George and a dragon, which appeared in front of the inn adjoining our house. The many inquiries put to our parents and other elders educed no satisfactory information, nor were later investigations much more successful. Dubious historical accounts indicated, as we learned, that St. George was martyred during the persecutions of Dioclesian. Certain it was that Greek, Roman, and Protestant churches had claimed him for their patron saint. With Gibbon we came to think that St. George was no credit to any church, but rather a disgrace. The Crusaders contended that their great victory at Antioch was gained through his intercession, but that claim was made in an age of unfounded faith, and therefore without evidence and of no account.

The most probable origin of the story of St. George and the

Dragon, I think, may be found in the "Tale of Beowulf," a poem of 6,000 lines. It is a Norse saga, its hero being a Danish prince who went out as a knight-errant to rid the earth of monsters. After many heroic exploits he was at length killed by a frightful earthdrake or dragon. Whether, however, the story be fact, fable, or fiction, or made up of all three, certain it is that it served me as an effective illustration in my youthful speech-making on the temperance question. Alcohol—I declaimed—was the fearful dragon, wildly and fiercely roaming over the world; rushing through poor men's cottages, lordly mansions, bishops' palaces, parliament houses, and through the very sanctuaries of God, seeking whom it might devour: while the great temperance cause, more heroic and triumphant than St. George of England, was enthusiastically pursuing, and would destroy the great dragon of strong drink, and so deliver mankind from unspeakable wickedness, wretchedness, despair, ruin, and death.

Some fifty yards to the north from the inn was the only day-school in the district. It was nearly surrounded by a garden, and was approached by a flight of steps. On my first visit, I found the room full of children, some at play, some in mischief, and some repeating lessons in the broadest and roughest dialect of Cheshire. In the midst of this village babel was Nanny Clarke, a thin, tall, gaunt, infirm old dame, with spectacles on nose, and birch-rod in hand. At frequent intervals the rod was heard going swish, swish, all round the school, when a little temporary order would ensue. Here it was my long pursuit of knowledge, under difficulties, began.

The uncouth sounds of letters and words I learned here, I had, with much effort, to unlearn in later days. Nor even yet is careful attention given to accent and pronunciation in the public or private school. In a speech delivered September 3rd, 1904, Bishop Casartelli said that the pronunciation of the English language in the day-schools was no better than it was fifty years ago. Hence it is so few good readers and speakers are to be found. Nor until something like Pitman's system of phonetic spelling is taught in the schools, will much improvement in this respect ensue.

Another bewildering experience I had when taken by my mother, on a certain Sunday night, to a prayer meeting held in the schoolhouse. The prayers were very earnest and the responses alarmingly loud, and souls, it was exclaimed, were being born again. By some means, two merry rollicking carters had been got into the meeting, when both became much excited and broke out into vociferous prayer. Very distinctly do I remember one of them, John Daniels, declaiming with astounding effect the following lines:—

> "Wrestling I will not let thee go
> Till I thy name and nature know,"

Then suddenly a great shout of triumph came, and jubilant hallelujahs made the rafters ring. Two souls, it was said, had been saved by the blood of the Lamb, and had found peace with God. The two parties were John Daniels and George Dodd, who had been lively, thoughtless young fellows, but not bad characters in any way. Such was my first wondering and puzzling experience of the Methodist way of saving souls. Even after my mother's anxious explanations I understood but little, while I pondered much. This event was the cause of many serious cogitations, which have not ended yet.

At the second house past the school lived Betty, Sarah, and James Hall, all of them elderly and unmarried. The work of silkwinding engines in a large upper room secured them an economic living. James Hall was an ardent student of the writings of Flavius Josephus. When going with my mother to the house I noticed that he talked incessantly about his favourite author Josephus. All the women preferred to sing the hymns with which they became familiar long ago, when they were together in the choir of Rainow Wesleyan Chapel. Still, the old man's praise of his favourite author led us into a costly undertaking in later years, when Billinge, the travelling bookseller, induced us to take in monthly numbers a finely-illustrated edition of Whiston's Josephus. The work when bound in half-calf cost 15s. 6d., an enormous sum to us at that time. My desire to secure the work was intensified by a controversy which was going on concerning the celebrated passage referring to the crucifixion and resurrection of Jesus Christ. In a dissertation included in the work, Whiston had undertaken to defend the passage against the charge of interpolation, and I was anxiously hoping to find his vindication conclusive and complete. Ultimately, however, and much against my will, I was forced to the conclusion that the insertion of the passage was one of those pious frauds so very common in early Christian times, and, indeed, in all Christian ages down to the present time.

At the next house, but nearer the highway, lived John Hooley, tailor and grocer. He was a low-set man with a quick footstep and a temper as quick. A true priest was this man; not by the laying on of prelate's hands, but by the inspiration of God's own spirit. He was an upright tradesman and a good Methodist withal. The sick and the dying he visited and comforted when no other could be found to do such blessed deeds. In my daily duty of watering cattle in Cliff Lane I often saw him quickly climbing the fields above and suddenly disappearing from sight. On one occasion, from childish curiosity, I followed him and, all at once, saw him in a deep dell down on his knees with hands uplifted, and heard an earnest whispering sound which I knew to be prayer. I turned quickly away, but he had seen me and shortly followed, saying, "Thou wilt not understand this just yet, but someday I hope thou wilt. I bring my cares and sorrows up here and leave them behind me, thank God." But even then I knew more about the needs and deliverances referred to than he supposed. Afterwards my experiences of both were neither few nor small. Only a short distance away was Ecton-top where, in the middle of an old quarry was a detached piece of rock which I called my altar-stone, where prayers were offered and blessings received during many years of my life. On my return to the neighbourhood, at the close of my Lancashire

Mission, I immediately visited this sacred and hidden shrine. The altar-stone itself was nearly buried in debris which had fallen from the heights above, but the memory of gracious influences, of blessed experiences, connected with the place—that was not, could not, be buried at all. That rich store of recollection, no upheavals of life, no rushing storms of time can either bury or obscure; nor would, even, the wreck of matter or the crash of worlds. Going one day to the favourite haunt, I had an unpleasant surprise. I found the quarry all alive with men cutting out stone and myself excluded from the sacred shrine. But happily I found at my next visit the stone-getting stopped, the men dispersed, and silence and quiet reigning as before. The altar-stone was gone, but two stone sheds, which I called tabernacles, were left. There should have been, I thought, three of these tents to be dedicated to the memory of Moses, Elias, and Christ, as also to Plato, Socrates, Buddha, and Confucius; as also again to the memory of a band of noble souls with whom I had held bright and sweet communion on that very spot. Here and around were Delphi, Parnassus, and Mount Zion over again, where inspiring oracles were received by devout, inquiring, and receptive minds.

Just beyond John Hooley's house was the lane leading to the deep valley, where was the famous Dodgmoor Well. The almost continuous procession of persons carrying cans and pitchers full of clear and sparkling water up the lane from the lovely dell, formed a romantic picture never to be forgotten by me who daily, for many years, carried water from this famous well. Here again I found illustrations and suggestions for my speeches at temperance meetings, and where I joined in singing with great glee the following lines:—

> "Bright crystal water, sparkling and free;
> Dancing and leaping so joyously.
> Bright crystal water foaming in glee,
> That is the best drink for you and for me."

Since that time the water has been drained from the old well in the field to a new well on the road side, but the water, I hope, is as clear and copious as before, and that in its musical flow whispers of inspiration may be heard by young and devout souls, now as then.

Close to our house was Cliff Lane end. Dear Cliff Lane! what bright hours, what happy times were spent there! What delightful meetings with playfellows, what joyous excursions, what romantic pursuits daily took place, for many years, in this natural people's park!

On either side of the lane from Hurdsfield Road to the cliff top—over a mile in length—were wide slopes of land with numberless uplands, knolls, and dells. Here grew blackberry, raspberry, and bilberry bushes containing abundance of fruit in season. The beauty of that fruit, the sweetness of its taste, and the sharpness of the appetite with which it was devoured, are rich heritages of memory to this day. Poor people's fowls, donkeys, ponies, and cows, also, found food and shelter in this natural park; but the children, the cattle, and the fruit bushes are no longer there. The slopes and little hills have all been levelled, enclosed and joined on to rich men's estates. The lane itself is a narrow water channel and little more.

About the end of my fifth year came a great change. Father had rented the Lower Fold Farm, consisting of three fields, a large garden, and an old dilapidated house. Here began a life of hard work. Father was mostly away in the daytime carting coal and stone to the town. Mother minded the three cows, managed the milk, and made the butter and sold it. My daily duty was, with sundry helps, to cultivate the garden. The toil and strain of delving and weeding that long-neglected garden, it would not be easy to describe. I was strictly injoined not to break the weeds, but to dig out the entire roots; and so I had to carry on a long and fierce struggle with masses of dandelions, each with a root at least twelve inches long—with clusters of nettles growing amongst gooseberry bushes, getting my hands both stung and scratched—and with endless growths of the wild convolvulus, with numberless roots stretching out in all directions, almost answering to Pollock's description of the tails of the worm that never dies.

At length, however, the stubborn glebe was broken; the weeds were cleared away; seeds were sown, and trees pruned; the garden bloomed into beauty; the harvest-time, with its glorious tints and maturing processes came on apace; and then the precious fruits were gathered in and stored for present and future use.

To go with my father on quiet Sunday afternoons over the farm and hear him talk of the wonders of Nature, and about the work of our own hands, became an experience of exquisite delight. Here, I thought, we might long continue to work and live without molestation or trouble from the outside world, but soon found out my mistake. Rough lads broke down fences in the fields, and stole fruit from the garden. With some of these I came into sharp collision, causing bruises and blood-letting on both sides. Less damage was done afterwards, and no more fisticuffs took place. This way of meeting difficulties I found was not a pleasant one, and I determined not to resort to it again, except from dire necessity.

One day, here in the old house, there happened an event which greatly influenced our course of life. A little stranger, it was said, had arrived. And there present, indeed, was a new immortal, with red face, chubby hands, and a forcible voice, demanding constant care. This was dear little Sam, to whom I was most warmly attached from his birth to his death. For years it was my willing duty to nurse and feed him when mother was away attending to the cows and dairy work. Often on these occasions I diligently rocked him in the cradle, until he was fast asleep, when I could get a little time for play. And thereby hangs a tale.

On a certain day, while the bright sunshine was streaming through window and doorway, and while merry children's voices were sounding outside, my endurance was put to the severest test. Could I not by some means rock the cradle and enjoy the play outside? Hunting up cords, and tapes, and pieces of thread, and tying the whole together, and fastening the long string to the cradle, I could rock away standing at the garden wall and enjoying the fun outside. For a time this was delightful; but alas—

> "The best laid schemes o' mice and men (and boys)
>   Gang aft a-gley;
>   And leave us nought but grief and pain
>   For promised joy."

For, just at a crisis of the play, there was a jerk of the string, and a loud shriek in the house. On rushing through the doorway, I found the cradle upside down, the blankets tumbled about, and poor Sam sprawling on the floor. To right the cradle, to replace the baby, and wrap him in his coverings, was the work of an instant, followed by a diligent rocking, which sent him again to sleep. Just then in walked mother and said, "I see he has been crying." I replied, "Yes, he was crying and I rocked him to sleep." But I was severely reticent as to to the cause of his tears. Energy, resource, and despatch have often been of service since then, but not always so successful in saving me from unpleasant results.

I ought at this time to have been making more progress in my education. But there was no day-school near, and if there had been I could not have been spared from work at home. There was, however, the much-loved Sunday school, my Alma Mater, within five minutes' walk of the house.

Entering the school in my fifth year, I remained regularly connected with it until my thirtieth year. In all the Bible classes at that time writing was taught. I worked hard and strove eagerly to get into one of these classes, and very soon did so. And then came the glorious times of straight strokes, pothooks, and ladles. How fascinating these elementary characters seemed! How, in admiration, I fixed my gaze upon them, and how easily, to my surprise, I made them! Then, more exhilarating still, came forth words, and sentences, and even my own name, written in large, strong strokes of my quill pen. No engineer, architect, inventor, discoverer, or commander could have felt more exquisite pleasure in their moments of conquest and triumph, than was experienced by me in mastering the art of writing. Nor was this a barren conquest, as victories innumerable followed in its train. There were certain favourite hymns which, from being frequently sung in the school, had become, imperfectly, impressed on the memory. By writing them down in my copy-book, they became a rich and lasting treasure. From Mr. Stead we have learned which are the favourite hymns of members of the royal family and of distinguished English men and women of all ranks, and which hymns, they say, have helped them. I feel sure no favourite hymn helped any one of those distinguished individuals more than I was helped by the first hymn I wrote in my book, and which contains the following lines:—

> "My God, the spring of all my joys,
> The life of my delights.
>
> . . . .
>
> Thou art my soul's bright morning star
> And Thou my rising sun.
>
> . . . .
>
> The opening heavens around me shine
> With beams of sacred bliss,
> If Jesus shows His mercy mine
> And whispers I am His."

From these words I learned that in contact with the divinely illuminated soul of Jesus my own soul obtains heavenly light; that in communion with Him sun and star with more lustre shine; and that when the sweet whisper comes that I am His, then the whole heavens are ablaze with the glory of God. The second hymn written in my copy-book, and into my memory at the same time, was sung in the School on several successive Sundays in the end of each autumn season:—

> "See the leaves around us falling
> Dry and withered to the ground,
> Thus to thoughtless mortals calling
> In a sad and solemn sound."

Here, again, we observe a divine voice is heard speaking through external nature to the human soul, and here too, in these simple lines we find an introduction to all the recorded religions of all the ages. In the closing verse the theme brightens with hues and tints from the Genesis narrative, and from the Apocalypse:—

> "On the tree of life eternal,
>   Man, let all thy hopes be stayed,
> This alone, for ever vernal,
>   Bears a leaf that shall not fade."

Thus, writing down and pondering over these plain Sunday School hymns, I was enabled feebly and faintly to touch the fringe, at least, of those sublime truths which have filled the minds of the greatest poets and thinkers of all time. The singing of hymns in the School, and the writing of them down seemed to fill my mind with sentiment and song. Working in the garden and in the fields, churning milk, or rocking the cradle, or running on errands, sweet words and tunes were continually passing through my mind like the zephyrs through an aeolian harp. By these writing exercises my mind was led out into ever-broadening streams of thought and investigation. In some book, belonging I think, to the School, I found a poem entitled "The Covenanter's Grave." I wrote it down, became deeply interested in it, and eagerly sought for further information concerning the Covenanters' sufferings and noble deeds. Very soon I became familiar with Peden the Prophet, John Brown, the murdered carrier, Graham, the bloody captain of dragoons, and with the final slaughter of the Cameronians, as they were worshipping together on the Moorlands on a bright sunny Sunday morning. An intense sympathy with martyred saints and as strong an antipathy to all religious persecution was fixed in my soul by the thrilling stories I read. Another poem, entitled "The Pilgrim Fathers," which I copied, greatly excited me. No rest could I have until I had learned more of these heroic people. The marvellous story of the May Flower, and the landing of the voyagers on Plymouth Rock, and the planting of a religious community in the American desert, was like a revelation suddenly bursting upon my view.

While listening, some years later, to the singing of some lines beginning, "Over the mountain waves, see where they come," I fell into a sort of enchanted dream of a free life in the American backwoods.

In my eighth year my attention was arrested by an address to the scholars in the Sunday School. The substance of the appeal, as I well remember, was something like this. "God wants constantly to speak to you and tell you how He loves you, and what He wants you to do. He spoke to the child Samuel in this way, and He speaks to you in the same way. Have any of you ever heard Him? Have you ever tried to hear Him? The way to get near to God is to go into a quiet place and pray. You must do this at once. Your welfare for ever may depend on this. Go straight home when you leave School. Go into your bedroom alone, and pray, and God will hear you and show you what to do." I went straight home entirely absorbed in the subject. Visitors in the house began to talk to me, but I passed on and went upstairs. But the shattered doors of the old house would not close and I was disturbed with the sound of voices coming from below. Escaping from the house, I wandered in the field just behind the house in search of an oratory in which I could hear God speak, and just there was the sacred place. At the foot of a large tree grew a dense mass of tall saplings. Drawing some of the young trees aside, I stepped into the circle and knelt down where no human eye could see me, and where no disturbing sound was heard. For a while I waited in silence, then the words "Our Father which art in Heaven" broke in an earnest whisper from my lips, and before the prayer was ended I seemed inspired and transfigured. The sunlight playing around me was not so bright as the inner light irradiating the soul. Outward voices there were none, but inward voices many. If God ever did speak to a child, He spoke then. If the heavens did ever open to an aspiring soul, then, flashing out new light, and creating new faith, and hope, and joy, they opened then, and indeed "Heaven lies about us (all) in our early days." What is imperatively needed is, that some wise instructor open the door and usher the young souls into the blessed abodes. Certainly my own life has been fuller, richer, brighter and better for the experiences of that sacred hour. The tree circle had become to me a sanctuary, whither I often wended my way with some book to read or hymn to sing, but suddenly and rudely these visits came to an end. A crisis in the family had come. For many months my father had been carting coal and lime and stone for certain builders and silk-men in the town who delayed payments to him and then became bankrupt with little or no assets. At once it was decided by my father to sell horses, cows, and the whole farm stock, except one cow, and one calf which were removed to a small croft near Cliff Lane end. After paying off all debts, we removed into a four-roomed house without cellar or back door, situated on the edge of the croft. My father became working farmer for John Broome, at Shores Clough, his wages being 7/- a week in winter, and 9/- a week in summer, including his meat, except at week ends, when he had his meals at home. No better wages could then be obtained anywhere about by admittedly the best farmer in the neighbourhood. Frequent and sad were the cogitations on the hearthstone at nights as to how the most meagre sort of living could be secured.

CHAPTER II

IN FACTORY AND FIELD

Although only eight years of age, it was regretfully decided that I must be sent to work at some silk mill in the town. On entering Green's factory in Commercial Road I shuddered. The close, impure air seemed to be stifling me. The clangour of machinery deafened me. I could hardly speak a word to any one. A girl was appointed to teach me how to fasten silk ends together, but my fingers trembled so much I could not use them. On being remonstrated with, I burst into tears. I was kindly taken away to sit on a stool in a corner until my emotion was overcome. After a while, I managed with great difficulty to find the topmost beat in a slip of silk. Somewhat more easily I found the end of the silk on the bobbin in front to which I tied the thread from the slip and so sent the swift, holding the slip, spinning quickly round. Shortly I had six of these swifts to keep going by myself. Then twelve, and then twenty and more, and thus I became fairly launched on this new and arduous course of life. Could I have begun my factory life as a half-timer, as children can in these later days, I should have got along cheerfully and safely enough. But my hours of labour were from 6 o'clock in the morning until six o'clock in the evening for the first few months, and then continued until 8 o'clock in the evening with intervals for meals amounting to one hour and forty minutes in the day. This was a murderous length of time for children to work. I managed to live somehow although my health was greatly impaired, but untold numbers went in this way to untimely graves. For this long and crushing labour I got 6d. a week the first month; 1/- a week for the next two months, and then 1/6 as a regular wage. At the end of eight months came emancipation, at least, for a time. Owing to serious difficulties of some kind the mill was closed, and about a hundred hands thrown out of work. At once my father sent me to work in clearing out brush-wood from a long, wild clough below the canal basin. This suited me exactly. In the day I cut down masses of briars and dug up the roots. At the night I was helped to pile up the rubbish and set it on fire. The bonfires were quite exhilarating, as I had never seen such masses of flame and smoke before. On patches of cleared ground I had to plant potatoes, and when ripe to carry them, in a bag, on my back, nearly a mile, on a steep road to our house. Then I had to wash and peel them, and, after boiling, to eat them along with buttermilk, with a relish impossible to describe. Some of the neighbours, hearing how good these potatoes were, wanted to buy some: then I had to dig up and carry some 60 pounds' weight during a single day. The selling-price was 6d. for 20 pounds, the proceeds being a very welcome increase to the family income. Amidst this hard labour there came, now and then, intervals of relief when I could walk around and survey the field of operations and indulge in waking dreams. How nice it would be to have a small house built in the clough and our family to live in it at a small expense. Or there might easily be a wooden hut put up in which I could have my meals for the day, and find shelter in stormy weather. I knew nothing then about Thoreau's solitary life in the backwoods. Indeed, he had not, as yet, pitched his tent, or wooden house on the banks of Walden Lake. Of this I am sure, that he had no greater delight in his woodland home, than I had in my pursuits in the woodland clough. The forest life of another notable character I had heard and read much about, and was greatly influenced by the account. My father had often talked about the doings of Robin Hood and Little John and their adherents with their bows and arrows. What harm could there be then in my getting a bow-and-arrows, and doing a little shooting here in the clough? Very soon these instruments were ready for execution, but what could I shoot? The birds, of course, for there were plenty of them, but not the wrens which I saw hopping about so briskly in the hedge. I had been too often charmed with their beautiful nests, so nicely roofed with moss, and with small entrance so artfully concealed that I could hardly get a sight of the cluster of eggs, or the brood of tiny, fluffy open-mouthed young within. Nor could I shoot the beautiful speckle-breasted thrush singing its rich and gushing song—nor the blackbird making the welkin ring with its clear, swelling notes—nor the lark descending from heaven's gate, where it has been so sweetly warbling and so long—nor the robin surely, which was my constant companion when digging in the earth, and had such trust in me and came so near to me that I could take it in my hand if I wished. No, certainly the redbreast must not be shot by me, for it is my mentor teaching me ever a lesson of trust in One higher than I. Nor must even that dun, plain, twittering hedge-sparrow be injured by me either, for it, too, reminds me of the One who takes care of both it and me. But what, then, could I shoot with my bow and arrows? There were rabbits and hares about in plenty, but for the sake of two tame rabbits I kept at home I would not hurt any of their kindred. The hares were safe enough, for I could not get near them. The quick-moving, beautiful, brown-backed, white-throated, diamond-eyed stoats I could not decide to injure. The water-rats on the brook side I might have aimed at, if I could have got a chance, but they too quickly got out of the way. My occupation, then, with bow and arrows was gone, or rather had not begun. Oh, why should not kindness to innocent and harmless inferior creatures be taught to all children in the home and in the schools? And why does not Christianity, so widely diffused, and at such an immense cost, create a universal humaneness towards such creatures, and forbearance and love towards all men; and why do Christians permit themselves to be so far inferior to Buddists in this respect; and how can they for shame to missionise Buddists when they the rather need Buddists to missionise them in these important matters; and why do not all religions combine in one grand Peace Society, and abolish the great standing armies which rest like horrid nightmares on the nations, and propagate the spirit of cruelty all over the world? Of course, as I knew then, there are noxious creatures that must of necessity be killed, just as there are creatures which ought not to be killed. The difficulty is in drawing a proper line. I was just then puzzled about the fishes I saw in the canal. There were shoals of them sporting near an inflow of fresh water. My idea was to catch some of them, and put them into a pool of clear water in the clough, and watch them until they got bigger. By tying worms to the end of long rushes I caught scores of them, and turned them into the large pools. To my disappointment they never got any larger. Well for them they did not, or they might have been caught, cooked and eaten. Finding that fishes eat one another, Franklin decided it would be right for him to eat them. This decision was urged on me by a lady when, after becoming a vegetarian, I was dining at her table on which were placed some fine, well-cooked fish, of which I declined to partake. I ventured to remark that Franklin's logic was limping. For did it not follow that if we must imitate fishes that eat each other—that then human beings must eat each other. I regretted having made the remark, as it seemed to have interfered with the relish of some of the party in the eating of, to them, a good dinner.

To my great but unavailing sorrow, my rural and free life once more came to a close. The awful factory imprisonment was looming before me, and so I had to say a sad farewell to my familiar birds, fishes, rabbits, rats, and stoats; to the trees, wild flowers, and green fields; and to the much-loved brook running from one end of the clough to the other end, sparkling and making music all the way.

Soon the fatal morning arrived, when at six o'clock I entered the bottom room of the middle factory in Hurdsfield Road. If I had read over the entrance door the words "Abandon hope all ye who enter here," I could not have felt a more intense despair. Taking me to the end of a side of swifts, the Steward, Mr. J. B., said, "Start here, and let us see what thou canst do." For a time my fingers trembled so much I could hardly do anything at all. "Humph!" exclaimed he to the Danter; he is not up to much." "Let him alone a bit; he is frightened," said the Danter. When he came again I had eight or ten swifts going round. "Set him a dozen," said the Steward. Next day, seeing all the swifts going, "H'm!" he exclaimed, "set him twenty swifts." In a few weeks he said to the Danter, "Oh, he'll do now; let him have twenty-five." The silk being inferior Bengal, that number of swifts was very difficult to manage, even by much older hands than myself, and the strain upon me from day to day was very great and very exhausting. My hours of work were from six o'clock in the morning until eight o'clock at night, with one hour and forty minutes allowed for breakfast, dinner, and tea; and my wages were one shilling and sixpence a week.

Had the half-time system been in existence then as now, as I have before remarked, my health might have been preserved and my education secured. But factory emancipation had not come, and this crushing slavery had to be endured. Hence my appetite failed, never to be fully regained; the ruddy colour left my face never to return; and chronic weakness took possession of my limbs, and retarded growth. But for the influence of the Sunday school, I think my health would have utterly broken down. The Sunday's lessons, and hymns, and prayers filled and uplifted my mind all through the week, and helped me to endure my long, arduous, and depressing work.

Just at this time there was a sensation in the school, and indeed throughout the township. This arose from the performance of the drama of "Daniel in the Lion's Den." Having to recite a psalm, I had a place on the large platform, and watched the various movements of the actors with wonder and awe. First there came marching along the platform a crowd of princes, clad in eastern robes. This procession included Benjamin Hammersley, James Moss, Joseph Davenport, John Clarke, and John Sutton. A very earnest discussion was going on in this company about a decree which had been signed by the king, and about the breach of the decree by Daniel the Jew. Then appeared King Darius himself, clad in a scarlet robe and with a glittering crown on his head, and took his seat upon an extemporised throne. This was Josiah Moss, who demeaned himself with so much majesty and dignity that it was declared that he seemed every inch a king. Immediately was seen the fine tall form of Thomas Newton, personating Daniel the Jew. Having been condemned to the lions' den, he was hurried into a dark hole at the end of the platform, and there shut up. After a troubled sleep, the king approached the den and exclaimed " O, Daniel, is thy God able to deliver thee from the lions!" and then in the complete hush of the audience came in loud sonorous tones the reply which rang through the whole building, " O king, live for ever: God hath sent His angel and hath shut the lions' mouths, that they hath not hurt me." This drew loud cheers from the audience. And then came the most fearful scene of all. The princes with their wives and children were all seized and dragged over the platform, and hurled pell-mell into the den of lions amidst the thunderous applause of the whole audience.

In these latter days when entertainments, with dialogues and dramas, go on incessantly at all our schools and churches, such a performance as that of Daniel in the lions' den would secure little notice, and less discussion. In those days the whole thing was a great novelty, and led to much conversation in the homes and workshops throughout the township. The far greater part of those present were quite delighted with the entertainment, and wished for more of the kind. Some of the more pious people said the Bible in such cases was treated with worldly familiarity and frivolity. Others said it was an excellent means of making the Bible understood. A few others expressed their scepticism as to the biblical facts of the case. How could an angel get to the lions, and in what way, they asked, could he stop their mouths? And if the angel saved the life of Daniel because he was an innocent man, why did he not save the wives and children of the princes for the same reason? These infidel surmises—as they were designated—were replied to by the authorities of the school, who said, "God moves in a mysterious way His wonders to perform." The wondrous works must be reverentially believed and the mysterious devoutly let alone. To doubt the Bible—which was God's own word—was exceedingly sinful, and would prevent the salvation of the soul. This settled the whole question, and shut the mouths of all objectors as effectually as the angel closed the mouths of the lions.

At the end of twelve months of my dangerous slavery, and notwithstanding continuously failing health, my wages were advanced to two shillings and sixpence a week, which sum was a great boon to my mother in her management of the home. Besides, I got now and then a penny as striving money. The first sixpence of this money I spent at a Barnaby fair in the following memorable way. Passing a bookstall on the market place, my eyes were fixed on a small book entitled "The Farmer's Boy," by Robert Bloomfield. Nervously I opened the book, was fascinated with what I read, and asked the price. "One shilling and threepence," said the man, and I walked sorrowfully away. The fair had no further interest for me, and I went in search of a companion who I knew had more money to spend than I had. Having at length found him and stated the case, he went with me to the stall and was pleased with the book. He would put fivepence to my fivepence (I had spent one penny) if the man would sell the book for that amount. "Here, take the book," said the man, "which at tenpence is dirt cheap." I bore away the book in triumph, but my companion was not so joyous as myself. I therefore promised to pay one penny weekly for five weeks, which

I did, and so made the book my own. My constant reading of the book intensified my craving for rural life, and I tearfully urged my parents to get me a place of work on some neighbouring farm. They, however, did not take a poetic view of the matter, and refused my request. The book served to brighten my hard factory life, and awakened hopes of deliverance from my drudgery in the time to come. Even now that deliverance was drawing near.

Before the end of the year, I was removed from the lowest to the highest room in the mill. This was a translation from darkness to light. An Elijah soaring in a brilliant chariot to heaven could hardly have felt a greater ecstasy than I felt on this occasion. The terrible piecing at swifts I had left for ever. Piecing at the cleaner frames I found easy and pleasant. Through a window near me I could see Paddlers' Wood, which was another clough scene to interest me; while far beyond I had glimpses of the Ecton range of hills, the Beulah mountains of my childhood days. My health began to improve, my spirits to rise, and my desire for knowledge to increase. I carried about with me as many small magazines and books as my pockets would hold. Reading was forbidden in the mill, but I must confess I continually broke the rule.

The first reading in my new situation was a missionary story, illustrated by a striking picture. Sitting in his house in an Indian jungle, a missionary saw a tiger enter the door, opposite which was a large mirror. Seeing, as it thought, another tiger, it dashed into the mirror, the crash of which so frightened it that it fled from the spot. The missionary affirmed this to be a great providential deliverance for himself. This I joyously believed, for had not even I experienced a great providential deliverance also. "But if the glass had not been there," asked a critical youth, "would not the tiger have killed the man?" "That question," I said, "did not apply, as that mirror was part of the providential arrangement for saving the missionary's life." This silenced the objector and satisfied myself.

CHAPTER III

THE MYSTICS — SUNDAY SCHOOL

To my few literary treasures at this time was added a book which perplexed me more than it interested me.

At the Sunday school annual prize-giving, I was presented with " The Imitation of Christ," by Thomas à Kempis. How it came to pass that such a book should have been given to a lad, hardly eleven years of age, was a puzzle both to myself and others. My teacher said it must have been intended for some older person, and given to me in mistake. The superintendent said there was no mistake. I had merited a good book, and I had got one. If I could not appreciate it at present, I should later on in life. These statements excited my curiosity, and led me to make many inquiries. Certain passages in the book clearly taught, I was told, the doctrine of Transubstantiation, or the real presence. That was ominous. The author, I ascertained, was a monk of the middle ages. That was more ominous. He spent seventy years, I learned, in a monastery, which seemed a wasted life. I was advised by wise preceptors to let the book alone, and for a time I did. Eventually, on hearing Kempis described as a Mystic, my curiosity was again excited, and I sought to know who and what the Mystics were. Hence ensued a protracted, but interesting research. A sufficiently comprehensive definition was difficult to get. Suidas derived Mysticism from the root *mu*, to close, and so the mouth of the Mystic must be closed while the soul was absorbed in lofty thoughts. The root *mu* with the letter "m" added forms the ordinary word "mum," which means silence. The Mystics, then, should inculcate and practise silence in order to aid the development of deep spiritual thought, but Carlyle inculcated silence in unlimited talk, and many of the Mystics pursued exactly the same course. This definition being too narrow, had to be widened in the following way. There were first the Intransitive or passive Mystics, and second, the Transitive or active Mystics. To this there needed to be added the statement that the same individual might be both an Intransitive and a Transitive Mystic, as, for instance, St. Bernard, who was Intransitive in the cloister and Transitive in preaching and travelling.

Ensuing investigation led to an acquaintance with many of the most remarkable individuals that ever existed, I thought, on the face of the earth. Living in all historic ages, and belonging to all religions, they wielded with great skill a persistent and dominating force. For good or ill they ever went on conquering and to conquer. Only brief glimpses of a few of these all-potent personages must be given here. He of the golden maxims—Pythagoras—may lead the way. His Esoteric circle of disciples constituted a religious brotherhood and a philosophical school. All initiates had to observe silence for a protracted period, and learn how to think. They discarded all flesh meat from their daily food, and lived strictly virtuous and studious and useful lives. A similar course of life was pursued by the Essenes. All flesh meats were banished from their communities, and they refused to attend any temple worship where bloody sacrifices were offered up. They cultivated the ground, and lived on the fruits thereof. Daily they attended to bathing, to contemplation, and to prayer. Thus a mystical enthusiasm was created which made their worship intensely devout. How fitting that John the Baptist and Jesus Christ should have come under the influence of the Essenes, as in all probability they did. The fine enthusiasm of these communistic Jews entering into Christianity at its beginning imparted to it an irresistible impulse and fascinating charm, but, turning into fiery fanaticism, it seized and has ruled the Churches through all the Christian ages with the most dire effect.

In our eager pursuit of the Mystics we could not help discovering those daring and wise men of the East, the Gnostics. These audacious, but inseeing, men rushed headlong into investigations and speculations about everything in heaven, earth, and hell. As the Pneumatikoi—the Initiated—the Inspired—they discovered, or thought they discovered, the mysteries lying beneath the letter of religious records. In their researches concerning the Infinite Being, they discovered the Aeons, the mediums between God and men, Jesus Christ being the chief of them. Their free treatment of the Biblical writings makes the higher criticism of these days seem feeble and insignificant in the extreme. Marcion set aside the whole of the Old Testament as having no binding force. Some of his disciples treated the New Testament books in much the same way, denying that they formed an authoritative code. But they were not only exclusive, but also adoptive in their treatment of religious books. Amongst the books selected for religious guidance were Prophecies by Cain, Psalms by Valentinus, Hymns by Marcos, and books of Enoch, Moseh, and Eliah. Very rash and arbitrary were such proceedings, no doubt, and yet not much more unreasonable than the orthodox treatment of the Scriptures in these reformation days. If modern orthodox theologians do not set the books of Scripture aside, they read into them their dogmas, confessions, and creeds, making a non-understandable mixture of Scripture and creed. Happily now, as in the days of the Gnostics, may be found many in the Churches who endeavour to live—not by the letter—but by the spirit of sacred books.

The Hindoo Mystics, we found, treated the Vedas in the same free and fearless way. When the literalisms and ceremonialisms of the sacred books hindered their spiritual aspirations, they decisively swept the impediments out of the way. Cleared of ancient literary baggage, they soared on beatific visions, and realised Eternity in Time. The songs and conversations of celestial choirs were heard, and their touches felt, they thought, as they passed through the air, and thus it would seem as if modern Spiritualism were ancient Hindooism writ large. The Neo-Platonist Mystics apprehended the Infinite in Ecstasy, as did our hero, Thomas à Kempis himself. In this state the Divine Essence was communicated to the devotee when he was no longer finite and earthly. Very much like this must have been the experience of the Mystic apostle Paul when he was " caught up into the third heaven into paradise," and " heard unspeakable words." As the best result of this heavenward ascent, Paul became a more able minister, " not of the letter, which killeth, but of the spirit, which giveth life."

That many of the successors of the apostle Paul in these days have had any such grand lifting heavenward, followed by such noble earthly work, we very much doubt. Chained to their gilded palaces; enthralled by courtly circles; holding fast to the nation's gold; clutching the children of the National Schools, and harnessing them to the Church's chariot wheels, how can Bishops, Cardinals, and Popes, have any mystic uplifting towards the heavenly spheres? Archimedes said that with a lever long enough he could lift the world, but how long and strong a lever would be required to lift our modern ecclesiastics to the third heaven?—and if let down to earth again, would each one become, like Paul, an able minister, " not of the letter, which kills, but of the spirit, which giveth life "? To these serious problems can any useful solution be found?

Our quest could not fail to lead us toward the Arabian desert and to the mountains of Hira, and to Mecca's cave where the prophet of Islam fasted, meditated, and prayed. Like all other Mystics, Mohammed heard divine voices speaking to him. As a special communicant he had the angel Gabriel himself. Somewhat of these revelations we find in the Koran, which contains an interesting series of romances, fables, and facts. Inspired imagination had free play in this book, as in the Bible and other sacred records. Under the momentum of these inspired words, Islam made rapid and overwhelming conquests. Of course, it was mightily aided by the sword, as was Judaism and Christianity. The blight of slavery has stuck to its garments, as was the case with Christianity. Both religions have inculcated fasting, praying, and abstaining from intoxicating drink. But while Moslems have remained almost entirely sober, Christians have largely taken to getting drunk.

As an antidote to the Mysticism of the middle and dark ages, Abelard confronted it with Scholasticism. With the most fiery fanaticism St. Bernard fell upon Abelard and vanquished him. "Search for the truth and teach it," said Abelard. "Faith believes but does not discuss," said St. Bernard. The result of the conflict was speedy and decisive. Abelard and his disciples had to hide their diminished heads. St. Bernard commanded the homage of kings, emperors, and popes. He founded churches, cathedrals, and monastic citadels. With fiery zeal he preached the great crusade, which led to numberless multitudes of armed men being hurled against the walls of Jerusalem and Jericho; which, however, did not fall down at the sound of trumpets, but formed a rampart of defence for the Moslems, while they vanquished and ultimately destroyed the crusading hosts.

But could not Mysticism and Scholasticism unite? Then truth and justice might have a hearing and, possibly, prevail. But was there any precedent of the kind to be found? Yea, certainly, in Socrates himself, who was the most complete embodiment of Mysticism and Rationalism the world has ever known. Consecrated by Delphic Oracles, attended by a spiritual guide, and heralded by heavenly voices, he entered on his great life work. Injustice was exposed, and righteousness set forth. The false syllogisms of the Sophists were shattered; hollow forms, empty ceremonies, and pretentious hypocrisies, laid bare: while, at the same time, the plain and simple truth of things was made to beam forth in splendour on the minds of men. But the pride of the ruling classes of Athens being peaked, their vested interests being endangered, and their power shaken, they doomed their greatest citizen to an ignominious death; which he met with unfaltering and sublime repose. Reversing the aphorism of Rousseau, we would declare that, while Jesus Christ died like a martyr, Socrates died like a god. Erasmus tried to follow the noble example of Socrates, but signally failed. To his Monastic mysticism he joined on the learning of the school men. He wished, sincerely enough, to reform the Roman Catholic Church, and indeed, laid the egg which Luther hatched. But he could not approve nor tolerate the daring rashness of Luther himself. Nor could Luther tolerate the hesitating speech, laboured disquisitions, and humorous satires in which Erasmus indulged. He plainly charged Erasmus with timidity and hypocrisy. To which Erasmus replied, that he had no inclination to die for the sake of truth. The career of the distinguished Mystic and scholar, Lamennais, was pursued on the same line as that of Erasmus, only with greater vigour and decision. In his early priestly fervour he became the foremost champion of the Church. Scholars, Bishops, and the Pope vied with each other in rendering him homage. A Cardinal's hat was offered him, which he refused to accept because, just then, he was beginning to get glimpses of the other side of things. Ultimately, he became revolutionary in his speech and writings. From being familiar with the interior of pictured palaces, he was doomed to become familiar with the inside of bare prison walls. "His Ecclesiastical career," it has been said, "was ruined because he had not the power, the negative capability, of shutting one of his eyes."

In Tauler we found a pantheistic mystic. "In Regeneration," said he, "God pours Himself into the soul as the sun into the air." The finite soul and the Infinite soul thus become one. A glorious thought, if it only admitted the individuality of the finite soul. The sentiment has pervaded many a rapturous hymn. Thus we read:—

> "With faith I plunge me in this sea (of the infinite being),
> Here is my hope, my joy, my rest."

And again:—

> "O Love, thou bottomless abyss!
> My sins are swallowed up in Thee."

An accommodating idea, but a questionable sentiment.

Tauler's idea of the soul's absorption in God is more clearly and more completely stated by the leading Persian Mystic, who says:—

> "All sects but multiply the I and Thou;
> The I and Thou belong to partial being;
> When I and Thou and several beings vanish,
> Then Mosque and Church shall bind thee nevermore.
> Our individual life is but a phantom,
> Make clear thine eye and see reality."

From Mystics militant, Mystics scholastic, and Mystics pantheistic and nihilistic, we turned to the Mystic pure and simple. Thomas à Kempis was the prince of all the Mystics. In a small convent in Cologne Province, he spent nearly the whole of his life of ninety years. "He was a little fresh-coloured man, near-sighted, with soft brown eyes, who never needed spectacles to the day of his death; short of stature, with a slight stoop. In chanting psalms he always looked upward, and rose and fell on his tip-toes. He never mingled with the world, knew no trouble (?) as we should say, loved little books and quiet nooks all his days, and used to steal away from the profitless talk of the monks."

In the quiet convent cell he noted down his most cherished thoughts, which have gone out through all the world. "It were good," he said, "to have good morning resolutions and evening examinations." No doubt he had read the golden lines of Pythagorus. But he gave impulse to the excellent precepts found there, and secured for them a wide acceptance attended by practical effect.

"Martyrs should be venerated," said he. But why the great dominant churches of Christendom should have been everlastingly engaged in making martyrs of the adherents of less dominant churches, our preceptor deponeth not. "The vanities of the world pass away," says our ascetic monk. But what about the vanities of the churches?—they go on for ever. In one endless procession they proceed through all the ages. "Let not Moses nor any prophet speak to me; but Thou, Lord, which inspirest all the prophets, speak Thou to me." Very finely said, O solitary monk! But the declaration places thee amongst the noble army of heretics who have ever been the salt of the earth. This sentiment approaches the higher criticism of to-day which enjoins the prophet to guide but not domineer; to advise but not enslave; to break the manacles which the churches have placed on the minds and bodies of men, and lead them to direct and free communion with God. Collecting the wisdom of the Mystic sages of the past, Thomas à Kempis transmitted it in a concentrated form to the Mystic sages of later days. From ancient dreamers beside Asian rivers—from monkish caves near the Egyptian Nile—from the oracles of God beside which fast flowed Siloam's brook—from Parnassus and Ilyssus, where poets sung the songs of all time, and philosophers enunciated the mighty thoughts which still move the world—and from the hermits' cells on Tiber's banks—came like a mighty rushing wind the mystic emotion which, flooding the mind of our sage and saint, formed the grand reservoir of sacred fervour and divine inspiration named "The Imitation of Christ." Overflowing thence, this holy afflatus entered the mind of Benedict Spinosa, making him "a God-intoxicated man." Striking the mind of Descartes, it enabled him to discover that when all prepossessions, alien accretions, imposed superstitions, and rubbish of all kinds were swept from the inner being of man, the intuition of God was written in characters of unfading light upon the soul. Under this influence, the Quietists and Quakers experienced a profound repose. In the same way the Moravian Brethren felt the witness of the Spirit, and were delivered from the bondage of sin and the fear of death. Sweeping through the minds of the Wesleys, this Holy Ghost woke up the dormant churches of Christendom, impelling their members to become missionaries of mercy and salvation to mankind—or, to become fiery fanatics ready to persecute such of their brethren as were led to differ from them a few hairbreadths in their dogmatic creeds. But the grandest effect of this divine overflow of the Mystic spirit was seen when it flooded the mind of Emerson, and enabled him to see into the deepest depths of spiritual existence and to declare that:—

> "Out of the heart of nature rolled
> The burdens of the bibles old;
> Like the volcano's tongue of flame
> The litanies of nations came."

Thus it came to pass that the puzzle-prize book of my early days led me into a long-continued course of interesting and important investigation. Trying to understand the Mystics, I ever approached the "Beyond man of Nietzsche." Or with John Pulsford I got into the region "Back of Theology," and felt with him that "one throb of God's life will do more for the soul than all the theology which the human brain has coined since the world began."

From twelve to fourteen years of age, my impressions at the Sunday School became unusually bright and vivid. Mr. Matthew Moss became, at this time, a teacher of the first class, and introduced a greatly-improved method of reading. Instead of carelessly gabbling out the words, we had to read deliberately, minding stops, accents, emphases, and pronunciations. Some of us took great delight in this new exercise, and made considerable improvement in our reading. This is just the improvement needed in our public day-schools at the present time. Shouting out words together in a great hubbub completely prevents natural, distinct, and sensible reading. Our teacher urged the importance of learning English Grammar, and some twenty-five lads formed a class and met together one night a week in the school. The time was from nine to ten o'clock in the evening, the long hours of work not permitting us to meet until so late at night. Lennie's Grammar, one-and-sixpence a copy, was fixed upon, and each scholar paid one penny a week until the purchase was complete. But oh! the sorrows of some of us, and the amusement of others in pronouncing definitions and making out the meaning of terms. Orthography, Etymology, Syntax, and Prosody, were the most puzzling and frightful words we had ever seen. Peter Mackenzie, when at the Methodist College, objected to his Grammar book because it was so unscriptural as not to mention even the name of the Lord Jesus Christ. Certainly we had not met with these strange technical terms in the Bible or we should have sooner grasped their peculiar meanings. Some of the learners attacked these bulwarks of words bravely and perseveringly, and fairly triumphed over them. Others failed and succumbed, and were never seen in the Grammar Class more. Our teacher obtained " Walker's Themes," and was sanguine enough—mistaken man —to think that a few country lads could make anything of such erudite things. " Man is Mortal " was the first theme treated. But the meaning was so obvious that when the terms were defined what more could be said? In several cases, after many severe mental throes, the essays were strangled at birth and never saw the light. Other essays were puny things, and brief life was here their portion. The whole undertaking was mortal without any possibility of immortality beyond. Walker's Pronouncing Dictionary was next secured, and was thought a very wonderful book indeed. During school hours it was incessantly used, and led to much investigation and discussion. This, again, paved the way to Phonography, which some of us rushed to learn on its first introduction by Mr. Pitman and other lecturers into the town. With still greater eagerness later on I, for one, went in for the adoption of Phonotypy and became a member of the Spelling League (Speling Leeg). Notwithstanding the adherence and advocacy of many eminent Philologists—including Max Muller—I regret to say that on the death of Mr. Pitman and Mr. Reed the League became defunct. It is, however, so great a necessity, that its day of success and triumph is sure to come.

Some of the disciplinary methods adopted by the managers

of the Sunday School were of an original and very peculiar kind. One of the rules enjoined that each scholar must come to school clean, washed, and combed at half-past nine o'clock in the morning, and at half-past one o'clock at noon. Finding it next to impossible to get this rule observed by persuasion, the following expedient was adopted: a rather high stool was fixed in the middle of the school, on which was placed a large bowl of water, with soap and a towel. The dirtiest boy and the dirtiest girl in the school were selected, and compelled to wash their hands and faces with all the scholars looking on. This caused a great sensation, and made a profound impression. It, however, rid the school, for the time being, of dirty hands and faces, and uncombed heads. On a certain Sunday, about the same time, news came to the school that football playing was going on in a field adjacent, and that some of the scholars were amongst the players. On the instant an expeditionary force was formed, when the ball was captured and hung up in the front of the gallery, where it remained for many months. The captured culprits were seriously lectured as they stood by themselves in the school, and a solemn warning against Sabbath breaking was given to all present. Another mode of punishment adopted, if somewhat severe, was certainly effective. An old stern man, who employed a number of asses in carrying coal, was appointed monitor in the boys' room containing two hundred scholars. He paced the room from end to end with a stout staff in his hand. Espying an unruly scholar defying his teacher and disturbing the class, he slipped quietly behind him, and applying his staff, the sounds whak! whak! whak! resounded all around, producing perfect quietness and attention throughout the school. Of course, some did not like this mode of operation, and complained, and wrote and posted skits about the old man's asses in the school as compared to his asses outside the school. The wit of these productions was too poor to find place in any permanent record of such kind of curious and humorous literature. Certainly there was no approach to such exquisite fooling as that recorded of Professor Blackie and his asses. After a vacation, the Professor posted a notice on the school door stating that on a certain day and hour he would meet his classes. A waggish student rubbed out the first letter, making it read "lasses." Seeing this, the Professor rubbed out the next letter, making the notice state that he would, at the given time, meet his "asses." It is to be hoped no one will attempt to spoil this story by questioning its substantial truth. Certainly the Professor would have enjoyed the erasures with the greatest relish, and the students would have done the same.

One Sunday the class was surprised by the entrance of a well-dressed, stout-looking, full-bearded, rather wild-looking gentleman, who had asked permission to come in and speak to the teacher and scholars. He proved to be a follower of Joanna Southcott, and talked about her dreams and visions and her mission and authority to the churches and peoples of Christendom, which had all wandered wildly and fatally away from truth and Christ and God. We had heard nothing of the kind before, and did not know what to make of it. After considerable controversy with our teacher, the man closed his remarks by propounding the following conundrum: "Is truth the most ancient or the ancient the most true?" The teacher did not see much wisdom or use in the question, but thought it might lead to useless quibbles. The discussion did, however, lead to serious cogitations on the part of one or more present as to truth in religion, and as to how and where it might be most surely found. As to Joanna Southcott herself, we found she was a lady who firmly declared and whose numerous followers firmly believed that she was on the point of giving birth to the Prince of Peace. Great was the disappointment when it was found that a dropsy was all she produced.

CHAPTER IV.

WAGES — BOOKS — RELIGION

AT thirteen years of age I was promoted to the spinning mills, when my wage was increased to six shillings a week, one shilling of which I had to myself. Sixpence went for books and collections, and sixpence went into my savings-box. This economic habit I formed in early life, and have continued it ever since. Hence the independence of my later days, very modest indeed, but adequate to my very limited wants.

Not many of my associates in the mills cared for books, or schools, or chapel, and hence my intimate friends were few. One of these, David Clayton, was a true, helpful and fast friend during many years. He was a fine, strong-built youth, taller than myself, and two years older. With a good memory and fine voice, he always distinguished himself at entertainments as the best reciter in the school. He lived in an ivy-covered house in Swanscoe Park. On fine Sunday mornings I went to meet him on his way to the school, and very pleasant and improving was our intercourse as we walked along the verdant fields and rural lanes. He frequently quoted Shakespeare, and I sometimes quoted Cowper, Thomson and Bloomfield, and very happy times we had. On a certain Sunday morning I found him absorbed in a volume of a new encyclopædia which someone had lent him. This great work, said David, included all knowledge, and I must join him in reading and studying it. On the way to school we had much tall talk on the subject, and freely indulged in dazzling dreams of our future conquests in the realms of universal knowledge. But alas! these glittering castles in the air soon tumbled into ruins. Inside the school itself influences were at work which brought my dear friend great trouble and checked his studious pursuits. A good-looking, amiable, virtuous maiden was in regular attendance at the school, to whom David became warmly attached, but who did not favour his suit. Many of his messages to her he sent by me, which I duly delivered. Suddenly, however, this process of communication came to an end. When—as Longfellow tells us—the maiden Priscilla received an offer of marriage from Miles Standish, delivered by John Alden, she " Said, in a tremulous voice, ' Why don't you speak for yourself, John?' " Just similar was the question put to me the last time I delivered a message from David to the maiden at the Sunday School. I was amazed and dumbfounded, while David received a shock from which he did not soon recover. For some months he absented himself from school, but at length he returned and our studies went on as before. Early in my sixteenth year, I was surprised and pleased when informed that I had been placed in charge of the Library in the Sunday School. I found nearly two hundred volumes on the book shelves, all of which I determined to read. One book at once arrested my attention, and kept it a considerable time. I had seen quotations from Homer's Iliad, but had never before seen the book. I plunged straight into it, and revelled in its exciting stories of gods, goddesses, and heroic men with great delight. David Clayton devoured the book as ravenously as myself. For some time Shakespeare's characters faded from the view. Cowper, Thomson and Bloomfield were thrust into the shade. With Menelaus we greatly sympathised, but Paris and Helen we severely condemned. The nod of Jove was awful, and the dignified mien of Juno magnificent. We loved Ulysses and returned the frown of Achilles as he sulked in his tent door. Ajax we admired for his prowess; but our greatest affection was for Hector and Andromache. Homer's vivid descriptions of these two fine characters friend David never ceased to recite. Their names were ever vocal in fields, woodlands, and highways. Hearing somewhat of the stir which the book was making in the school, the authorities looked into it, disapproved of it, and condemned it. "How did such an objectionable book get into the Library?" inquired the censors. I simply replied that I found it there. "But how could you commend a book containing tales about gods and goddesses and their wicked intrigues with men and women on earth?" they again inquired. I humbly hinted that the Bible itself told of the visits of spiritual beings to the earth. "But, surely you know," said they, "that the Bible is sacred and the Iliad profane." That settled the question. The book disappeared from the Library, but not its contents from our minds, nor the determination to read it again when the opportunity came. Another book in the Library which caused me much trouble was George Combe's "Constitution of Man." The author, said the censors, wrote too much about the laws of Nature, and too little about the laws of God, which was disrespectful to the Creator and Ruler of all things. The statement in the book that in a wreck at sea the most moral man would as soon drown as the least moral, they said, was rank heresy. "Someone in the school," they continued, "had said that a Missionary would sink as fast in a wreck at sea as a heathen, a heretic, or a sceptic." This, it was contended, was an impious statement, and I was to be blamed for recommending a book which led to such dangerous discussions.

In closing the controversy, the censors summoned forth Cowper, the poet, to vanquish Combe, the philosopher, by means of his poem beginning with these lines:—

> "God moves in a mysterious way
> His wonders to perform:
> He plants His footsteps in the sea
> And rides upon the storm."

The most popular book in the Library was Pollok's "Course of Time," the central figure of which is the worm that never dies. In the description of this worm of hell there is presented one of the most awful and revolting pictures ever conceived in the mind of man. This enormous monster has a horrid convolution of tails each tipped with a frightful sting, and in the midst of this awful coil is seen a swollen, bleeding, quivering human heart. And yet this shocking thing was a favourite theme for lessons in the class and addresses in the pulpit. That it might be an aid to conversion, as affirmed, I have no doubt. A guilty soul made afraid of death and hell might be converted to anything that would save him from the fearful doom thus set forth.

Having gained access to the Library of the Useful Knowledge Society, I soon became deeply interested in many of the books I found there. The first book I obtained was " Consolations of Travel, or the Last Days of a Philosopher," by Sir Humphry Davy. Here I found topography, history, science, and general literature finely blended together in the form of dialogues by certain learned men. Seeing me in possession of this book, a member of the Committee commenced the following conversation:—

C.—Do you read philosophical books of this kind?

R.—I have read this particular book.

C.—Do you understand it?

R.—Yes, for the most part.

C.—What particular subject in the book has interested and impressed you most?

R.—The vision which the author had when sitting amid the ruins of the Coliseum at Rome.

C.—What shape does the vision take?

R.—In the first place there is presented a splendid panoramic view of the procession of the numerous races and nations of men which gradually became absorbed into the great Roman Empire of the past. In the second place we are presented with a view of the author's imaginary brilliant flight through the stellar regions, in which he passes from planet to planet and from comet to comet, until he arrives at glorious regions where seraphic beings—who were once denizens of earth—are now living in indescribable splendour and bliss.

C.—But surely the author presents something more tangible and useful than dazzling visions like that?

R.—O yes, the reader is taken on a delightful excursion through the wide and glorious realms of science, during which the author dwells at great length on the wonders of the science of Chemistry, which is the queen of all the sciences known.

C.—But, seeing that you work in the factory from early morning until late at night, how do you find time for reading books like this?

R.—By rising at four o'clock in the morning in summer, and at five o'clock in winter, and sitting up two hours before midnight I secure three to four hours each day for reading and making notes of what I read.

Soon after this conversation, although so young in years, I was appointed by the Committee to teach a class in the Institution, which I did on two nights a week during fourteen years, with much benefit to myself as well as to others.

Even in the mill amongst the spindles my books were continually the means of bringing me to account. My library there, consisting of magazines and a few other volumes, was under a large revolving box, called a drum. Great was my consternation on one occasion to see the Steward (Mr. B.) rummaging amongst these books, and reading in some of them. "What is this lot?" he asked rather sternly. "I read a little during breakfast and tea," I said. "It is against the rule," he said, and walked away. A day or two later when I was helping him in the stove-room, he suddenly said, "Have you read the volume of 'Rollin's Ancient History,' which I saw under the drum?" "Most of it I have read." "Do you believe what you have read?" I was puzzled, and replied, "Yes, in a general way." "The story of Romulus and Remus being fed by a wolf and a woodpecker, for instance?" "Well," I replied, "we read in the Bible of Elijah being fed by ravens, and one account may be as true as the other." Smiling, he replied, "But a Bible fable cannot prove another fable to be true. An English statesman," he continued, "spoke of the large array of historic volumes on his shelves as his 'ancient and modern liars.'" To some extent historic works are liars, as I found later on. I began to think it was very difficult indeed to get the exact truth in any narrative, or in anything else.

In referring on one occasion to " Paley's Natural Theology," the Steward said the very title of the book was a misnomer. " Nature had no theology in it. Priestly parties had made up a deleterious mixture of their own conjectures, and tried to stick it into nature, or fasten it, at all hazards, on nature. But it was a defacement of nature, or an excrescence on nature, making ugliness where only beauty should be. As to that story," he continued, " about an unmoved stone on Salisbury Plain, it was quite ridiculous. Had not the stone been spinning round daily with the earth moving on its axis? And had it not, at the same time, gone in a mighty sweep with the earth in its orbit round the sun? The story about the watch had no cogency nor any direct bearing on the point in view. When a watch was shown to a savage islander who had never seen one before, he inquired if it was to eat. On hearing the tick, he was frightened, and dashed it on the ground, saying it was alive and dangerous. Mankind had no more knowledge of a great Designer of the Universe, whom they had never seen, than the islander who had never seen the maker of a watch." "There," I said, " you trench on the argument between Aristodemus and Socrates. Said the former to the latter, ' We never see the gods at work in the world around us.' ' Neither,' said Socrates, ' dost thou ever see thine own mind, which, however, guides and directs all the movements of thine own body.'" To this my opponent made no reply, and hence I concluded I had the best of the argument.

Although often perplexed and sometimes hurt by statements made during these continued discussions, yet I could not but respect the man who made them. Like myself, he had been trained in Methodism, from which, after much reading and study he had advanced into utter scepticism. He was evidently sincere and honest in his professed convictions, and his life was without reproach. I had frequently heard preachers very earnestly declare that unbelief was a clear proof of mental and moral obliquity. But clearly it was not so in this case. I afterwards found many cases of sceptics whose lives gave the lie to the sweeping denunciations of the preachers. And now, after much observation, I conclude that the lives of sceptics as well as the lives of heretics in general, will compare advantageously with the lives of professing christians.

Being removed from the mill-room into the warehouse, these interesting discussions came to an end, to the mutual regret of the parties concerned. Although I had obtained what was considered a promotion, my wage was not advanced until the end of the year, when I got seven shillings a week. My mother somehow managed to let me retain two shillings a week. Of this sum I spent sixpence for books and school and chapel collections. Repair of my clothing took another sixpence, while one shilling went into my saving-box, and ultimately into the saving bank. In this way I continued the habit of economy in the use of money and all other things with which I was concerned which has proved of the greatest benefit to me through the whole course of my life.

During my intercourse with Mr. B. of the mill-room, there were frequent references to the writings of Thomas Paine. Since then I had been anxious to obtain some able book written in refutation of Paine's writings. In "A Reply to Paine's Age of Reason," by the Rev. Thomas Scott—with many quotations from Bishop Watson—I got the very thing I wanted. I read the reply again and again, but without much satisfaction. In many cases the quotations from Paine seemed too clear and strong for the two clerical assailants. Paine seemed to be rather refuting the clericals than the clericals refuting him. I began to suspect that the great ecclesiastical guns of the churches were not so formidable as I had been led to suppose. Uneasy fears and doubts began to crowd upon the mind, and I began to ask myself and others what truth was, and where? Sceptical tendencies were, however, effectually checked by events which now occurred.

A revival was just breaking out at Sunderland Street Chapel, where on Sunday I statedly attended. Many young persons were greatly influenced by this movement, and I did not escape. Numbers went to the penitent forms, and got converted there; but I never could be persuaded to act in the same way. The preachers spoke of this kind of reluctance as being the result of pride and obstinacy. Sometimes I felt guilty in this respect, but could not overcome my reluctance. Since then I have concluded that there may be more pride and vanity shown in going to a penitent form than in keeping away from it. The public penitent is the observed of all observers. He has the sympathy of all the congregation present. He has the uttered and unexpressed prayers of a large number of very devout people. If he gets successfully through the process of conversion in this public way, he has the congratulations and caresses and praise of many excellent individuals. If he then joins the society and becomes a member of the inner circle of the church, he is quite a distinguished individual, and finds the entrance to interesting circles which otherwise he would never have been able to approach. Has not then the public penitent much more temptation to pride and vanity than the private penitent? However, under the strong religious influence which prevailed I was induced to join a class which was held in the Sunderland Street Chapel vestry, at eight o'clock, on the Sunday morning. The class consisted of young men exclusively, and was conducted by Dr. Birchenall, one of the most intelligent and devout Methodists in Macclesfield. At the two first meetings I had nothing to do but listen to the experience of others, no question being put to me by the leader. At the third meeting I had quite a shock. "Well, dear brother," said the leader turning to me, "what is the state of your mind?" This question found me entirely dumb. I could not possibly give an intelligent reply, and so I spoke no word. At the next meeting which I attended—rather reluctantly—the question put to me was in another form. "Well, dear brother, have you found peace?" "No, I fear not," I replied. "But you are earnestly seeking peace?" he asked. "Oh yes, I am," I said. "Praise the Lord!" exclaimed the leader, in which the other members joined—to which was added the injunction, "Persevere, dear brother, for they that seek shall find."

Many months passed, and I had no better testimony to give. I daily prayed and wrestled and agonised without any satisfactory result. I read books on conversion, but could not get converted. I listened intently to the expositions of the preachers, but got no light. I had private conversations with experienced Methodists, but found not the desired peace. Every day the question, "What is the state of your mind, brother?" struck me like a gunshot. The question, "Have you yet found peace?" was like an arrow piercing the heart. During the week I kept saying to myself, "Sunday morning is approaching and I have no satisfactory answer to give." Sometimes I went part way to the meeting, and then suddenly turned back. I have got to the very door of the vestry, and then rushed away, and hastened home. Sometimes I resolved to go to class no more until I had some satisfactory testimony to give. Then yielding to persuasion, I attended again, still with the same burden of agony in my soul. In some moods I gave myself up to reasoning on the whole matter. "What is the exact nature of this saving faith I am required to have?" I asked myself. I know well enough what faith in man means. I know what is faith in the existence and attributes of God. I have no difficulty about faith in its ordinary application and acceptance. Where, then, is the difference? And why, if there is a difference, cannot I see it? Or again; if this special and saving faith is the direct gift of God, why is it not given to me who have prayerfully sought for it so long? And what exactly is conversion which is so persistently urged upon me? I have all along, as far back as I can remember, been going through certain processes of mental and emotional change. In throwing off erroneous notions from time to time, I have, surely, become converted. In getting hold of new truths which have greatly influenced my life, I must have undergone a process of conversion. What then is the difference? Where is the distinction between the conversion with which I have always been familiar and this other conversion which I am so earnestly seeking and cannot find?

What, again, is the exact nature of the "witness of the Spirit," about which I have heard so much and waited for so long? I have heard some converts speak of this witness as being obtained by the divine spirit's voice within the soul; while others have spoken of the voice coming through the senses from without. Have we not, say, in the latter class, the case of Saul of Tarsus, whose conversion was effected by voices from heaven? "My reasonings," said my friends, "were carnal, and suggested by the devil for the ruin of my soul."

I am glad to say that through this dark period of my life, I was treated with kindness by the members of the class. The Doctor himself—habitually so serious and solemn—was always patient and forbearing with me. Otherwise, indeed, I should have left the class and given up the conflict. As it was, I was frequently on the verge of doing so. But then, again, would come a rush of solemn thoughts about the everlasting destiny of the soul. Lines and sentiments in the hymn-book which had fastened on my memory in early life came back upon me with overwhelming force. Such sentiments as those in the lines:—

"Will angel bands convey their brother to the bar,
Or devils drag my soul away to meet its sentence there,"

would fall like an avalanche on my mind, and plunge me into conflict and almost despair again.

At length, however, the conflict reached its highest point, the battle culminated, the great crisis came. On an ever-memorable Sunday evening, I was at Sunderland Street Chapel sitting in my usual seat in the gallery in front of the pulpit, when I became entirely absorbed in a very searching sermon preached by the Rev. Alexander Strachan, one of the circuit ministers. His subject was the healing of the man with the withered hand. "When Jesus Christ commanded the man to stretch forth his hand," exclaimed the preacher, "what did the man do? Did he begin to reason with himself, and say 'I cannot do that; it is impossible to do that; I cannot move my arm in the least.' Or did the man reason with Jesus Christ himself, saying 'Why dost thou ask me to do what is impossible? Why dost thou not perform an operation on my withered limb and heal and restore it?' No!" thundered the preacher, " when Jesus Christ exclaimed ' stretch forth thine hand,' he, on the instant, made an effort, stretched forth his hand, and was healed. And thou," continued the preacher, " poor, doubting, reasoning sinner, is what thou at this instant hast got to do. Stretch forth the hand of faith now, and find healing, and rest, and peace to thy diseased and troubled soul." Of the rest of the sermon I knew nothing. I sank into a profound reverie, which passed into ecstasy. In this state of absorption I walked home and into my bedroom. There, in a sort of vision I saw faith materialising. In the form of a hand faith seemed stretching itself from me, through boundless space, passing through brilliant and endless stellar worlds, resting nowhere until it reached the materialised hand of God itself. I felt the effort must certainly prevail, and so it did, as I conceived. The hand of faith was grasped by God's own hand. And then at the same time came a vivid impression of words saying, "Child, what would'st thou?" "That I may be made whole," was my reply. And then— O blessed moment!—in some way came the merciful response, "Be it unto thee even as thou wilt; thy sins, which were many, are all forgiven thee." I rose from my knees, left the house, walked through the field behind the house, along Cliff Lane, on to the top of Ecton, stood for a while beside the altar-stone in the quarry, with the stars shining brilliantly overhead. In these quiet places I communed, prayed, and praised until midnight had come. I felt that the world, the flesh, and the devil were beneath my feet at length. I must now go forth conquering and to conquer sin in every form. New purposes were formed, new plans were laid, and a new and diviner life, I felt, had begun.

In describing the experiences of that memorable Sunday night, I find words utterly fail me. Only by actually passing through a similar process of faith can even a faint conception of such experience be known. In meditating on this event, as I have often done since then, there arises a question as to the *rationale* of such an event, or operation, or experience. In the first place, is the event real? Only such as have never gone through the process can question the reality of such conversion. But was the event only subjectively real? Subjectively real it certainly was, but not subjectively only. Was it then objectively real also? Certainly it was objectively as well as subjectively real. It was my own soul in conscious contact with what Emerson designates the oversoul. I was then knowingly, sublimely, ecstatically, one with the Father of all. But was the event, or experience, or process natural or supernatural? And here comes in the old puzzle—which ought never to have puzzled anyone—as to the distinction between the natural and the supernatural. This distinction I long sought for but never found. For what is there in existence not included in the natural? The physical is natural, and the spiritual is natural. Matter is natural, and all the forces of matter are natural. The soul or spirit of man is natural, and consequently the infinite soul or spirit is natural also. What then becomes of the hypothesis of the supernatural, and of the hypothesis of the miraculous? No place is left for either. No reason exists for either. No use remains for either. They vanish, they disappear, oblivion absorbs them. At least such is my own conclusion after long and careful study and research.

What then is the exact *rationale* of the conversion of a soul? Simply this—the discovery by the human soul of its relation to the infinite soul, and the conscious and loving union of the two. From various circumstances, from observation, from meditation, from praise and thanksgiving, and from personal appeal, the soul obtains vivid intimations of the presence of the infinite, feels the drawings of the infinite, and then in rapture clings to the infinite one, and the soul's conversion is complete. From that moment a purer, nobler, more sublime life begins; fed and nourished by the constant aspiration expressed in the words:—

> "Nearer, my God, to Thee,
>   Nearer to Thee!
> E'en though it be a cross
>   That raiseth me;
> Still all my song shall be—
> Nearer, my God, to Thee,
>   Nearer to Thee!"

One result of this new experience was to increase in me an intense spirit of devotion. I had, indeed, from very early days been subject to strong religious emotion. The fervent preacher, if also intelligent and clear, moved me strongly. An earnest and instructive teacher could always impart to me his own enthusiasm. Impressive religious books always awakened strong emotion. But now all these agencies acted upon me with greatly-increased force. Religious fervour seemed as a mantle to enwrap me. Airs from heaven, as blasts from hell, seemed freely to sweep around me. Life, at once became more sweet and solemn, entrancing and awful. And so time passed with me, bearing me nearer heaven along the road passing by the mouth of hell. My attendance at school and chapel was more constant than before.

On Sunday, from 7 to 8 a.m., I was at the prayer meeting at Sunderland Street Chapel. From 8 to 8.45 at Dr. B.'s class in the vestry. From 9.30 to 12 noon at Hurdsfield School. From 1.30 to 4.30 p.m. at the School. From 6 to 8 p.m. at the Old Chapel, and from 8.30 to 9.30 at prayer meetings at different places.

Sometimes in the evening I was very much tired. But what matter to me if I had spent the whole day in feeding the soul on the bread of heaven, and drinking deep draughts from the waters of eternal life.

I was now more eager than ever to read and study eminent books of a devotional kind. Amongst my mother's heirlooms, brought from the little farm under the shadow of Pym Chair, in the Derbyshire range of hills, were Hervey's "Reflections on a Flower Garden," and "Meditations among the Tombs." I had cursorily glanced through both these works previously, but I now read them with care. Little influenced by the Calvinistic dogmas of the author, I was yet strongly influenced by the gloomy and also glowing sentiments the works contained. Pictures of earthly frailty, of heavenly glory, and of hellish gloom seemed painted on my mind. Spiritual imaginations overshadowed my whole being, and, I think, aided me to escape from the snares and follies of youth.

Another of these heirlooms was Baxter's "Dying Thoughts," which also absorbed my mind with solemn imaginations. In prospect of death and eternity, earthly things seemed to fade from the sight of Baxter and to be considered of little account. And under his influence I also became entranced in eternal things, and for the time cared little (too little) for life, or time, or the things of sense.

My attention having been directed to an edition of the whole works of John Wesley, I had an intense desire to possess the lot; but there were fourteen volumes, at four shillings and sixpence each, and it seemed impossible for me to raise the money. I learned, however, that one volume a month could be got from the preacher's book-room at the Allen Houses. I decided at all hazards to secure them in this way, but with a terrible strain on my resources. My wage at this time was ten shillings a week with three shillings and sixpence a week for myself for clothing, books, and collections. In fourteen months the volumes were my own, in the reading and study of which I had an exceeding great reward. The very style of the language came to have a great charm for me. Then how strikingly concise I found most of his statements. No circumlocution, no verbosity, no beating about the bush, could be found in these writings, but short, pointed, direct statement.

The Journals I liked best of all. In ten or twelve lines might be found a comprehensive review of some important book. The very gist of a treatise is sometimes put into half a dozen lines. And what a large number of books he continually read, and on what an amazing variety of subjects! Theology, philosophy, science, politics, domestic economy, physics, and novels were all taken up, studied, mastered, and criticised or corrected and explained. The picture of the great and good man reading books continuously on horseback as he travelled thousands of miles from one preaching station to another was exceedingly interesting and stimulating to me at the time. Then very sweet and touching and confidential indeed, are his letters to his friends. And how keen and trenchant, and cutting—and yet fair—his letters concerning his foes! His letters to friends are such as we would like to cherish as our own; but those to his foes we would rather to be sent to anyone but ourselves. So permeated did I become with the unearthly spirit of Wesley, that I could heartily exclaim with him:—

> "Nothing is worth a thought beneath
> But how I may escape the death
> That never, never dies."

Under this overpowering fervour I seemed qualifying to become an energetic revivalist minister. Not few were the hints and suggestions which I received in that direction from influential parties.

CHAPTER V

THE PEOPLE'S CHARTER

BUT other and powerful worldly influences broke at this time upon the minds of all classes of persons in the United Kingdom. Chartism suddenly burst from the political heaven and kept the country in an excited rush of emotion and action for ten years. At Newport, in Wales, a murderous conflict took place. An immense crowd of Chartists, headed by Frost, Williams, and Jones, resisted the authorities, and a savage battle ensued, when ten persons were killed and hundreds wounded. The three leaders were tried for treason and condemned to death. Happily, they were only imprisoned for a few years, and then set free. The details of this conflict as told by numerous fiery orators roused the whole country to fury. Arming and drilling in Lancashire and Yorkshire were going on daily and universally. Even poor and spiritless Macclesfield was mustering its Chartist forces and drilling them on Eddisbury Hills in full sight of the people in the town. I could not say, as some of my religious brethren said I ought to say, " None of these things move me." These movements did move me very deeply. Our family had suffered much and continuously from dear bread, low wages, and long hours of labour. I could not for the life of me adopt the sentiments of my mother expressed in the words :—

> "The rougher our way, the shorter our stay ;
> No matter what cheer
> We meet with on earth ; for eternity's near."

But why should there not be rewards, when deserved, all along the way? Here were patriotic men leading the Chartist hosts, who earnestly contended that the rewards of labour could and must be obtained. Several of these great leaders were received with great enthusiasm at a large demonstration on Parsonage Green. There was Feargus O'Connor, with his herculean form, majestic head, sandy hair, and splendid voice—though husky with constant use. "Bad governments, bad laws, and bad monopolists," he said, "had reduced the working-men of the United Kingdom to abject slavery. But," continued the fervent orator, "the great revolution is at hand." There must be a run on the savings banks. There must be entire abstention from all excisable articles. There must be a month's holiday for all working-people. The land must be made accessible and available to the lower classes. A monster petition must be signed and a great convention held, and the imperial Parliament compelled to adopt and put into practice the six points of the People's Charter without delay. These statements were received with the wildest enthusiasm by the immense assembly. But, in my judgment, the most keen and pungent and eloquent speech of the meeting was that of the Rev. J. Rayner Stephens, Wesleyan minister. During his discourse he delivered two or three most marvellous perorations, each of which was a compound sentence taking several minutes to speak. The minor sentences fell like sword cuts, or dagger thrusts, or pistol shots. The Prime Minister of the day, with the leading members of both sides of the House of Commons, the Bishops and Clergy generally, the lordly and ducal and squirearchical monopolists of the land, with all slave-driving masters and millionaires, were oratorically cut and slashed and gashed in the most fierce and terrific manner amid thunderous applause. There was one man on the platform whom I was surprised and pleased to see there. To most dwellers in Hurdsfield the form of Mr. John Richards, Schoolmaster of Rainow, was a familiar one. Every Saturday he might be seen walking with steady and measured steps from Rainow, through Hurdsfield, to the town, and in a few hours returning thence in the direction of home.

Usually he had a parcel of books as he went and another parcel of books when he returned. He was rather over middle height, and rather stout of build. He bent forward somewhat in his walk, and moved his legs rather heavily, as if they were touched with rheumatism or neuralgia. His face was of a ruddy colour, his head was large, and round his neck was a white tie, which gave him the appearance of a parson. His clothes were neat and clean, but somewhat seedy. The same dress was evidently worn a long time, being old-fashioned and preserved with scrupulous care. But few persons knew he was a Chartist or that he meddled with politics at all. Yet there on that platform, surrounded by a surging and noisy crowd, stood that modest, quiet, and retiring man, self-possessed and serene. His speech was historical, interesting, and instructive. It showed that he had read and studied the descriptions of the Utopias of the past. The prophecies and dreams of sages, patriots, and martyrs were now, he said, to be fulfilled. A new and real and universal Utopian realm was now to arise, in which men of all classes and races should dwell in prosperity, harmony and peace. The state of things he pictured was as impossible as it was beautiful. And yet such visions had cheered the man's mind through a long life of severe privation. So charmed were several youths at the meeting, including myself, with the elderly Schoolmaster, that we decided to attend his evening school two nights a week. We found him living in a small house, the largest room being used as a day and evening school. The forms and desks were old and rather rickety. The white-washed walls were nearly bare, only a few plain, unframed prints of sages and reformers hanging on them. We got glimpses of a much smaller room as bare and plain as the school-room itself, in which he got his food. If any other people lived in the house, we never saw them. Here the venerable sage spent his obscure but useful life. Only on a very few occasions did he figure in public life, but then with a self-possessed and dignified mien. Some of us were at the time learning recitations for an entertainment at Hurdsfield School, and we wished for him to train us. With upright figure and book in hand, and with a clear and distinct voice he went through the several pieces in a very impressive and instructive manner. We got so weather-beaten as the dark and stormy nights of winter came on, that we were compelled to cease attending the school. For many years he managed somehow to make a living from the income of his poor school. Then the worthy man passed into the eternal silence, noted only by a few who had known him and loved him. But beyond the bourne we are sure he would hear the welcome words, " Good and faithful servant, enter thou into the joy of thy Lord."

The Chartist demonstration was not without strong and lasting effect. Many meetings were held in the town to consider the propositions which, at the larger meeting, had been made. The discussion as to the run on the savings banks was quite ludicrous. No one would own to having any deposits. I had a small amount in the bank, but said nothing about it. But if every penny had been withdrawn from the bank in the town it would not have affected the Government in the least degree. Neither would withdrawals from banks in other towns have touched the Government in the least. The discussion of this subject proved therefore to be a mere farce. As to avoiding excisable articles, that proved a farce, too, for some attending the meetings were smoking their pipes, and others smelt of strong drink. What interested me most at these meetings was the question of the Land, which was earnestly discussed. My father had always the earth-hunger upon him, and so had I. Should I ever be able to possess a few acres of freehold to make into an earthly paradise? This was a question I pondered over frequently and long. Chartist orators and writers contended that a family might be maintained from a few acres of well-cultivated land. But this cannot be done, except on the very richest soil in the very best of weather. Several small estates, however, were secured by the Chartist leaders, and divided into plots of two and three and five acres each. Many of these plots were taken by working men and partially or wholly paid for.

Unfortunately, monetary difficulties arose, and the Land League was broken up, and many hundreds of pounds, paid as purchase money for land by working men, were lost. The monster petition to Parliament was signed by many thousands of townsmen, but many of the signatures were practical jokes. The names of all sorts of odd characters, as well as the names of leading Tories and churchmen, figured on its pages. In London and elsewhere the names of the Queen and members of the Government and of Lord Wellington were found to have been written scores of times on the petition. One-and-a-half millions of signatures were found on the petition, which was so large and heavy that several men were required to carry it into the House of Commons, where it was received with laughter and derision. As to the universal holiday, that was actually some years later carried out. As in other towns, so in Macclesfield, every mill was closed for at least a week. When the mob from Stockport approached the middle factory (Brocklehurst's) the excitement amongst the workpeople inside was intense.

When the leaders thundered at the front doors, I was one appointed to meet them. "Where are the masters?" they inquired. "In the counting house," we replied. "Show us the way in," they said. We took them in, as we had been instructed to do. From the masters they inquired, "Will you turn all the workpeople out of the mill?" "Yes," was the reply. "Will you let us see the engine fires put out?" "Yes, if you do no injury," was the reply. And so out went the fires and out went the workpeople into the streets. My week's holiday was the longest I had ever had, and I enjoyed it intensely. I got far away from the crowds, and with book in hand visited all my favourite haunts on mountain and valley and beside musically-flowing brooks. My appetite increased, and my health greatly improved during that precious holiday-time.

All too soon these emancipation days came to an end, and we were imprisoned again within factory walls. But this great mob movement produced great and good effect, which, however, the mill-owners did not like. The hours of factory labour had already been shortened for women and children. And now very soon came the time for shortening the hours of all workers where machinery was employed. Unfortunately, I had been removed into the warehouse, where no machinery was in use, so that there was no shortening of the time for me. In a few years the shortening of the time reached even the warehouse, and the day's work ended at seven o'clock. On the first evening I rushed past our house and up to the top of the Cliff in frantic joy to see the sun set from thence. I could now easily get to Institution meetings at eight o'clock, which had been impossible before.

Several other reforms might have taken place at this time had not the reformers become divided amongst themselves. The Free Traders said "We want to secure cheap bread for the people." "And then," said a large section of the Chartists, "the masters will reduce their wages." A great meeting of Free Traders attended by Richard Cobden and John Bright was held in the old Fence School. In the most simple and convincing way Mr. Cobden entered into a calculation of the cost of living of a family of six persons under the present rate of taxation. Then he showed most clearly how Free Trade would reduce the cost of bread and lead to the reduction of the price of tea and sugar and clothing, as well as bread. The saving in such a family would amount to five or six shillings a week. "Now," said John Bright, "study carefully that statement and then say if you will bear such crushing burdens any longer." With the most convincing logic and most convincing facts Mr. Cobden made the subject clear as the open day. John Bright, with burning eloquence, drove the matter home to the mind and heart.

The visit of the great Free Traders produced much excitement, which did not soon abate. Many public meetings were held, when sharp debates took place. The fiery orator, John West, fiercely attacked the Free Traders. In language rushing like a cataract he denounced them as middle-class traders seeking to increase their own wealth by keeping down the working classes. Their object was to secure long hours and low wages for the poor workers and riches for themselves. The fine-looking Timothy Falvey in sonorous, deliberate, clear, and eloquent language showed that Free Trade would benefit all classes and in many ways. John West, the pessimist, remained a poor weaver all his days, the latter part of his life being darkened by his addiction to drink, his poverty being relieved by the charity of his friends.

Timothy Falvey, the optimist, worked his way from the weaver's loom to a newspaper desk, became a writer of leading articles, and then editor of a Southampton newspaper, and made it and himself popular and successful. Civic honours were conferred upon him, and he spent his latter days in competence, in independence, in comfort and in peace. Both the Free Trade movement and the Chartist movement became in varying degrees successful. The ranks of the Free Traders were rapidly swelled by recruits from all parties, and became suddenly victorious under the leadership of Sir Robert Peel, who, as Disraeli said, "had clothed himself in the garments which he had stolen from the Whigs whom he found bathing." Numerous and valuable were the Parliamentary reforms which quickly followed. Sometimes these reforms were carried through by the Whigs and Liberals themselves; and sometimes by Tory governments, who systematically imitated Sir Robert Peel, and stole the garments of their Liberal opponents. But, at the same time, there was this difference between Sir Robert Peel and the later Tory leaders as to the methods by which they obtained other people's garments: while Sir Robert Peel frankly acknowledged the theft, Disraeli, in the face of the most palpable evidence against him, denied the theft, and said the garments were his own.

CHAPTER VI

NIGHT SCHOOLS — BOOKS — TRAVELS

CONTEMPORANEOUS with the Chartist agitation were the many attempts made to enlighten the minds of the masses of the people. Evening schools, called Mechanics' Institutions, were formed in many localities and patronised by the wealthier classes. Cheap periodicals of a really useful kind were published and extensively circulated. The Society for the Diffusion of Useful Knowledge, with Lord Brougham as Chairman, issued *The Penny Magazine*, which was deservedly popular. I bought and read it from the beginning of 1836. Many of the articles were very interesting, and furnished one with excellent material for use in the Sunday School, as also in the Mechanics' Institute. In one of the earlier numbers appeared a rather fine view of the Castle of Chillon, accompanied with the following lines from Byron:—

> "Chillon ! thy prison is a holy place,
>   And thy sad floor an altar—for 'twas trod,
> Until his very steps have left a trace
>   Worn, as if the cold pavement were a sod,
> By Bonivard ! May none those marks efface !
> For they appeal from tyranny to God."

These lines led both myself and others, to whom I mentioned them, to learn more about the prisoner, and to read more of the writings of the poet. This we did in face of the Index Prohibitorium of our betters. "Childe Harold" we revelled in; but as to "Don Juan," we were willing it should remain in the Index aforesaid.

Most deeply interesting to us was an article on the "Nibelungen-Lied," which we had never heard of until then. With its picturesque scenes, savage warriors, and greatly daring women, we were fascinated, if not altogether pleased. Did not Tennyson get from this romantic poem some of the materials used in the " Idylls of the King "?

At the same time was being published the *Saturday Magazine* by The Society for Promoting Christian Knowledge, evidently with the intention of giving to its records a religious and sectarian tone. I took in the weekly numbers from January, 1836. An article on Erasmus, with the representation of a rather fine statue of the man, arrested my attention. When, as a young man, he got any money, he first bought Greek books, and then clothes, said the writer. This came directly home to myself. I did not buy Greek books, but I bought English books, and afterwards clothing, the latter being much patched before laid aside. As to his connection with the Reformation, it was said, " He laid the egg which Luther hatched." Diverse as were these two great men, the united efforts of both were needed in the breaking down of the mighty tyranny of Rome. Erasmus, it would seem, never formally seceded from the Romish Church. But his refusal of a Cardinal's hat proves, I think, that he had broken entirely with the intolerant spirit and murderous proceedings of that iniquitous Church.

A picture of Snowdon and its surroundings in a later number made me quite restless until the next midsummer holidays, when I started off to see with my own eyes these wondrous sights. After lodging a night in Manchester, I went, early in the morning, in a fly-boat on the Bridgewater Canal to Runcorn, and thence in a vessel to Liverpool. I was just in time for a ship sailing to Carnarvon. I had no company that I knew, and wanted none. At once I was absorbed in the observation and contemplation of the objects of nature. Around me was the gloriously gleaming sea, which I gazed upon for the first time. Soon my eyes beheld the two Orme's Heads, which seemed to rise majestically from the sea. Then dark and solemn-looking Penmaenmawr came into view, associated, as I knew, with the English massacre of the Welsh Bards. The Straits of Anglesea, with the Mansions set in the woodlands on either side, I thought might have formed the pattern of Swedenborg's descriptions of the Mansions of the blest in heaven. Several passengers were talking earnestly about a great open-air meeting of the Welsh Methodists then being held at Carnarvon. I followed them, and soon came to a great gathering of some ten thousand people with four or five preachers speaking from different platforms. The effect of the preaching was simply overwhelming. Every individual seemed deeply moved. Some were in fearful convulsions. Many fell prostrate on the ground and lay groaning in agony. Others knelt down beside them, praying for them with great fervour. Now and again an individual rose from the ground in ecstasy, uttering shouts of triumph. I was deeply moved myself, although I did not understand a single word that was spoken.

After the meeting I got lodging in a house—or rather a cave—near an old ruin, which I found clean and comfortable. For a supper of hot milk and bread I paid threepence, and for the same fare at breakfast another threepence, with sixpence for a bed. This very low charge suited well my limited means. I then made my way to the foot of Snowdon, charmed with the wildness and beauty of the scenes by the way. Not venturing to climb the mountain alone, I travelled on to Beddgellert. On the road I conversed with a Welshman who could speak English well, and questioned him about the numerous and perplexing double "Ds" and double "Ls" in Welsh. "They were," he replied, "the great adornments of the language." "But would not," I asked, "a simple phonographic spelling, such as that just published by Mr. Isaac Pitman, very greatly improve all languages?" "For such an irregularly-formed and altogether imperfect language as the English it might be of service," he said, "but it would simply spoil the Welsh, which had the best alphabet and best orthography known, and was indeed the finest language spoken on the face of the earth."

Having visited the grave of the noble dog Gellert, I returned slowly and wonderingly and devoutly, amidst the romantic scenery, to Carnarvon. I occupied the same lodging on the same terms as before, and in the morning sailed back to Liverpool. I got home late in the evening, tired in body, but exhilarated in mind, and with rich stores of memory never to fade from the mind.

On the 4th of June, 1837, was commenced "Ward's Miscellany of Literature, Science, and Religion," for which I regularly subscribed. This was the ablest magazine I had known, and contained much information for which I had been in search. "The Cosmogony of Moses" was continued from week to week, and riveted my attention from first to last. The treatment of the subject was quite novel and somewhat heretical.

Writer.—Creation, as described by Moses, did not comprehend the whole Universe. Did not Job say that "the morning stars sang together when the foundations of the earth were laid"?

Reader (myself).—But that is Job's Cosmogony, and not that of Moses. No doubt Job believed that the stars were made before the earth, but Moses believed the earth was made first.

W.—May we not imagine the creation of mankind intended to fill up the thrones of the revolted angels, after a trial of their (men's) obedience in some distant world?

R.—An ingenious and interesting suggestion. Such a thing is easy to imagine, but impossible to prove.

W.—"No one of sound mind," says Origen, "can imagine that there were an evening and a morning without a sun."

R.—What a vast number of unsound Christian minds there must have been in Origen's time, and since, if that dictum were true.

W.—"The darkness which covered the earth before the appearance of light," says Saint Basil, "was owing to a density of atmosphere too thick for the penetration of the sun's rays."

R.—That is a stark, staring gloss. Basil thus softens the condemnation of Origen and saves the sanity of Christians, ancient and modern, who have accepted the Cosmogony of Moses as against that of Job.

W.—The "Encyclopædia Brittannica" says there is a probability that the Creation, as described by Moses, was not confined to the earth alone, nor extended to the whole universe.

R.—That idea, at the time, was rejected with scorn. But in these later days the theory has come boldly to the front. The great scientist, Alfred Russell Wallace, is to-day presenting such an array of facts and arguments in favour of the theory of a limited universe, as will prove difficult, if not impossible, to set aside or resist.

W.—"When Alexander the Great entered Egypt the priests professed to show him out of their sacred books an account of the Macedonian and Persian Empires through a period of eight thousand years."

R.—The writer quotes this Egyptian chronology in order to set it aside in favour of Bishop Usher's "Chronology of the Bible." But both chronologies have been superseded by overwhelming evidence since then. Monumental evidence, enormous in extent and irresistible in force, has swept Archbishop Usher's Biblical Chronology into the great dust bins of past time, from which it shall never return except as a ghost betimes revisiting the glimpses of the moon.

In the same magazine "A Scottish Sabbath," in a rural district, was most graphically described. After a calm night's rest, a devoutly-minded individual rises early on a fine Sabbath morning. Bible in hand, he climbs a moorland hill side where he reads, meditates, and prays. On his return walk he is arrested near a cottage by the sound of a hymn being sung by a family circle. At another cottage he pauses to hear a fervent prayer uttered by the good man of the abode. After a frugal breakfast he journeys along through wild but beautiful scenery to a rustic church, filled with devout worshippers, and feels a benediction which seems to descend on all. A plain dinner partaken of, and he eagerly fares forth again in search of further blessing, which, in large measure, he finds. Tea over, many of the worshippers meet together in groups or single families, when note-books are produced with reports of the services of the day. Hymns are sung, prayers are made, and then follow many edifying comments and keen catechisings with a view of deepening the solemn impressions made during the several services of the day.

At the time I read this very interesting account my own Sunday experiences were of a somewhat similar kind. Early in the morning I walked a distance of one-and-a-half miles to Sunderland Street Chapel vestry, where a prayer meeting was held, beginning at seven o'clock. At eight o'clock commenced Dr. Birchenall's class of young men, to which I belonged. After solemn searching of hearts and lives for three-quarters of an hour, I and Matthew Moss walked home together in serious conversation. Now and again the Doctor took us to breakfast with him. And how calm and quiet that meeting was! A verse or two being sung, tea was served. Brief and devout were the remarks made. In partaking of the food supplied, the Doctor would say a few words as to the necessity of partaking of the heavenly manna and of the water of Eternal Life. "Had the dew of heaven visited our souls in the morning services?" he would ask. Or "Had we been seeking for the holy Spirit's influence to guide us while teaching the scholars in the Sunday School?" Or "Were we going to pray that the word of God spoken by the preachers during the day might lead to the salvation of many souls?" Then, after a silent clasp of the Doctor's hand, we made our way to the School, thinking only devout thoughts and speaking only devout words.

Then came in succession teaching in the Sunday School, twice—two plain meals—two half-hour walks in the woodlands with Testament or hymn-book in hand—evening service in Sunderland Street Chapel—band meeting or prayer meeting—walk home at ten or eleven o'clock at night. I was sometimes told that I was a Sunday slave, and that I ought to take rest after the hard toil of the week. But indeed I took the best kind of rest I knew. The clamorous cares of the past week were hushed, and I felt fortified against the harassing pursuits of the week to come. Magazine reading of this kind is sometimes depreciated as being a great hindrance to methodical study. But it is not necessarily so. If an eclectic method be adopted, and a note-book be constantly used, such reading may prove of inestimable value. And indeed, some such method is necessary in mastering completely any literary work. The leading ideas must be discovered, the gems of thought secured, and the whole be systematised in the reader's mind. In this way I began the study of Thomson's "Seasons," which was one of the books approved of and quoted from in Methodist circles. Its ideas and sentiments soon began to fasten on my mind. I read the work at early dawn going to work and by the evening firelight when the long day's work was over. Its language I thought much more glowing than that of Bloomfield. Its description of natural scenery I considered equal to that of Cowper, and freer from theological gloom. One of the ruling sentiments of my mind I found expressed in the lines :—

> "Retirement, rural quiet, friendship, books,
> Ease and alternate labour, useful life,
> Progressive virtue, and approving heaven."

Instinctively I fastened on such passages as these :—

> "To steal from the degenerate crowd
> And soar above this little scene of things,
> To soothe the throbbing passions into peace
> And woo lone quiet in her silent walks."

Some of the author's female characters I thought exquisitely drawn, both in their persons and surroundings. "Musidora at the bath" rather startled me, but Lavinia suited me exactly, who with her widowed mother

> "Lived in a cottage, far retired
> Among the windings of a woody vale;
> By solitude and deep surrounding shades,
> But more by bashful modesty, concealed."

In later days, when in the midst of the hurly-burly of city life, how helpful was the recollection of the lines :—

> " I just may cast my anxious eyes
>   Where London's [Manchester's] spiry turrets rise,
>   Think of its crimes, its cares, its pain,
>   And shield me in the woods again."

True, there were not then any near woodland haunts to shield one from the rushing crowds of men. But I knew of such blessed haunts far away to which I hoped to return, and to which, happily, I did return. And now at the end of life, how cheering is the memory of the poet's closing lines:—

> " The storms of Wintry time will quickly pass,
>   And one unbounded Spring encircle all."

John Milton was patronised by the members of the Authoritative Circle, and so I could with safety read his works. I began with " Paradise Lost," the influence of which became a lasting treasure. I soon found that the familiar extracts taken in their connections shone with a new and more brilliant light. The numerous gems of thought fairly blazed with an enchanted radiance as set in their places by the master's hand. As if commencing a philosophical essay, Milton states his aim to be:—

> " That to the height of this great argument
>   I may assert eternal Providence,
>   And justify the ways of God to men."

That is the noble expression of a noble intention, and is connected with a noble invocation in these lines:—

> " And chiefly Thou, O Spirit, that dost prefer
>   Before all temples the upright heart and pure,
>   Instruct me, for Thou know'st."

The departure of Adam and Eve from Paradise is touchingly described thus:—

> " The world was all before them, where to choose
>   Their place of rest, and Providence their guide."

At the time I took this to be the literal statement of a unique fact, but afterwards came to the conclusion that it was the poetic description of a universal experience. In the magnificently splendid descriptions of heaven, earth and hell, and of the terrific battles of angels, devils and men, we have further illustrations of a universal experience. Very clearly is this shown in these lines:—

> "The mind is its own place, and in itself
> Can make a heaven of hell, a hell of heaven."

At the suggestion of a Quaker acquaintance, it is said, Milton wrote "Paradise Regained," with which I did not become so enthralled as in his former work. Over many passages, however, I was compelled to pause, linger and muse. An eager desire to become acquainted with the glorious land of Greece was awakened by the following lines:—

> "Athens, the eye of Greece, mother of arts,
> And eloquence."

> ". . . The olive grove of Academe,
> Plato's retirement, where the Attic bird
> Trills her thick-warbled notes the summer long;
> Thence to the famous orators repair,
> Those ancient, whose resistless eloquence
> Wielded at will that fierce democratie,
> Shook the arsenal, and fulmin'd over Greece,
> To Macedon, and Artaxerxes' throne."

> "Socrates, . . .
> Whom, well inspired, the oracle pronounc'd
> Wisest of men."

In the shorter poems of Milton I found the same lofty sentiment and the same beauty of expression as in the longer poems. In "Il Penseroso" I seized on the following glowing lines:—

> "Then let the pealing organ blow,
> To the full-voiced quire below,
> In service high and anthem clear,
> As may with sweetness, through mine ear,
> Dissolve me into ecstasies,
> And bring all heaven before mine eyes."

Here we have the full, sweet, flowing, musical emotion so much needed to subdue the distractions of the world, and to make holy peace in churches and homes.

In "L'Allegro" we have the same musical theme and the same rich expression:—

> "And ever against eating cares
> Lap me in soft Lydian airs,
> Married to immortal verse;
> Such as the meeting soul may pierce
> In notes, with many a winding bout
> Of linkèd sweetness long drawn out."

On hearing of the persecution of the Vaudois Protestants, Milton wrote the strong invocation beginning with the lines:—

"Avenge, O Lord, Thy slaughtered saints, whose bones
Lie scattered on the Alpine mountains cold."

At the same time he sent to the persecutors sharp missives with an intimation that they might be followed by Cromwell's sharp swords, which checked the persecuting tyrants in their murderous career.

My excursions into the prose writings of Milton were not extensive. In the "Areopagitica," "a flame of eloquence at which one may warm one's hands yet," I seized upon and feasted upon the following memorable words:—"As good almost kill a man as kill a good book; who kills a man kills a reasonable creature, God's image; but he who destroys a good book kills reason itself." "A good book is the precious life-blood of a master spirit embalmed and treasured up on purpose to a life beyond life." "Methinks I see in my mind a noble and puissant nation (under Cromwell) rousing herself like a strong man after sleep, and shaking her invincible locks; methinks I see her as an eagle mewing her mighty youth, and kindling her undazzled eyes at the full mid-day beam."

Unfortunately, the period of the Commonwealth was too brief for the realisation of this brilliant dream, and we have made but few and slight advances since. True it is that in the nineteenth century the People's Charter became law; that Free Trade was secured; that Revivalism kept Dissenting chapels on a blaze, and that Ritualism kept the Established Church up to the boiling point. And yet there is not the slightest indication that the Millennium is at hand.

In the heated controversy between Milton and Salmasius very hard words were used on both sides. Milton's "storm of eloquence and abuse threw his opponent into a terrible fit of chagrin, which led to his death." Equally severe was the assault on Milton, but he was made of sterner stuff than Salmasius and could not be killed by a storm of words.

That Milton could make a sharp repartee, when provoked, was manifest in his reply to the insinuation of the Duke of York. Visiting Milton in his blindness, the Duke asked him if he did not think the loss of his eyesight was a punishment inflicted on him for what he had written about the late king. "In that case," said Milton, "the displeasure of heaven must have been much greater against the king, for I have only lost my eyes, but he lost his head." Great indeed must have been the courage of Milton to have made such a dangerous reply. Hastening to the King, the Duke advised that Milton should be hanged. "But said the King, "if, as you say, he is old, and poor, and blind, he is miserable enough in all conscience: let him live." Happily, Milton was not so miserable as the King thought. His frugal habits and moderate desires rendered him indifferent to the smiles and frowns of fortune. "He is withdrawn," says "Chamber's Encyclopædia," "from the ordinary world of men, as an Alp is withdrawn, by vastness, by solitariness of snows, by commerce with heaven."

CHAPTER VII

HEALTH—EMIGRATION—METHODIST MINISTERS

ALL through this period of five years, ending with my twentieth year, the hours of work at the warehouse were from six o'clock in the morning until eight or nine o'clock in the evening. Then came attendance at classes and other meetings, so that I did not get home until eleven o'clock, after which came supper and an hour's reading. At midnight I went to bed, but not to sleep soundly enough to secure even moderate health. Daily pains in the chest became troublesome, which, I was told, arose from indigestion. My attention was directed to Dr. Andrew Combe's " Physiology of Digestion," which I found interesting as well as useful. The work was based chiefly on the experiments of a Dr. Beaumont on a discharged soldier whose stomach had been penetrated by a large bullet, leaving an opening only covered by a piece of movable skin. Giving the soldier a certain amount of a certain kind of food, the Doctor carefully observed, through the aperture in the stomach, the process of digestion. A great variety of foods were experimented upon in the same way: the whole of which were tabulated, showing the time taken in digestion in each case. As the result of long and careful study, Dr. Combe contended that most people eat too much food, and too rich food, and drink too much strong and stimulating drink.

Although I learnt from this book to make dietetic alterations, I had not much to learn with respect to the importance of living on plain food. In our home in early days, this was a necessity. Our staple food was oatmeal with milk. Bread was stinted, and butter more so. On baking day a number of dough cakes were made with gooseberries inside, which served for us to take to the factory for breakfast and tea. These cakes were so small as to be far from satisfactory for hungry stomachs. On Sunday only we had a grand treat at dinner, consisting of a limited amount of beef and potatoes, and apple or gooseberry dumpling. This course of living had been nearly followed up to the time I read Combe's book. I had heard nothing of Vegetarianism then, and Dr. Combe said nothing about it. Otherwise I might sooner have experienced the benefits of that system of living. But my stubborn indigestion was not so much from the food I ate as from my hard and grinding work at the warehouse from twelve to fourteen hours each day, with the early mornings and late nights devoted to reading and close study. A radical change, I was told, was necessary. I needed to be less in confinement, and more in the open air. This I knew and felt, but what could be done? I had read more or less of life in Utopia, but could not find the way into it. Just at this time much was being said about a new Utopia being formed in America. The first start was at Brook Farm. Hawthorne, Emerson, Alcott, Channing, Margaret Fuller, and other parties were joining it. They were to be a community of thinkers and workers. Each member was to be a farmer, and besides, might be teacher, preacher, scientist, or literary writer, according to individual gifts and tastes. What a grand community it would be! If I could only get into it, the cherished ideal of my life would be realised at once. Seeing no possible way of access, I was almost in despair. When some years later I read Hawthorne's "Blithedale Romance," I saw that my despair would have been still greater if I had managed to join this community of literary saints. About the same time, however, I found there had been launched a far more practical scheme of American backwoods life.

The British Temperance Emigration Society had secured large tracts of land in Wisconsin, near the township of Milwaukie. The land was divided into sections of eighty acres each, ten acres of which were ploughed and partly planted. A frame-house with wooden out-buildings was placed on each lot ready for the arriving emigrant. Later, I became a member, as did several other parties in and near Macclesfield, all of whom, with myself, paid down the requisite purchase money. My brothers could not join me for want of means, nor could my father and mother, who would, otherwise, have liked to have gone with me. But if I prospered, and could send aid, some, if not all of them, would join me at Milwaukie. I gave notice to leave my work at the warehouse, and was very busy collecting materials and making arrangements for my departure. I got maps of the land and of the route leading to it. I was almost in a frenzy of delight at the thought that I was about to leave the Old World with its oppressions—the old mill, with its long hours and dingy rooms, and bad air—for the broad and open and sunlit prairies and extensive woodlands of the Far West. In the New World I was to be preacher, teacher, surveyor and farmer. New and effective methods of education could be struck out and brought into successful operation. Literary societies, in however humble a way, could be formed, and meetings held including opportunities for music and song. In religion, mammon worship would find no place. The words of Jesus Christ would be gloriously fulfilled: "The hour cometh and now is when the true worshippers shall worship the Father in spirit and in truth." The first poem of Emerson had just made its appearance, and exactly expressed my feelings and anticipations when on the point of escaping from the world, the flesh, and the devil:—

> "Good-bye to Flattery's fawning face;
> To Grandeur, with his wise grimace;
> To upstart Wealth's averted eye;
> To supple Office, low and high;
> To crowded halls, to court and street;
> To frozen hearts and hasting feet."

As if set to notes of sweetest music, the following words were continually floating through my mind:—

> "O, when I am safe in my sylvan home,
> And when I am stretched beneath the pines,
> Where the evening star so holy shines,
> I will laugh at the pride and the lore of man,
> At the sophist schools and the learned clan;
> For what are they all, in their high conceit,
> When man in the bush with God may meet?"

Then it was, sad to say, that amidst this most blissful anticipation that a great darkness came. Then I beheld Satan, like lightning, falling from heaven—or elsewhere—and crushing out of existence our great emancipatory movement, and closing the gate of our western paradise just as we were about to enter in. I felt my own case to be far worse than that of my namesake, Adam the first. He was within the Eden gate for a considerable time, and fed on angel's food, and conversed with heavenly beings, and with God Himself. In bowers of roses he held delightful dalliance with Eve, his spouse. The climate was heavenly, labour was easy and short, and the periods of rest and leisure long. These easy terms of life indeed led to the undoing of the happy pair by giving the Tempter opportunity of securing their too frequent attention, ending in their fall. But I had no opportunity of entering the promised land and proving how by hard and constant exercise of both body and mind Satan might be vanquished, and for ever overthrown. Unspeakable was the anguish of the hour when the direful missive came. The title deeds of the plots of land in Milwaukie could not be obtained. English lawyers and American lawyers were at swords' points over the matter, and English claims could not be sustained. The shareholders might go over and make individual claims there. That meant all the members of the Society were placed between the devil (lawyers) and the deep sea. Crossing the ocean in such a case would have been sailing between Scylla and Charybdis in a tempestuous sea, with the imminent danger of being engulfed in the roaring waves. Some few I heard of went and faced all risks, but had better, like myself, have stayed at home. Mr. Thompson, late of Eddisbury Hall, with his father, went to Milwaukie and sold their plots of land, but at so low a price that it did not pay their expenses in going and coming back. I had to settle down to my thirteen or fourteen hours a day work in the warehouse as before. My money was gone, and my hopes of deliverance from slavery were gone too. An indescribable sadness seized me and held me for many weary weeks and months and years. I tried to find comfort in the words:—

> "No foot of land do I possess,
> No cottage in this wilderness;
> A poor wayfaring man.
> Yonder's [heaven] my home, my portion fair;
> My treasure and my heart are there,
> And my abiding home."

Here, I tried to believe, were title deeds better and safer than any that earth can give. Ah me! but they were of a rather misty kind, and a long way off.

I was just now in danger of sinking into a deep and settled melancholy. Hope, as regards this life, seemed to be taking its departure. My earthly ideal had vanished quite. Paradise was lost, with no prospect of its ever being regained. Hard and incessant work, however, kept back approaching despair. Evenings were all taken up at the Institution classes or in the close reading of books, mostly of a religious kind. With an increased seriousness I instructed my scholars in the Sunday School. Any uplifting words of the preachers at the chapel came with great force to my mind. Any deep pathos, any picturesque descriptions of a heavenly life beyond the grave, and true and lofty eloquence of the speakers made me forget my troubles for a time. In every brief opportunity I sought to converse with my mother about her early religious experience. I learned much that was interesting and edifying about the ministers who regularly visited the Cooper family in their mountain home at Hooley Hay. On these occasions fervent prayer meetings, searching class meetings, and comforting love-feasts were held, and rousing sermons were preached. Over mountain tops and through long-stretching valleys came crowds of persons to Hooley Hay. In open-air services they made the welkin ring with their loud and hearty songs of praise. A most welcome minister was Rev. Charles Burton, who was exceedingly fond of hymnal music. Some half-dozen members of the Cooper family had all good voices, and most could play on the harpiscord, violin, 'cello, and other instruments. Hence Mr. Burton would have many sacred concerts during his visits. These mountains and moorlands, he declared, were on the verge of heaven. The ladder which Jacob saw in a vision at Bethel, he said, might be seen there by the eyes of faith, while the presence of angelic beings could be felt by all loving hearts. "Once more," he exclaimed, "the prophecy of Isaiah was fulfilled which saith: 'The wilderness and the solitary place shall be glad, and the desert shall rejoice and blossom as the rose.'"

On leaving Hooley Hay at her marriage, and settling in Higher Hurdsfield, as she told me, she regularly attended Methodist meetings. When I was only a few years of age, she always took me with her to service. My father would go with us to hear a popular preacher, but could never be persuaded to become a member of a Methodist class. By no means could he be induced to approach a penitent form or a confessional room to the day of his death. My mother was much grieved on this account, and, at one time, so was I. But I came to think that, from the high tenor of his life, he had as good a chance of heaven as any religious zealot that ever lived.

The first Revivalist I knew was Rev. Robert Pilter, whose visits roused the neighbourhood. Great was the excitement during his sermons, many and loud were the cries for mercy, and as loud were the shouts of triumph when the devil was vanquished and souls were saved. Objections were made to the methods pursued at these times, and to some extent fairly so, but still, the effects, to a large extent, were good. Frivolity, indifference, and sin were driven out of many hearts and minds, and impressions made which were blessings extending over the whole of life. This was so in my own case, for while I talked with my mother about these bright and happy days and events, the clouds which then enshrouded me were pierced by light from heaven.

The great revival excitement was followed by a period of exhaustion, of quietness, and peace. The chapels were no longer crowded, many of the converts having gone back to the world. But from the year 1831 to 1833 another great personal influence was felt throughout the circuit. This new life came with the advent of the Rev. John Farrar, whom I could well remember. He was in the vigour of early manhood, of middle height, and strongly built. His hair was black; his eyes dark and piercing, and sometimes fascinating. His voice was sometimes strong and sometimes soft, and always melodious. His themes were heaven and hell, death and judgment. His descriptions were solemn, awful, thrilling. The glooms of hell and the effects of damnation frightened and appalled my young soul. But my mother was too absorbed with the splendours of heaven to be affected by such dark and terrible things. For was there not in heaven the great white throne with God sitting in the midst of it? And were not the trumpets of praise sounding while the heavenly hosts were casting their crowns before the throne? And were not the redeemed there from all kindreds and peoples and nations and tongues? And oh! enrapturing thought! would not she and I and every member of the family, with all dear ones, be gathered there!

While I in my present depression looked at the dark side of events, she, bearing heavier burdens, looked at the brighter sides of events. In this way she not only uplifted her own mind into a happier state of experience, but she exalted my own state of mind as well. In our conversation about a still later and much greater revival than any of the previous ones, my own experience was more extensive than her own. This revival commenced on the arrival of the Rev. John Rattenbury, a real boanerges, a true son of thunder. This fine preacher was tall, thin, lithe and wiry, and far on the nearer side of the summit of life. His method of discourse was simple, direct and powerful. In every case his audience listened to picturesque descriptions and earnest persuasion. He placed his hearers in the position in which John Wesley found himself when he wrote:—

> "Lo! on a narrow neck of land,
> 'Twixt two unbounded seas I stand,
> Secure, insensible;
> A point of time, a moment's space,
> Removes me to that heavenly place,
> Or shuts me up in hell."

"That is the exact position," the preacher would say, "of my hearers now. At this very moment you are on the verge of heaven and of hell. What are you going to do? Wait for a more convenient season? It will never come. This is the most convenient season you will ever have. Just till to-morrow, are you whispering to your soul? To-morrow you may be dead and damned, or dead and saved: and whether saved or lost, depends on your decision now. O my dear friends, by the God who loves you; by the Son of God who died for you; by the Holy Ghost who is now pleading within your souls; by the prayers of your ministers and teachers; by the entreaties of a dear father or mother, perhaps now in heaven: I beseech you, O, I beseech you, crowd to the penitent forms and be saved to-night!"

And they went. In troops they marched to the forms, and bent their heads in agonizing prayer. For three years this revival went regularly on. And if one-third of the converts remained members of society, the permanent in-gathering of souls was great, and justified the continued and triumphant shouts of harvest home!

"And all that time," said my mother quietly, "you held back, and would not humble yourself and be saved at the penitent form." "My time was not come, and I felt it would not come in that way," was my reply. And then with her soft voice and sweet smile she said, "I knew the time would come," and, thank God, it did.

After the great revival came the inevitable lull. This my

mother regretted, thinking revivals should extend and go on until Methodism should cover and control the whole world. Many Methodists of the imaginative kind thought the same, but my thinking was of a different kind. Some of the wiser elders contended that some educational efforts should now be made to train and firmly secure the younger converts who had been brought into the church. And just at the time appeared the man to institute and carry on the work. From 1837 to 1839 the controlling influence of Methodism in the circuit came from the Rev. Alexander Strachan.

I attended his first lecture on "The History of the Alphabet, with Side-lights on the Bible." On entering the room, we found the walls hung round with pictures of an uncouth kind. Rude figures of animals were seen interspersed amongst these curious representations. Directing attention to the face and horns of an ox, we were informed by the lecturer that there was the original of the first letter in the alphabet. Then came elaborate disquisitions on Phœnician, Greek, Roman, Anglo-Saxon, and Hebraic letters and literature: the latter containing the most sacred and illuminating records in the world. Amongst the hearers, some were repugnant, some were perplexed, and some wished for more instruction of the same kind. In a subsequent lecture on the "Celtic Elements in the English Language," we got some curious information. The word "Britain," we were told, came from *Prydd* (rich) and *Tan* (country).* The word "Cockney," as applied to Londoners, we were informed, was a corruption of "Cocagne," a French word derived from the Latin *Coquina*, a kitchen. "In a remarkable and very ancient poem," said the lecturer, "London is called the Land of Cockaine, and is described as a city of beef and pudding. The poem shows that in those days John Bull was a gross feeder, as, indeed, he is now. He had then, as now, a great and gormandizing paunch, and with it a great and gormandizing ambition. Hence the English people have ever been

* Bockhart derives Britain from the word *Baratanac*, "the land of tin." Others deduce Britons from the Gallic *Britti*, "painted," in allusion to our ancestors' custom of painting their bodies.

amongst the most rapacious land and gold grabbers on the face of the earth."

Outside the lecture-room a devout Methodist said to me, "These lectures, with those odd pictures, seem rather heathenish." "But," I said, "they are instructive, and very interesting." "Not very likely to convert souls," he replied. "But may prevent," I said, "some late converts from getting unconverted. These lectures," I continued, "may set them thinking as well as feeling, and so give them stability in their new course of life."

The minister very soon proved himself to be a man of deep feeling as well as of deep thought. Such as heard him relate his rich experience at various love-feasts could not easily forget his moving words. As a child he was brought up in connection with the Scotch Kirk. In early youth he was persuaded to go to a Methodist meeting-house. On entering the room, he was offered a hymn-book, which he looked at and thrust aside. Singing from that book instead of from the Psalms of David would be profanity, he would not do it. Nevertheless, he was moved by the singing, and more moved by the preaching. He could not help going again and again. Nor could he resist the Holy Ghost, which came upon him like a mighty rushing wind, converting his soul and making him a new creature in Christ Jesus. Only by regular attendance at Methodist worship could his precious new-born peace be secured.

Every Sunday he walked ten miles to get to the nearest chapel. On the wild moorland roads he found snug, quiet woodland nooks, where he rested and meditated and prayed. In this way his mind was prepared to receive the blessing of God at the service of the day, which he never failed to get. On his return at the same nooks he sought God's grace to guide him through the coming week, which also he never failed to receive. How deeply this story affected me, I cannot tell. Had I not sacred field and woodland walks, and hidden places where I communed with God? Yea, indeed, and was thenceforth more attached to them than ever before. Having gained so great an ascendancy over my mind and heart, there is no wonder that Alexander Strachan should be the means of my new birth into the Kingdom of God. No event in my life had given my mother such joy as this new birth, which she was so well acquainted with at the time. And nothing gave her greater comfort now in her declining days than our conversation about the great event. With one of her far-off but angelic looks she said, "Your brothers will be under your influence and charge, and you will have to lead them safely to heaven." I had seen the touching picture of Monica in conversation with Augustine after his conversion to a better and more peaceful life. I remarked that in a small and obscure way our own case was somewhat like. And I think that Monica's peace and joy were not greater than my mother's; nor were the peace and joy of Augustine greater than my own.

CHAPTER VIII

TEMPERANCE—THREE ANGELS—SCIENCE STUDENT

BUT I was not to have a peace of inactivity. An enthusiastic Teetotal movement commenced, and I was at once drawn into it. Crowded meetings were held in the large School and elsewhere. A band of young men, including myself, went through the audience with books and pencils writing down the names of such as would pledge themselves to abstain from intoxicating drinks. Many broke their pledges in a short time, but many, also, kept their pledges and became active workers in the Temperance cause for many years. The whole town seemed to be agitated more or less on this important question, and much discussion took place. One day, several young men living in Hurdsfield came to me in a state of great excitement, saying that a band of Moderation men in the town had sent a challenge of discussion to them, the meeting to be held in the open air. Would I undertake to meet the party and defend Teetotalism? I shrank from the duty for a time, but at length undertook it. A field at the foot of Ecton Woods was fixed upon for the meetings, the platform of the speakers being the stone steps of a stile.

On the first night I undertook to prove that drunkenness was the chief cause of poverty. My opponent attempted to show that poverty was the cause of drunkenness. About fifty young men were present, and the votes were about equal. On the second evening I contended that drunkenness was the chief cause of crime, my opponent contending that poverty was the cause. Over one hundred persons were present, and a large majority voted on my side of the question. On the third evening I maintained that drunkenness greatly increased disease, and that teetotalism greatly favoured health. Some hundred and fifty persons were present, a majority, not a large one, being in my favour. Some complaint of trespass by a farmer prevented more meetings being held. Although there was much excitement in the neighbourhood and at the meetings, yet fairly good temper and good behaviour were maintained from first to last. Good was done, and some pledges secured. The parties won over to Teetotalism were mostly young people, the older ones being hard to persuade. With old and hardened drunkards nothing could be done. To certain friends with artistic tastes the varying scenes during the discussions were picturesque and interesting indeed. "As the late twilight faded and the stars or the moon revealed the glory of the sky, and as the sound of the winds sweeping through the fir trees blended with the earnest voices of the speakers, both scenes and sounds were entrancing, making an impression never to be forgotten by such as had eyes to see and ears to hear." Such are the words written by one present at each of the meetings held.

Amongst the habitual drunkards I tried at this time to reclaim, was George Turner, living in a house—now taken down—near the end of Cliff Lane. Once or twice in the week he came home drunk, and always under the influence of delirium tremens. As he walked slowly along the road he incessantly talked, sometimes quietly and sometimes savagely, with invisible beings. He would argue with them, strike at them, kick at them, or run at them, howling and swearing. On arriving home, his poor, haggard-looking wife had to flee and hide herself until he had sunk into a helpless, drowsy state of mind. When sober, he would talk to me in a civil, sensible way. Under the influence of my persuasion he made several strenuous efforts to keep entirely from strong drink for a certain number of weeks. But he invariably failed to keep his pledge. For one or two weeks, at most, he would keep sober, but all the time he was in a wretched condition. His craving was so intense for the old and customary indulgence that he rushed headlong, "like the sow, to his wallowing in the mire."

The other case was that of John Oldfield (called Old Jack), living on the way to the Well Lane. His was a more hopeful, and at the same time, a more tantalizing case. He would take the pledge, and remain sober for several weeks or months at a time. I managed, at times, to get him to attend the Sunday School and Sunderland Street Chapel. During some revival he became—it was thought—soundly converted. Both I and others greatly rejoiced over him, concluding that he was a brand plucked from the burning. But alas! for human hopes and efforts, and also for converting grace, the poor fellow was tempted into a public house, got thoroughly drunk, and was heard cursing and swearing in Hurdsfield Road. Again he signed the pledge, and again—after several weeks—he broke it. We would not give him up. To chapel again he went for several Sundays and seemed greatly moved. One of the sermons he heard had reference to the drunkard's death and consequent punishment in hell. This horrified him, and induced him to come to me for explanation. He wished to know if, when he was a drunkard, he had died, would he have been now in the flames of hell. I said, "I did not like to answer, but I could not go against the preacher and the Bible. Take care to keep from drink as you are now doing, and then you will not need to fear a drunkard's death, nor the hell that follows it." Shortly afterwards, about midnight, I was roused from sleep, as were all in the house and nearly all in the adjoining houses, by a loud, raucous howling voice sounding in front of our house. I soon perceived it was Old Jack drunk, who, for an hour continued cursing Methodist preachers and Sunday School teachers in general, and a Methodist preacher and myself in particular, and consigning the whole lot of us to the flames of hell. After this exploit I left the poor fellow severely alone, having concluded that neither the still small voice of persuasion nor the thunders of damnation would save him from a drunkard's life and death.

Before my discussion in the fields I had sometimes been called upon to ascend the pulpit in the Sunday School and begin the service by prayer and to close the School with a brief address. This latter exercise I always entered upon with considerable trepidation. But now I had to engage in these duties more frequently. When the Christmas Tea Party came, I had to ascend the platform with Matthew Moss and other speakers. Taking note of the hundreds of faces directed towards the platform, I began to feel it would not be so easy to address the audience there as it had been to speak to the people in the fields by moonlight. I began nervously by referring to a tall heap of stones which several of the young men present had piled up on the highest peak of Ecton, and which they had named the Tower of Freedom. Speaking of the noble efforts of saints, sages, and heroes to secure freedom for mankind, I quoted the words, "If the Son therefore shall make you free, ye shall be free indeed." Then, referring to Beeston Rock which could be seen from the Tower of Freedom, I spoke of some of the battles which had been waged there. "But far more interesting than the sight of Beeston to me," I said, "is the sight of this Sunday School so prominently visible from Ecton summit. This is the spot where our battles have to be waged. Here our arduous conflicts with ignorance and falsehood and sin have to be continuously carried on. Here our young people should learn how to put on the whole armour of God. Here it is they should learn how to gird themselves about with truth; here they should learn how to defend themselves with the shield of faith; and here they should grasp the sword of the Spirit, and go forth conquering and to conquer, whatever monsters of evil should oppose them on the road of life." This deliverance—briefly stated here—surprised many present, but myself most of all. Much I intended to say was left out, and much I had not intended to say was, somehow, said. Mr. Matthew Moss rose and said that having been my teacher for several years, he had been expecting some such speech as this. He had now only to say that henceforth

I must increase, but he must decrease. I did not feel flattered by these words from my old teacher, for I was much troubled with the thought that in any further attempts at speech-making I should be quite uncertain as to what I should say. That difficulty, however, was overcome as time went on.

Coming events at this time were beginning to cast their shadows athwart our homestead, which, hitherto, had always been a happy one. Trouble and persecution and oppression enough we found outside the home, but inside there was comfort, sympathy, and help. But our mother's health, it was sadly too evident, was fast breaking down. In case of the worst happening, what then? Who could step into the dreaded vacancy if it should occur? Father was living chiefly on Aunt's farm at Butley. What could I and my two younger brothers, all engaged in the mill, do, if left alone? I had been too busily engaged in work and study and religion to let a certain cherished ideal take practical shape. That ideal was founded chiefly on a poem and a picture. The poem contained these lines:—

"Far in the windings of a vale,
Fast by a sheltering woods,
The safe retreat of health and peace,
An humble cottage stood."

In describing a virtuous maiden living with her widowed mother in that woodland abode, the poem says:—

"The sweetest blush that nature spreads
Gave colour to her cheek;
Such orient colour smiles through heaven
When May's sweet mornings break."

These lines awakened, at times, a vague, dreamy state of mind, which might have been continued indefinitely without producing any serious result. But the picture—a present from my mother—brought matters to a crisis at once. This was a small, framed engraving representing the beautiful forms and faces of three angels praising God.

I had never seen any earthly beings at all like the beings represented on the picture, until a certain Sunday morning when I went to hear a noted minister preach. He had gone through a long, earnest, solemn, and inspiring prayer. He had read the two lessons in a most solemn and impressive way. Rising to sing the hymn before the sermon, I turned to look towards the orchestra, and was fairly startled at the scene before me. Just in front of the organ stood three good-looking female forms earnestly singing. There was my picture over again. The centre figure was the taller and finer-looking of the three, as in the picture. The centre figure in the engraving had always been my favourite one, and I felt the same preference for the central figure standing in the orchestra now. In the worship of that day my heavenly ideal faded, and the earthly ideal reigned supreme.

Interviews followed of quite an idealistic kind. According to arrangements these meetings were few and far between. I had not much time to spare, and I did not wish her to be otherwise than well employed. In conjunction with another pair of friends we had rather long local journeys at holiday times. Over Ecton we went, visiting and moralising at what I had designated my altar and shrine. We scaled the steeps of Kerridge, and traced out interesting places connected with noted persons. On the Rainow side we looked down on the house and garden and sanctuary of James Mellor. There was spent a long and active and quiet life. Much in the life and character of this eccentric man we admired, but we all agreed that in one respect he had made a great mistake. He had never married and hence he was lopsided, short-sighted, maimed, and altogether incomplete. Alderley Edge was visited, its caves examined and its myths discussed. Gawsworth Church was visited and the numerous effigies of the Fitton family surveyed and speculated upon. Johnson's grave in the wood suggested many resurrection theories which were earnestly considered. Some of the party thought the old gentleman was quite sensible in deciding to be buried in such a beautiful place. From an orthodox point of view it was agreed he had proved himself cautious and wise. He had certainly taken a just precaution to secure on the judgment day what unquestionably belonged to himself. In picnic fashion, on these excursions, some snug woodland retreat was secured in which refreshments were partaken while conversation, wisely or otherwisely, went rattling on. So far all seemed bright and fair, but clouds were gathering, when true love did not so smoothly flow. Various educational aims were proposed which the females of the party did not very decidedly adopt. The mutual reading of useful books did not successfully proceed. A few novels proved fascinating and attractive to all, and became ground-work for improving discourse. But a taste for the best literature of ancient and modern times had not been and could not be formed by the females concerned. At evening classes advancement in elementary knowledge was but slow. Scientific lectures could not be understood, and did not interest. Theology was an enigma, and only a few formulæ found a lodgment in the mind. Conducted to the foot of the ladder of aspiration reaching from heaven to earth, only feeble attempts were made to ascend. They sought no acquaintance with, and so gained no help from, the angels ascending and descending that heavenly road. The ideal suggested by the picture of the three angels praising God became dimmed and, for the time, entirely obscured. The glowing radiance of the dawn of love faded into the light of common day. The evening, with its gleams and glooms, came on apace. Then the thick darkness of night descended and buried all. Had I then been pursuing an Ignis-Fatuus all this time? But even that is a real thing, only delusive and dangerous. Seen at a distance it is beautiful and attractive. Pursued too eagerly it vanishes away, while the pursuer finds himself in the dark, and sticking in a morass. But surely all ideals do not vanish when approached. My class leader is a real concrete being. He is a veritable saint; I will get near to him in spirit, and will hang upon his words spoken in the class. My literary saints are real too, and I will drink in their burning words. My dear friend, Edward Davenport, is the noblest scientific saint

I have known, and I will imbibe science with the same fervour as himself. Finding him at the Institute with an air-pump and furnace, and retorts and phials around him unweariedly at work, I said experimenting in this way was a somewhat tedious affair. "What," he exclaimed, "now that Dr. Dalton has demonstrated his Theory of Atoms? Now that we can analyse and synthesize almost all things? Now, when we are finding out how worlds are made and unmade, and re-made? Tedious—to find out the glorious secrets of the Universe!" Poor fellow! He very nearly analysed the life out of himself. Watching very closely the formation of a gas in a retort, the glass burst into fragments, a large piece cutting into the middle of his face. He was lifted from the floor stunned and bleeding, and looking like a dead man. For two days he could not see, On the third day he could see with one eye; and in a week he could see, more or less, with both eyes. But a broad, red scar, reaching from his brow and crossing the nose to the cheek, remained through life.

CHAPTER IX

PLAN OF MUTUAL STUDY—SEVEN TEXT-BOOKS

AMONGST my periodicals at this time was "The Youths' Instructor." In January, 1841, "Letters to the Young" were begun. The preface stated that these letters were "on the means of improvement for a youth whose opportunities for acquiring knowledge have been, and still are, very few." "Just the very thing for me," I thought, but I would first see what Edward Davenport said about it. He was delighted with it, and we decided to begin the prescribed course of study, conjointly, and at once. Seven works were recommended for study, the first obtained being " Mason on Self-Knowledge." This proved to be a confessional without a priest, or a sort of Methodist class-meeting without the presence of the leader. The conscience must be constantly probed to its deepest depths, but only by its individual owner. Daily conduct must be carefully scrutinized and true verdicts concerning it given: but only to the inner self illumined by the light of heaven.

In reading aloud one of the chapters, Edward paused at the following lines:—

> " And having plunged the gulf, you love to view
> Succeeding spirits plunged along like you,
> Nor lend a helping hand to guide them through."

He closed the book, and we read no more that night. But we entered into a solemn compact that the one of us which first passed the boundary between time and eternity would, if possible, communicate with the one remaining on earth, or, at least, watch and wait for, and help him with outstretched hand as he passed into the eternal bourne.

Our second book was "The Improvement of the Mind," by Dr. Watts. On a few occasions I had heard parties refer to this important book, but had not met with anyone who had read it. Since then I have met with many hard-reading men who knew little or nothing about it. The neglect of this most valuable book is much to be regretted. It can hardly be superseded by anything of the kind. Nothing finer, and certainly nothing so complete and extensive, can be found in Todd's "Students' Manual" or the writings of Dr. Blackie, Dr. Channing, or Mr. Smiles. Its careful study would surely tend to prevent the omnivorous, desultory, and utterly useless reading so common at the present day. Such was its effect on ourselves and, I think, on some other parties whose attention we directed to it. Many of its rules and illustrations became firmly fixed in our memories, and formed the ground-work of much profitable conversation and discussion. We never forgot how "Plumeo skimmed over the pages of a book like a swallow over the flowery meads in May"; nor how "Plumbinus read every line and syllable, but did not give himself the trouble of thinking and judging about them"; nor, especially, of "Studentio who gained facility to judge of what he read by his daily practice of it, and who made large advances in the pursuit of truth." Nor, again, have I myself ever met with anything that has had greater influence over my own career than the injunction expressed in the lines found in the book:—

> "Seize upon truth where'er 'tis found,
> Amongst your friends, amongst your foes,
> On Christian or on heathen ground;
> The flower's divine where'er it grows:
> Neglect the prickles, but assume the rose."

The third book in our course of study was "The History of Greece," which painted pictures in our memories never to be erased. We seemed to stand at Thermopylæ and gaze with wonder and admiration at Leonidas and his brave three hundred as they perished there; at Salamis, when Themistocles with his few vessels swept the enemy's mighty fleet from the Grecian seas; and to hear that great admiral exclaim, when news came to him that the enemy's ships darkened the sky, "Then we will fight in the shade." But more interesting to us than her warriors were the orators of Greece. From the sea shore where Demosthenes spoke with the pebbles in his mouth, we followed him to where he stood amid the surging masses of his countrymen, who, inspired by his fiery eloquence, exclaimed with one mighty voice, "Lead us against Philip of Macedon!" And yet greater than the warriors and orators, to us, were the philosophers of Greece. With the disciples of Plato we seemed to walk in the groves of the Academy, entranced by the great teacher's words; with Socrates in the market-place of Athens, as he tore to tatters the specious, plausible and deceptive reasonings of the Sophists; and with him as he calmly and triumphantly went to a martyr's death.

Rousseau is said to have exclaimed, "Socrates died like a martyr, but Christ died like a god." But is not the reverse of the statement nearer the truth? While Christ in His tremor cried out, "My God, My God, why hast Thou forsaken Me!" Socrates cherished unfaltering trust in God to the last moment of his life. Nor did we fail of admiration and homage for the architects and sculptors of Greece: Phidias and Praxiteles becoming and remaining with us honoured names. Thomson, the poet, in reference to one of the matchless sculptured forms of Greece, exclaims, "So stands the statue that enchants the world!" We extended the apostrophe, and exclaimed, "So stand the temples, palaces, and sculptures that enchant the world!" In the religions of Greece we had less delight. Olympus, we thought, contrasted unfavourably with Zion Hill; the oracles of Delphi seemed frivolous beside those of Sinai's hoary summit; Delos was not so sacred as Patmos Isle; nor had Ilyssus such rich memories as had Jordan's stream.

Severe in our judgment of the quarrels of the Grecian goddesses and gods, we did not think, just then, of the Biblical angels who kept not their first estate, but who, after long wars in heaven, were hurled into gulfs of unquenchable fire. With Homer's deities who fought on the side of the Trojans at one time, and on the side of the Greeks at another time, we had but little patience. But how much more trying to the patience is the Biblical account of Jehovah sometimes aiding his chosen people, the Jews, and sometimes helping their enemies to vanquish them, we did not consider. Somehow, our comparisons all leaned one way: a very common method, as one has learned since. At the fount of Parnassus, as we read, Grecian poets were inspired with prophecy and song. Ah! but the waters of Babylon, Jordan, and Siloam inspired Jewish poets with far grander prophecies and songs! The strains of Æschylus and Sophocles, indeed, were pervaded by a wild, wierd, and awful sublimity; and yet, must be considered somehow far inferior to the strains of Isaiah and the psalmist David. Grecian poems, we said, were full of grand and solemn warning, but had little if any of the comforting, uplifting, joy-giving inspirations of Hebrew prophecy and psalm. The hosts of fairy beings with which the Greeks peopled earth and sky, river and sea, were, to us, unreal, vain, and useless things; while, at the same time, we held to all ghosts, angels, and devils described in Bible words. Thoughts did sometimes intrude as to whether, after all, there might be some rather close relationship between Greek Mythology and Jewish Story. Had Edward's life been a little more extended, he might, with myself, have been led to apply the words of Byron to Greece and Palestine alike:—

"Where'er we tread, 'tis haunted, holy ground;
No earth of thine is lost in vulgar mould,
But one vast realm of wonder spreads around,
And all the Muses' tales seem truly told."

The fourth subject of study was "The History of Rome." The story of Romulus and Remus, with the account of the flight of the vultures and the suckling of the twins by a wolf, was briefly disposed of, and with but slight respect. The story of the ravens feeding Elijah might be treated with reverence because found in a sacred book, but the story of the wolf and the Roman twins, being found in a profane book, might be profanely treated. Certain remembered statements in Combe's "Constitution of Man" awakened in me serious doubts as to the soundness of our method of comparing things. Edward, however, had no hesitation in drawing a clear line of demarcation between sacred history and profane. The story of the Sabine Rape, from the circumstances of the case, seemed credible enough, as also did the tragic and characteristic story of Tarpeia, who, to obtain the bracelets which had dazzled her eyes, betrayed the fortress to the enemy. The laws of Numa, it was agreed, displayed great wisdom, but were not, of course, equal to the laws of Moses. The Alban War, with the combat at the bridge of the Tiber, awakened only a passing interest. That interest, however, was intensified when Macaulay, in his glowing martial lines, told—

> "How well Horatius kept the bridge
> In the brave days of old."

Of course, in the second Punic War came to light some of the great generals of Rome. We watched with interest the impetuous Scipio and the Cunctator Fabius, as with opposite and yet united tactics they saved Rome from destruction by the Carthaginians led by their redoubtable leader Hanibal. Taken to a shrine by his father, Hamilcar, we found this same Hanibal compelled, at nine years of age, to swear eternal enmity to Rome; the carrying out of which oath brought that great kingdom to the verge of ruin. But, resting too long at Capua, the conquering soldiers of Hanibal were themselves vanquished, not so much by the armies of Rome, as by the luxury, sensuality, and licentiousness into which they had fallen. Still greater men crowded on our view and excited our imagination. Antony, Pompey, and a Cæsar himself, after many an heroic and triumphant conflict on the field of battle, we saw fall nerveless, demoralized, and subdued into the arms of that brazen and yet fascinating creature, Cleopatra of Eygpt, and who was, at length, herself voluntarily and fatally vanquished by a poison asp.

Julius Cæsar, pausing at the Rubicon and making a picture for many future historic painters to copy, we could not forget; nor his memorable despatch from a victorious battlefield, "I came, I saw, I conquered," which has passed into all literature; nor his tragic exclamation, "And thou, Brutus," as he fell dying at the foot of Pompey's Pillar, pierced with twenty-six wounds from the daggers of Brutus, Casca, and others. Still nobler figures were those of the Royal Philosophers, Antoninus and Marcus Aurelius: the former memorable for his tolerant treatment of the Christians, and the latter becoming so distinguished for his extensive learning and great ability that his Godhead was decreed by the Senate: an act of profanity, as we thought then. At a later time the question with me arose as to whether it was not just as profane for Christians to decree the Godhead of Christ. We loved the elder Pliny because of the fine example he set of a close, exact, methodical, and industrious study, both of the works of Nature, and the works of man. We should have liked Pliny the Younger better if he had used more of his great influence with the Emperor Trajan to prevent the persecution of Christians. Interest in Cato was increased by the lines of Addison, beginning "The Soliloquy" thus:—

> "It must be so, Plato, thou reasonest well,
> Else whence this pleasing hope, this fond desire,
> This longing after immortality?"

and ending with the lines:—

> "The stars shall fade away,
> The sun himself grow dim with age,
> And nature sink in years;
> But thou [the soul] shall flourish in immortal youth,
> Unhurt amid the war of elements,
> The wreck of matter, and the crash of worlds."

The religion of ancient Rome, at its best, was of an edifying and ennobling kind. Its Priests, Augurs, and Vestals would compare favourably with the official devotees of other religions. With the increase of age and wealth, as we saw, it sank into formalism, inanity, intolerance, and pride. In performing the prescribed rites, the priests sometimes laughed in their sleeves and at each other. But what of that? It was not peculiar to them. Max Muller thinks that similar things take place at the present time. He knows of certain church dignitaries, including a bishop, who made light of dogmas they now teach, and of ceremonies which they now perform. In looking askance at the worship of the Lares and the Penates, were we not condemning ourselves, seeing that all around us was going on the worship of the saints, the worship of Jesus Christ as God and of Mary as the Mother of God? Wondering, as we did, at the all-embracing inclusiveness of the Pantheon at Rome, why did we not feel ashamed at the striking exclusiveness of all the great churches of Christendom at the present time? When will this great and ever-boasting Christendom build its great memorial temple enshrining the statutes of Buddha and Christ; Bede and Ulphilas; Origen and Hypatia; Bernard and Abelard; Luther and Servetus; Baxter and Biddle; Swedenborg and Wesley; Penn and Channing; Keble and Martineau; Davis and Ingersoll? Until then may Confucius live and teach and reign; Mohammed raise his voice in restraint of the savage hordes that bear his name; Zoroaster stir up and keep bright his purging fires; and the Pantheon of Rome still radiate some rays of embracing charity and truth to penetrate the thick darkness which enshrouds this haughty Christendom—which dominates and terrifies the world.

The fifth subject of study was "The History of England." The question which had arisen as to the authenticity of historic records had been met with no reassuring replies. One authority affirmed that such records were "will-o'-the-wisps." Hume says that Saxon history resembles the scuffling of kites and crows. Macaulay makes little of any English history before the Revolution of the 17th century. The most scathing judgment of such records is that of Walpole, who would say, when asking for an historic volume, "Bring down that liar from the book-shelf." Still, we remembered the pleasure we had got from reading even legendary stories when of an interesting kind and of literary value. We determined, however, to discriminate, as far as possible, between fact and fiction; between truth and falsehood; and between what was useful and what was of no value.

Beginning with the Picts, Scots, and Celts, our judgments were greatly strained in trying to distinguish between the one lot and the other lots of these obscure aboriginal tribes. One sublime form, in the person of Queen Boadicea, rose out of and above the darkness of Britain's early ages, that form being the more horribly attractive from the streams of blood flowing from her delicate limbs, gashed out by the Roman scourge. The scourging of this noble lady and the outraging of her noble daughters throw a blood-red stain over the Roman rule in these British Isles. Another magnificent form arose in those dark ages and amidst so-called savage tribes, in the person of Caractacus, who, when taken a prisoner to Rome, could only ask in astonishment why his captors living in palaces should envy him a hut in Britain: and we wondered how many Asiatic, African, and other chieftains had asked the same question, as they, and all belonging them, successively fell into the hands of their English captors. How grandly loomed in the twilight of a later day the heroic forms of Arthur and his Knights of the Round Table! and how fine a preparation was the reading of this dim passage of history for the profitable study of Tennyson's "Idylls of the King." Of the same heroic type appeared the noble Saxon whom Kingsley afterwards immortalized in his "Hereward the Wake." But these heroes had, however, to yield precedence to one greater and more real than themselves. This was the cake-burner, the harper, the singer, the philosopher, the statesman, the warrior, the hero who vanquished the Danes, and reigned as king, and has been worthily called Alfred the Great. For William, the Norman, and his marauding hosts, we had only feelings of detestation; while for Harold and his army we felt the greatest sympathy and regret.

The field of Runnymede, and Magna Charta, of course,

interested us greatly; but not much insight was required to perceive that here was no victory for the people at large, but only for the Bishops and Barons against the weak and worthless and priest-ridden King John. But few of the sovereigns of England gained our admiration and esteem. Henry IV., who scaled the throne, was no doubt a very able and successful ruler, but he was a usurper, bold, unscrupulous and miserable. In his struggles with the Welsh our sympathies were altogether with Owen Glendower and his heroic soldiers; while for the Bards who fanned the flame of Welsh patriotism we had an almost worshipful regard.

In the great Scotch conflict our judgment took a similar direction. What mattered the military skill and success of Edward I. to us? Our hearts were away with the patriotic and heroic Wallace and Bruce in the Scotch mountains. With as much fervour as Professor Blackie himself we could have sung:—

> "See approach proud Edward's power!
> Chains and slavery!

> "Lay the proud usurpers low!
> Tyrants fall in every foe!
> Liberty's in every blow!
> Let us do or die!"

Concerning the Stuart Kings it was difficult to form a judgment in brief. Did they deserve pity or reproach? Condemnation or commiseration? Perhaps a mixture of all. James I. was vain, foolish, conceited, and superficially learned, and with an itch for scribbling and printing books. Duke Sully said he was the most learned fool in Christendom. Charles I. was domesticated and religious, but proud, pompous, deceitful, and treacherous. Persistently acting on the idea of his divine right to do outrageous wrong to his subjects, he lost his head on the scaffold at Whitehall. For a large number of the best and most patriotic men in the kingdom this was a most fortunate event, for, had the King not lost his head, these men would certainly have lost theirs.

To describe the chief feature in the character of Charles II., as also the character of his court, the word "licentious" only need be used. England got well rid of the whole lot of the Stuart kings when James II. was driven from the throne, and William, Prince of Orange, reigned in his stead.

The noblest and greatest ruler England had ever had, in my opinion, was Oliver Cromwell, and this, as I afterwards found, was the opinion of Thomas Carlyle. On this matter I and Edward differed somewhat, as might have been expected, he being a Churchman and I a Dissenter. My own contention took the following direction:—Early in life Cromwell became intensely and sincerely religious, and largely succeeded in communicating the same fervour to others. He was a determined and disinterested patriot, and his influence in this direction was singularly contagious. Being intensely real himself, he made short work of pretences, shams, and all hypocrisies. He had the gift of seeing into the main points in movements and events, and the power of getting to the centre of things. He could not waste time in beating about the bush, but went straight into the bush itself and discovered and made clear what was there. Time and force he ever economised by directness of thought and action. In illustration of his decisive method of procedure, there is the case of an Englishman imprisoned by order of the Spanish government: the charges against whom were mostly frivolous, but including that of heresy. Cromwell demanded his immediate release. The Spanish government hesitated and shuffled. Cromwell then threatened military force. The Spaniards replied, "They had no responsibility in the case, as the man was imprisoned by the Holy Inquisition." "Then," replied Cromwell, "I at once make war on the Holy Inquisition." That was enough: the man was immediately released. In the same way, under the advice of Milton, the Royal persecutors of the Waldenses got sharp remonstrances and were checked in their murderous career. As a commander of armies Cromwell was one of the ablest and most successful the world has ever known. Out of rabble followers he made good soldiers. Even awkward squads he made effective. As to the Ironsides, they became, like himself, invincible. On every battlefield he was victorious. Over every Parliament he was master either by words or swords. If arbitrary sometimes, it was when he was in conflict with mischievous and interminably talking tongues. His impatience of endlessly protracted speech made him, it must be admitted, sometimes intolerant in his deeds. And yet civil and religious liberty were enjoyed throughout the whole country as never before.

What a revelation, what a prophecy, what an exposition of the great Puritan conflict there is in David Neal's picture of the meeting of Cromwell and Milton in their earlier days! There stands Cromwell in an ante-room in Milton's house, clad in a rustic garb, lost in thought and absorbed in the sounds of the organ which Milton is playing in an adjoining room. In these two men extremes, indeed, met, and with wonderful effect. That music of Milton we may imagine as awakening the dream of Cromwell, stealing its way into the very heart of the country, arousing the flame of patriotism, kindling the fires of revolution, stimulating men to deeds of heroism on the battlefield and in the council chamber, and, finally, as calming the passions of men, and aiding them in establishing peace and security throughout the land.

CHAPTER X

SIXTH SUBJECT: THE HISTORY OF CHRISTIANITY

ALTHOUGH Edward and I differed more widely on this than on any preceding subject, we never failed to preserve the best feeling to each other from first to last. At the outset of our present study we were perplexed with the question of religious persecution. Not only did Pagan Emperors and their subordinates persecute Christians, but Christian Emperors and Bishops, with their subordinates, persecuted members of Christian sects. What was the cause of such inhuman proceeding? Did it arise from a sincere conviction of the divine right of an Emperor, or a Pope, or a Bishop to suppress all opinions at variance with the opinions of the powers that be? Or was it the result of ignorant popular enthusiasm fanned by priests behind the public scenes? Or was it a question of vested interests, as in the case of Demetrius, the silversmith and the image-makers of Ephesus? We concluded that persecution arose from a mixture of all the three causes, mixed in different proportions in different cases. Looked at in themselves, the several heresies which have so greatly agitated the Churches in various ages seem so innocuous that it is amazing they should have awakened any severe hostility at all. If the Ebionites did wish to unite Moses and Christ; to give precedence to Matthew's gospel; to hold that Jesus Christ was inferior to God the Father; to contend that the Son of God was a creature, and not the Creator—what then? They might have been, and according to the best accounts, were, equal to their opponents in character; and in their love and fidelity to truth were greatly superior to them. If, again, the Gnostics did hold that God governed the world by Aeons, or inferior gods, what harm was there in that opinion? And when John (?) had written his Gospel to refute these notions, why had not the orthodox more faith in such refutation than to continue their further refutations by imprisonment and death? If, again, Mani, the leader of the Manichæans, did teach that the world was ruled by good and evil, or by God and the Devil, where was the unpardonable offence? And yet Mani was actually flayed alive: such monsters of cruelty as his tormentors existing amongst the Christians of that day.

The most widespread and exciting of all the so-called heresies was that of Arianism. Of the two champions for and against this heresy, I, at least, thought Arius the more worthy character. Athanasius, no doubt, was learned and able, but terribly overbearing and unscrupulous. Had not Arius suddenly died, as some contend, by poison, his views would in all probability, have prevailed, and then Arianism would have been orthodoxy and Athanasianism heresy. Watching the theological battle as it went on after the death of Arius, our attention was specially arrested by the very curious war-cries with which the combatants rushed into the conflict. "Homoiousian"—meaning similarity of substance (in reference to Christ)—was the decisive word used by the Oriental, or eastern, Bishops and their followers who defended the views of Arius. "Homoousian—meaning sameness of nature—was the watchword of the Occidental, or western, Bishops and their followers who adhered to Athanasius. At length the more violent western party prevailed, and so Arianism became heresy and Athanasianism became orthodoxy.

The persecution of heresies then became fast and furious; and yet they multiplied and spread through all Christian countries, and continued through all succeeding centuries. The honour of adopting the finest and most numerous selection of heresies fell to an Englishman. This was Edward Wightman, of Burton-on-Trent, whose death-warrant was signed by James I. This warrant charged Wightman with holding the ten heresies of Ebion, Cerinthus, Valentinian, Arius, Macedonius, Simon Magus, Manes, Manichæus, Photius, and of the Anabaptists. Hail! all hail! to Wightman, then, the truth-lover, truth-seeker, truth-finder, truth-liver, sage, saint, and martyr!

In regard to the influence of Constantine the Great on the Christian Church, I agreed with the statements in a lecture which I had just heard by the Rev. Dr. Binney in Roe Street Chapel. "In the State Church," said the lecturer, "constituted by Constantine there was little pertaining to Christianity except the name. Henceforth power and pelf were the main objects of the Church. Spirituality was asleep, if not dead, while worldliness was fully alive and awake." Edward, on the other side, contended that the Church in its connection with the State was protected from popular fluctuations, and so enabled to extend itself more widely and do its work more efficiently than when separated from the State.

With the mission of Augustine, sent by Pope Gregory to make the Angles into Angels, we were interested, of course, but with the methods adopted we were not favourably impressed. Fixing altars in heathen temples, whitewashing walls and effacing heathen symbols, and dipping people in rivers of water, seemed all that was thought necessary in the way of conversion. And what beside nominal Christians have missionaries made of heathens from that day to this? In some cases there may have been improvement in life and conduct, but in other cases quite the reverse, from what travellers and writers say. Are not the words of Jesus Christ, addressed to the missionaries of His day, directly applicable in some cases at least, at the present time, "For ye compass sea and land to make one proselyte, and when he is made, ye make him two fold more the child of hell than yourselves." The mission of Augustine, powerfully aided by Ethelbert, King of Kent, and Queen Bertha, no doubt, made rapid progress; but the statement that ten thousand persons were baptised in one day in the river Swale seems an enormous exaggeration. One wondered how long it would have been before the water in the Swale would be clean enough for the cattle on its banks to drink after such extensive operations had taken place. But missionaries, like other people, may sometimes be very inexact in their figures. Amongst a host of notable personages who came into our view was one who rose head and shoulders above all the rest. This was Abelard, the eminently learned scholar and mentor, who, after completely vanquishing St. Bernard by his unanswerable logic, was himself vanquished by fanatical saints under the directions of a persecuting church. In Abelard's connection with Heloise we both repudiated him and sympathised with him. Such a thrilling tale of love, philosophy, and religion, the world had never heard before or since. The letters passed between the lovers were such as none but themselves could have written. For the time, both Abelard and his writings were crushed and effaced. But the higher criticism of religion which he created has risen from the dead and is making the most delightful havoc of the theology of both Rome and Canterbury at the present time.

Edward and I, being village youths, had neither time nor means—and never, probably, would have—of visiting and identifying distant places connected with important personages and important events about which we read. In our plan of study, therefore, we found a given spot on the map, and then, from written description and our own imaginations, made a picture of important persons and events connected with that spot; and then criticised the picture, philosophised about it, and thus tried to understand all about it. At Canossa, for instance, we saw in 1077 the proud Emperor Henry IV. standing bareheaded and barefooted for three days in the outer court of the palace of the Pope. Inside the palace was the haughty Gregory, deliberately starving and humiliating his foe. When permitted, the Emperor pretended humbly to ask forgiveness, when the Pontiff pretended graciously to bestow it. After which each proceeded to continue the struggle by which both were ultimately crushed.

Such was the picture which drew forth the following critical questions:—Which is the most dangerous to human welfare—

an Emperor ruling by an assumed divine right, or a Pope ruling by an assumed infallible authority? Are not both destructive of civil and religious liberty? When the two authorities happen to co-exist, is it not very desirable they should be in active hostility to each other? Should not religion be kept free from the State and free from the Pope?

In Martin Luther as a street-singing lad at Mansfeld; a close student of Augustine and the Vulgate at Erfurt; a keen logician nailing his ninety-five theses on the Church gates at Wittenberg; taking a bold stand in the Diet of Worms with the high representatives of principalities and powers and spiritual wickednesses in high places around him; and as spirited away to the castle in the black forest, there to vanquish the Devil with an ink-pot: we saw one of the most picturesque personages that history presents to view. In the enthusiasm of the moment we thought Luther had led the way to the mental and spiritual emancipation of mankind. Later on it seemed clear enough to me that while Luther was breaking down the infallibility of a priest, he was establishing the infallibility of a book; that, while dethroning the Pope, he was enthroning the Bible in his stead: the consequence being that Book-Popes innumerable sprang into life.

Upon the reforming efforts of Henry VIII. and his minions we looked with much distrust; while upon the doings of Calvin we looked with utter disgust. Zwingle we thought as learned a man as Luther and much broader and tolerant in his religious views. Had he lived longer, his influence on the Reform movement would have been beneficial in many ways; but, fighting against the hereditary foes of freedom, he fell and died on the field of battle.

We hailed the appearance of Wycliffe, " The Morning Star of the Reformation." By translating the scriptures and sending a number of poor men throughout the country to read them to the people, he greatly relaxed the Popish grip on England. His plain, pointed, and direct speech, both spoken and written, must have produced great effect. " The Pope," he wrote, " is

Anti-Christ, the proud, worldly Priest of Rome, the most cursed of clippers and purse-kervers" (cut-purses). He was cited to Convocation, and went, bearding the Popish lions in their den, and somehow managing to escape their sharp teeth. Many Bulls were sent out against him, but in some way he managed to avoid being seriously gored by the long horns of the fierce brutes. His books were burned to ashes, but his body escaped the trying ordeal by fire.

Slowly emerging from oblivion, two notable figures rose dimly into view. Both had passed through the fires of martyrdom, and with priestly curses had been consigned to the flames of hell, whence, it was hoped, the smoke of their torments would ascend for ever and ever. They had been neither Popish, Lutheran, nor Calvinistic, but truth-seeking pilgrims and wanderers on the face of the earth, finding no rest to the soles of their feet, and ever denounced by priestly parties as the off-scouring of all things. One of these remarkable men, Servetus, we found as a youth studying Law at Toulouse, when he became excited by the theological controversies which prevailed, and determined to penetrate dogmatic foundations. Hearing that Bucer and Capito and others were expounding Reformation theology at Strasburg, he hastened there, hoping to enter the school of the prophets, and be initiated into the arcana of truth. Happening, however, to question the doctrine of the Trinity, he awoke a storm of rage among these eminent scholars, who denounced him as "a wicked and cursed Spaniard." He fled for his life and took refuge at Paris where he studied Medicine and took his degree as a physician with honours. It was said "he had a restless intellect which enabled him to *hit* truth." A gift both noble and rare. Amongst the truths he *hit* was that of the circulation of the blood. Harvey, credited with this discovery, was not yet born. The life of Servetus was spent in expounding and defending his advanced theology, both by speech and writing, and in fleeing as a refugee from place to place. While quietly passing through Geneva he was pounced upon by Calvin and his minions and condemned to be burned to death in a slow fire. This barbarous verdict, procured by the savage and brutal Calvin, was carried out to the letter. Amid long-protracted and indescribable agonies the great and noble-minded Servetus perished at the martyr's stake.

An even less known and less regarded heroic martyr was Bruno, who, with his piercing glance into the nature of things was continually bringing new or obscured truths to light. To the clerical fraternity with large invested interests in stereotyped forms and ceremonies such a man was dangerous, and must be crushed. As a youth he had to fly from a Dominican Convent because he confessed to having ceased to believe in transubstantiation and the Immaculate Conception. From Geneva he was driven by the bitterly persecuting Calvinists because of his rational views of things in general. At the University of Paris his logic was too keen for the clerical Aristotelians there, and so he was compelled to leave France. Two years in England—during which he enjoyed the friendship of the amiable and gifted Sir Philip Sidney—seem to have been the happiest years of his life. But here, again, he incurred the displeasure of the Clergy by his heretical writings, and was compelled to leave the country and become once more a homeless wanderer. Settling for a time at Venice, the officers of the Inquisition pounced upon him, and conveyed him as a prisoner to Rome. Seeking by savage persecution for two years to wring from him some form of recantation, in vain, he was burned to death at the stake on the 17th day of February in the year 1600.

But the implacable foes of honesty and truth could not burn his powerful ideas which had got afloat in the world. Benedict Spinoza caught his inspiration, and became, as he was designated, a "God-intoxicated man." Descartes was penetrated by his thought, and hence exclaimed, "Clear out of the human mind the accumulated theological rubbish of ages, and then shall clearly and unmistakably be seen the hand-writing of God upon the soul, explaining the universe within man and the universe without." Emerson caught up his idea of the immanence of God in nature by which man becomes divine and the universe divine, and added the statement that trade and commerce also would be divine when men yoked their market waggons to the stars.

After much investigation and study, I came to the conclusion, at a later time, that in the great and glorious army of martyrs, there were none greater and nobler than Bruno and Servetus.

The story of the great Crusade to recover the Holy Land from the Mohammedan infidels seemed to us to be romance converted into reality. By the injunction of Pope Urban II., the words "God wills it" were made the war-cry of the great enterprise. After travelling and preaching the most fiery discourses throughout Christendom, his main subject being the necessity of being at Jerusalem at the Judgment Day which was at hand, Peter the Hermit led 600,000 men in the direction of Palestine. During a seven month's siege of Antioch the army was so reduced by battle and disease that great numbers deserted, including poor Peter himself, who was making his way as fast as possible homewards when he was arrested and taken back by the soldiers of Tancred. The miserable remnant of the great army reached Jerusalem and took possession of it. To make secure the possession of Palestine and Syria, a second Crusade was preached by the eloquent fanatic St. Bernard. As the result, a mighty army of 1,200,000 men, as reported, was raised, and marched for Palestine led by the King of France and the Emperor of Germany, in the year 1147. After a vain attempt to take Damascus, the mere relics of this mighty host returned to Europe. Thus perished, without reaching the Holy Land, nearly a million of men, vociferating with their latest breath the Pope's watchwords, "God wills it." Had, indeed, God willed this awful carnage of the Christian hosts? And if not, what becomes of the Catholic judgment as to the Pope's infallible words? The most ignorant of men could not possibly, we thought, have uttered more false and disastrous words. More Crusades succeeded, more mighty hosts marched towards the Holy Land, more great battles were fought, more awful carnage ensued, until the whole Christian armies were utterly vanquished, and the Saracens were left in full possession of Jerusalem and the whole of Palestine.

Amongst the prominent commanders in this great warfare, was that of the bold, able, and fanatically religious Richard Cœur de Lion. His career was made the more interesting from the story told of his rescue from a dungeon by the aid of his minstrel Blondin. But the grandest figure of the whole Crusade was that of the brave, able, merciful, and magnanimous Saladin, the Saracen general. His treatment of the Christians on his taking of Jerusalem was sublime as viewed in contrast with the ferocious treatment of his countrymen by the Christians when they, previously, took Jerusalem by assault.

If we may estimate the comparative effects of the sacred books of each party in conducing to the final result in this great Crusade, then the triumph of the Koran over the Bible was complete.

In the case of the Scotch Covenanters the scenic effects were alike vivid, arousing, and enduring. As to the hidden forces at work, our views were sometimes divergent. Peden, the prophet, seemed to me a spiritually-intoxicated man. The temptations of the devil were as real in his case as in that of Christ, and the ministry of angels was as effective in the one case as the other. He lived in constant communion with the spirit world, and seemed to bear about with him "airs from heaven and blasts from hell." What, again, but immediate communion with heaven could have enabled John Brown to have faced martyrdom with such a holy calm? With the muskets of the dragoons pointed at his head he prayed for his murderers and calmly commended his wife and family to the care of God. Not less startling was the heroism of his wife who stood close by him when he was shot dead. "What do you think of your husband now," said the brutal Claverhouse. "I always thought well of him," was her reply, "but never so well as I think of him now." Then, gathering into her apron the scattered brains of the murdered man, she remarked, "You will have to answer at the bar of God for this day's work." But might not Claverhouse have been animated by a sense of duty? Yes, indeed, as was Milton's Satan, who thought it better to reign in hell than serve in heaven. The martyrdom, by slow drowning in the river Solway, of the heroic aunt and niece displayed a religious fortitude which made them angelic; while on the part of their murderers was displayed a religion which was fierce, brutish, and devilish.

No fiction could be so exciting and thrilling as the story of the Pilgrim Fathers. Even under Queen Elizabeth persecution fell heavily upon all who did not conform implicitly to the ceremonies of the Established Church. With great courage Robert Brown of Ipswich stood for Nonconformity on many particulars. His disciples increased and acquired the courage of their leader. James I. determined to make such parties conform, or they should be harried from the land. The Pilgrim Fathers were amongst the first to be harried across the sea. John Robinson, of Norfolk, suggested the formation of a New England on the American shore. Some 130 persons embarked in the small frail ship named the "Mayflower." What a daring band! What a forlorn hope! What a romantic scheme! What terrible sufferings they endured! and how great a triumph ensued! Tossing on the wild waters for months, they missed their way, landed on an inhospitable shore, could find but little subsistence, were in danger from roaming Indian bands, and in several months found their numbers reduced by nearly one half.

Any dreams of their old homes, any desires to return on the part of the survivors were entirely vain: they were fixed on the spot to live or die. They had sought free homes and a free church, and they had them. They had come to found a New England, and by God's help they would. And by God's help they did, and that same New England has had the freest homes and the freest churches down to the present time. True, as pointed out by Edward, these New England Puritans did not always allow to others the freedom which they claimed for themselves. But the intolerant party had no connection with the company of the "Mayflower," but were a mixed party of emigrants who arrived in New England at a later period. Subsequently it was that William Blaxton was banished into the depths of the distant forest. "Having fled from My Lord Bishop in England," he said, he had now "to flee from My Lord Brethren in America." Roger Williams, also, had to flee to the far-away wilderness of Rhode Island because he had freer and nobler ideas than his brethren, but which they would not tolerate to any extent.

Quakers were persecuted, and so-called witches were in large numbers cruelly put to death by these freedom-seeking Puritans being all the time enslaved by the literalisms of the Bible, which they made the rule of life, both civic and religious. When reading, at a later time, "The Courtship of Miles Standish," by Longfellow, my delight in the poetic narrative was intensified by the recollection that Miles Standish, John Alden, and Priscilla, the Puritan maiden, were all included in the Mayflower Pilgrim Band.

In the early history of the Waldenses we found the garden of Eden over again. Peter Waldo, a retired merchant, made another attempt to secure an earthly paradise. The hills and valleys of Savoy were the localities fixed upon, and the simple and guileless inhabitants were the elect people of God. For a time freedom and justice and happiness prevailed. Waldo's ideal was being happily reduced to the real. But alas! for only a very limited period. Romish demons from hell penetrated these happy regions and marred their peace. Rome, through her ever-eager emissaries, threatened, and then sent armies to destroy the fair fruits of honest industry, and to murder the people. An earnest protest, drawn up by Milton and sent in haste by Cromwell to the Dukes of Savoy, checked these destructive expeditions for a time. But when, later on, Louis XIV. revoked the Edict of Nantes, persecution was renewed and carried on with greater fierceness than before. The angel of deliverance on this occasion was the brave and noble-hearted Henry Arnaud. Under his guidance the Waldenses wrought deeds of almost superhuman valour. Army after army launched against them were overthrown and annihilated, while amidst appalling sufferings they maintained their ground for many years. But devils with devils damned firm concord hold; and so Pandemonium, France, and Rome prevailed, and the Waldensian Paradise was lost. Deeply moved by this thrilling narrative, the love of civil and religious liberty was greatly strengthened in both our minds, and no divergent criticism ensued.

In proceeding to study the treatment of the Huguenots in France, we met with the culmination of tragic horrors. Black Bartholomew's Day, or the Blood-wedding Day, was, surely, the most terrible day ever known in the history of mankind. In painting the terrors of the French Revolution, Protestant and Catholic preachers have vied with each other, while at the same time they have passed lightly over or altogether misrepresented the more enormous massacre of Bartholomew's Day.

One of the finest figures amongst the Protestant party, we thought, was Prince Conde, who fell in the conflict. The noblest personality of all was Admiral Coligny, who, after displaying great ability and great fidelity to a worthy cause, was lured into the fatal trap laid at Paris and there perished. Henry of Navarre was conspicuous on both sides of the struggle, being either Catholic or Protestant just according to his plans. Really, he held tolerant sentiments, and secured the Edict of Nantes favourable to the Protestant cause. The most fearful figure, the most treacherous and cruel of all the miscreants of that fearful time, was that she-wolf, the Queen Mother Catherine de Medici. And then, as the last awful figure in that panorama of human blood, stalked forth the Hierarchy of Rome, singing the Te Deum and proclaiming a year of jubilee in commemoration of the massacre of at least twenty thousand human beings.

In the proceedings of the Westminster Assembly of Divines

and Scholars we were interested and perplexed. For some of the individuals present we had much more admiration than for the numerous and mysterious propositions which the Assembly formulated and inserted in its Catechisms and Confessions. The way in which the learned John Selden with his Greek Testament upset many favourite renderings of Scripture texts must have been as galling to the solemn Divines as it was amusing to Cromwell, Milton, and other laymen present. Amongst the Divines I most admired Philip Nye, who, now and again, contended that some reliance should be placed on human reason as well as on the Word of God. Going through the Assembly's propositions Henry Ward Beecher compared to the tramp of a convict climbing the tread-mills, with some preference for the latter. In this judgment I now fully concur, and think the comparison applicable to three-fourths of all the theology I have read.

Previous to the time of the Commonwealth civil liberty had been fought for, and, to a limited extent, secured; but religious liberty had only been dreamed about in England until then. Cromwell held advanced ideas on both points, and Milton more advanced ideas still. George Fox tried the principles and patience of Cromwell greatly and yet met with much forbearance. John Biddle, the earliest of the English Unitarians, met with much indulgence from the same ruler. Richard Baxter gave great and constant trouble to the Protector who made continued efforts to conciliate him. The restless Baxter could not manage to remain a Churchman although he tried hard to do so. He succeeded no better in trying to be a Presbyterian. And, strange to say, although so independent himself, he could not work with the Independent party. Standing thus alone, he entered with great zest into controversy with all comers. Happily for himself and others, he was even more eager to soar into the lofty region of a fervent devotion. While his controversial writings have sunk into obscurity, his " Dying Thoughts " and " Saint's Rest " have continued to nourish devout and tender and humble souls.

Having found that during the 18th century all the churches had gone to sleep, it was a pleasant thing for me to point out that Wesley and Whitfield were called to wake the slumberers from their dangerous and fatal dreams. My companion raised no objection as to the work done by these great evangelists, but would rather they had remained within the Established Church, and indeed, rather thought they had never left it. For the noble stand made for a rational religion by Priestly and Channing we had but little admiration at the time: and little did I think I should ever become one of their earnest disciples, although I had long had leanings in that direction.

CHAPTER XI

SCIENCE

THE seventh subject in our plan of study was science. Science in general and chemistry in particular had long engaged the close attention of my friend. The text-book I best liked was Joyce's " Scientific Dialogues." There may have been works displaying the circle of the sciences in as clear and interesting way as this, but I have never met with such. If a new edition of these Dialogues could be published, thoroughly revised and brought up to date, it would be found to be one of the finest text-books of science in existence at the present time. Plunging headlong into an account of mechanical forces, we soon made acquaintance with Archimedes, some of whose formularies the world had not and would not let die. If, however, he had known of the forces that kept the earth spinning round on its axis, and which sent it rushing at a mighty speed through its orbit round the sun, he would never have uttered his memorable desire for a fulcrum and a lever by which to move the world. But then we would have been deprived of a unique and very interesting figure of speech in continual use ever since. But far more memorable still were the words " Eureka ! Eureka ! " which he uttered in a frenzy as he rushed through the streets in a state of undress. Puzzling his brains to discover the amount of alloy mixed with the gold in King Hiero's crown, he entered one of the public baths, when, observing the amount of water displaced by his own body, a flash of thought made the solution clear. Careful experiment proved the theory to be correct, and hence the discovery of the specific gravity of all bodies, so important to all scientific investigators and so beneficial to mankind at large. We made a pleasant acquaintance with Sir Isaac Newton sitting in his garden and inferring universal gravitation from a falling apple; with him in his study experimenting with a glass prism and forming a new theory of light; with him when comparing the sublime achievements of his life to the diversions of a boy gathering pebbles and shells on the sea shore, with the great ocean of truth lying undiscovered before him. The lines of Pope we thought striking and appropriate in which he says:—

"Nature and nature's law lay hid in night;
God said: 'Let Newton be!' and all was light."

With Dr. Dalton and his Atomic Theory, as also with his many experiments, Edward was quite familiar. And so while he experimented and demonstrated I looked on or listened with pleasure and profit. Even so dry a subject as that of the divisibility of atoms of matter could lead, it seemed, to wonderful discoveries of the secret forces of Nature, as well as to practical and useful results. With the guidance of the Herschels we pursued our astronomical studies under the starlit skies. With the names and movements of the larger heavenly bodies we became familiar. Concerning nebulæ, comets, double stars, and erratic bodies only revealed by the telescope, we learned from the text-books. But neither reflecting nor refracting telescopes, nor the discoveries made by them, were known then. Nor did we learn of any indications that some at least of the constituents of the sun and other heavenly bodies were similar to the constituents of the earth. Nor, again, could we learn that the movements of the magnetic needle were intimately connected with the movement of the spots on the sun. Nor still, again, had we heard it declared that within the Pleiades was situated the heaven of heavens with the throne of God in the midst. This picturesque story was lately told in a sermon by a popular London preacher, the great difficulty about the narrative being the entire absence of evidence in its support. Just the same difficulty there is about that other picturesque story given us by the Greeks concerning the same constellation: in which we are told that the seven daughters of Atlas were placed in the heavens after their departure from the earth, six of whom shine brightly because of their alliance with the gods, and the seventh shines dimly because of her marriage with an earthly mortal. Anyway, the two stories may each serve to point a moral or adorn a dull discourse.

In the study of electricity we, of course, met with the beautiful story of Franklin seizing the lightning with his kite. But there was not the least prospect, in those days, of yoking the same force to a train of tram-cars to be pushed along the streets, nor of harnessing this terrific power by threads of wire to carry instant intelligence all round the world, nor was there any idea of Marconi methods. Proceeding to the Mechanic's Institute, Edward took possession of the air-pump and Torricelli's tube, and performed many interesting experiments in connection with atmospheric air and gases of various kinds. Here the great name of Priestley came into view. In the discovery of oxygen, which, however, he gave another name, he awakened the jealousy and oppotion of many of the Savants of the day. At the same time, by his heretical theological writings, he awakened the fierce hostility of the Clergy. This bitter savagery being communicated to the rabble in the streets, his house in Birmingham was stormed by mobs of infuriated men, his furniture broken to pieces, and his books and scientific instruments scattered in the streets. Just escaping martyrdom himself, he escaped to America and then spent his life in usefulness and peace.

For nearly two years we had steadily pursued our arduous, self-denying, fatiguing course of study. Besides gaining a large amount of useful information, we had formed habits of thorough, continuous and close study. At the same time we had managed to get through a great deal of miscellaneous reading in religion, science, and general literature, including novels. This desultory reading we did with a good conscience, knowing we were doing other and better work. Two or three nights a week, also, we had spent at the Useful Knowledge Society. Even Sunday did not afford us much rest. Edward was in attendance at Church and School. I was at the old Chapel in the morning at the 7 o'clock prayer meeting, at the class meeting from 8 to 8.45, and at School from 9.30 to 12.30. In the afternoon I was at School from 1.30 to 4.30, at Chapel from 6 to 7.35, and at after meetings until 9.30 or 10 o'clock. Seeing that at the same time we were working more than seventy hours in the six days in the warehouse, it is clear we were injuring our health by doing too much of good things. Afterwards we felt we were suffering from bodily weakness and mental strain. Indeed, poor, dear Edward shortly broke down completely. Reluctantly he gave up his work, hoping soon to resume it. He rallied a little, and we were hopeful, but he soon relapsed and our hopes of recovery gradually faded. Calmly he met the coming change. Serenely the earthly life ended, and brightly the heavenly life began. But what an indescribable shock to his poor father and to myself! He had lost the only family tie he had left, and I had lost my dearest friend.

Past scenes, conversations, studies, confidences, and endearments continually rushed through my mind for many days; and indeed, have never ceased. In a sort of solemn dream I attended the funeral. Familiar conversation was passing in the company present in which I could take but little part. The processon along the tree-shaded roads to Prestbury churchyard I tried to think a triumphal march. And such it must have been to his conscious spirit. To me, since then, it has ever seemed as the taking to its last resting-place of the dust of a young hero, of a conqueror, of a veritable saint.

I must have been some months over twenty-two years of age and Edward about twenty-three when this sad parting came. My greatest comfort was the remembrance of the sacred compact into which we had mutually entered. And now he waits joyfully *there* and I wait hopefully *here* until that compact shall be literally carried out. Patience then, my soul: get on with thine earthly work. When that is complete, then the outstretched hand, as agreed, shall be there to help thee through the gloom of the valley of the shadow of death. I could not but feel lonely for a time. When talking with ordinary acquaintances I felt as if they were almost strangers. Happily, in a while and by degrees, a new and confidential and comforting presence was discerned. My brother Samuel was then some fifteen years of age, and was becoming thoughtful and studious. He had been going through hard experiences such as I had gone through myself. He was in the silk mill at nine years of age, and very soon was confined through long and slaving days. He began to look pale and sickly and sorrowful, and could eat but little. I knew the malady and spoke encouragingly, when the tears would start from his eyes, showing how terribly he felt the grinding and crushing effect of factory laws and regulations. To the Sunday School we had gone together for many years. Very attentive was he to his lessons, and learned them quickly and well. At the Useful Knowledge Society he was regular and attentive, and soon developed a love of history in particular, and the higher literature in general. Here our tastes and sympathies met, and we became warm-hearted and constant companions. This happy union of hearts grew stronger and closer from year to year, and remained without a break until the day of his death. Thus in a comparatively brief space of time I had lost one dear and true friend, and gained another. And so the vicissitudes of life have ever kept sweeping on. Always I have been losing the best of persons and the best of things, but never without compensations of the richest kinds. Surely then I ought to feel by this time that—

> " I stand amid the eternal ways,
> And what is mine shall know my face.
> Nor time, nor space, nor deep, nor high,
> Can keep my own away from me."

CHAPTER XII

OWENISM — VESTIGES OF CREATION — RITUALISM

WHILE going through my late course of study I had paid but slight attention to a new public movement which was spreading rapidly throughout the country. It was variously described as Owenism, Socialism, and Communism. Several young men in the warehouse were smitten with it. John Perry sought every opportunity to argue the matter out with me. " Man's character is formed for him and not by him," was his leading proposition. I contended that both factors entered into the formation of characters. " The new party were intending to make a ' New Moral World '," said my opponent. " But," I replied, " by leaving the Christian religion out the party were endeavouring to form an Immoral World." Here I was wrong, as my opponent did not fail to show. Owen had formed large Day Schools and carried them on with great success, it was stated. " Such secular teaching might be good as far as it went," I said, " but would need supplementing by dogmatic Christian teaching, or one side of human nature would be left altogether untrained. By living in Mr. Owen's New Communities mankind would escape the evils of the old outside immoral world, it was said. " That had to be proved," I replied. But Owen was a great philanthropist, having spent fortunes in benefiting mankind. I thought much of his money had been spent in vain and unwise schemes. But all such small discussions were overshadowed by a great discussion in the large Sunday School during three successive evenings, attended by great and crushing crowds

The assailant of Owenism was a Dr. Brindley, a fluent, forcible, and somewhat unscrupulous speaker. He dealt largely in sarcasm and invective. On one occasion he gave a most ludicrous account of the formation of Mr. Owen's scheme of moral and social reform. "It was during a serious affliction, when he had to be dosed, and purged, and poulticed," said the speaker, "that the idea of a new moral world was borne in upon his mind": thus showing that this revolutionary and Godless scheme originated in physic and gruel! Of course there was neither argument nor sense in such statements, but they greatly amused the crowded audience.

The Owenites secured an able champion in Mr. Lloyd Jones, equal, in most respects to Dr. Brindley, and in some gifts greatly his superior. He had a fine presence, a good voice, and an imposing manner. His able defence of Owenism greatly troubled many Christian minds, my own included. Terrible rents, it was apparent, were made in Dr. Brindley's armour, which he seemed unable to repair. Many began to see and to say that no good would come to the Christian cause from the protracted discussion, and I was of the same opinion. "You speak," said Jones, "of the deleterious influence our principles would have on the masses of the people. But what are the influences of your own Christian system on the masses of the people? Look at the countless number of drunkards in your midst; at the armies of criminals, aye, juvenile criminals; and at the tens of thousands of prostitutes swarming your city streets: and then say what your principles have done to save the masses of the people." From the large School the discussion was carried into the mills, warehouses, and workshops of the town. The questions heard on every side were— "Has man a free will, or does he act from necessity?" "Does he form his own character, or is he the creature of circumstances?" "Would co-operative life in communities be better than life under the grinding tyranny of capitalist employers?"

I entered earnestly into these discussions, being often pitted against John Perry, the ablest of the Owenite disputants. The result on my own mind was a decided conviction that the truth was not altogether on either the one side or the other.

Quite as keen, and far more widely spread was the controversy which arose on the appearance of the remarkable book entitled "Vestiges of the Natural History of Creation." Scientific men and literary men with theological casts of mind joined the mighty hosts of irate clerics who rose up in arms to do battle with this terrible book. One of the most moderate assaults on the work I found in "The Student" for the year 1844. "We have perused the Vestiges," says the writer, "with mingled feelings of gratification and pain—of gratification from the lucid exposition therein contained of some of the most interesting subjects of human research—of pain, because amidst so much that is talented and commendable there is a tissue of hypothesis deserving the reproval of the Christian. Whatever may have been the intention of the writer, it is clear from the reception of the Vestiges that the result has been evil. The interests of truth and religion demand an expression of the most unqualified disapproval that the author should have directly assailed the Mosaic books, and thereby attempted to disturb the foundations of all revelation. Development is the most subtle and the least perfectly known of all questions connected with the study of life."

Of course the critic of "The Student" did not see that the Mosaic books themselves were full of hypotheses; nor that the Christian religion was only one religion amongst a number of equally authorised religions; nor that Nature itself was a revelation, and the only direct revelation, that man has within his reach. Nor did I myself at that time see these things except through a glass darkly. As to that bugbear of a word, Development, which had so frightened the critic of "The Student," it was simply the herald of the far more potent word Evolution, indicating a force which was sweeping through all fields of investigation, and aiming to hold the whole realm of knowledge within its grasp.

Contemporaneous with the excitement over this revolutionary

work was the ecclesiastical sensation attendant on the secession of Newman to Rome. By his discourses at Oxford University, he had been turning the heads of the students during many years. Spoken in a low, soft, solemn, and monotonous voice, his words pierced like dagger-points the hearts and minds of his hearers, causing them involuntarily to turn their faces towards ritualism and Rome. He not only pointed out but led the way towards the hoary citadels reared in the darkest ages, and from which, for a thousand years, had been fulminating the thunders of doom against all noble freethinking and free-speaking men. Crowds of disciples, with the greatest enthusiasm, followed on to the very verge of the Rubicon, but there proclaimed a halt! With the greatest courage their leader, with a straggling few, passed the stream of destiny, but the clerical crowd still halted on the hither side. That region in front seemed bare, barren, rugged, and uninviting—their Goshen was behind. What! leave their historic episcopal palaces, noble abbeys, richly-endowed churches, beautiful manses, aristocratic and royal patronage, with annual millions of pounds sterling from tithes, rates, and fees? Nay! that could never be. It was impossible; unthinkable. But could they not have Romanism at home? Yea, it must be planted firmly in the heart of the Anglican church itself. Thenceforth their course was clear. A new historic past must be found for this new-fangled church. Tract No. 90 would render most valuable help in that direction. Suitable extracts must be made from the ancient church fathers; care being taken that the puerilities and foolish fancies of these ancients be kept well out of sight. The Book of Common Prayer must be so learnedly and skilfully manipulated as to make it a strong bulwark of the reconstructed church. Bible texts, also, might be shown strongly in its favour, provided that other texts were kept hidden from view. Keble could furnish any quantity of suitable hymns to be set to Gregorian tunes which should fascinate the musically-minded and win them to the church. Of course latitudinarian churchmen would mildly complain and gently wail. Simeonite clergymen would first protest and then resignedly tolerate the new Dagon set up. Amongst the Philistines —otherwise militant non-conformists—would be heard wailing and gnashing of teeth. But what mattered such puny things as these to the fanatical refurbishers and whitewashers of a decaying church, who felt the rising tides of a ritualistic sea bearing them mightily on to fortune and great success?

CHAPTER XIII

FAMILY EXPENSE — MOTHER'S DEATH — USEFUL KNOWLEDGE SOCIETY

SERIOUS coming events, of a domestic kind, had for some time been casting their shadows before them. Uncle Houldbrook, according to custom, had placed a young life on his farm at Butley, at the cost of all his farming capital. In a short time the young man had died, and a large rent charged on the farm, which meant ruin for the farmer. After much persuasion, my father undertook the arduous task of managing the farm and saving Uncle Houldbrook from bankruptcy and from being ousted from the place. By hard work, and with little remuneration, he kept the farm going for many years, and until both uncle and aunt had died.

In the meantime mother's health was failing fast, which necessitated an immediate change. The little farm stock at Cliff Lane cottage was sold off and the proceeds kept in reserve to pay the expenses of a certain event of which we did not like to think, but which she felt would soon come. As soon as possible, we removed to the small house adjoining the Sunday school, where we had to manage housekeeping on a strictly economic scale. After much thinking and careful planning, the weekly balance came out thus:—

INCOME.

My Wage	£0 15 0
For Teaching at Useful Knowledge Society, etc.	0 5 0
Brother Samuel's Wage	0 8 0
Brother Enoch's Wage	0 6 0
	£1 14 0

EXPENDITURE.

House Rent and Rates	£0 4 0
Coals and Candles	0 2 0
Food	0 12 0
Sundries	0 2 0
For Clothing, Books, Collections, Charities, and Deposits in the Government Savings Bank	0 14 0
	£1 14 0

In this way we secured the necessities of life, kept out of debt, maintained our independence, and were enabled—like Longfellow's village blacksmith—to "look the whole world in the face," for we owed not any man.

It is written that Alexander the Great asked the chiefs of certain tribes he had conquered what they most desired. "We want," they said, "to live on, and not die." Ah! and how unspeakably strong was our desire that the one so dear to us, her sons, and who had done so much for us, should live on some years and experience repose of both body and mind, of which she had known so little during her arduous life. But alas! this was not to be. At the beginning of March, 1846, her health was failing so fast it became doubtful if she would live until the end of the month.

To realise my own keen and vivid experience at that time, as well as my mother's triumphant experience, I must quote literally from the written diary before me:—"Sunday, March 1st.—Mother is sinking fast into the arms of death, Uncle Adam and John Hooley (her class leader) both present. A glorious prayer-meeting, lasting nearly through the afternoon. Next day, just after awaking from a dose, she broke out in a rapture of praise and thanksgiving. Calling the family and several visiting friends into her room, she described, most joyfully, God's special message of grace to her soul. 'All fears and doubts,' she exclaimed, 'had disappeared,' and she could now rejoice with a joy unspeakable and full of glory. When John Hooley called next day and was told the exact time when this great manifestation of the grace of God took place, he declared that just then he was at prayer on her behalf, and that rising up he exclaimed to his wife that Martha Rushton was either released from the flesh or made unspeakably happy in God."

Sitting by her bedside, I showed her the class ticket which had just been sent to her. "Yes," she replied with a smile, "it is the last." I asked if she remembered when she got her first ticket? "O yes!" she exclaimed, "it was during a revival in Saltersford when I was twenty-one years of age and living with my parents at Hooley Hey. And oh," she continued, "how those hills and valleys resounded with prayer and praise." Speaking to Samuel, Enoch, and father, she hoped they would, like myself, join the Methodist society, so that we might all travel together to the better land.

About half-past twelve o'clock on the morning of March 6th, 1846, I went to bed, not to sleep, but to think and pray. Very soon I was summoned back to mother's bedroom, and found she was dying. As she fixed her eyes upon me, I said "Is all well now, mother?" In a distinct whisper she replied, "Aye, Lord," three times; and then, finding she could not complete the sentence, she lifted up her right hand and waved it, as if in triumph, while a bright light glittered in her eyes. We all then—father, Samuel, Enoch, and myself—knelt down by the bedside while I whispered a parting benediction, during which her breathing gently subsided, and all was still—the spirit had fled.

I copy the following words from my diary just as they were written on the day of her death:—"Death! Death!! O Death! and hast thou executed thy commission upon our dearly-beloved mother? Hast thou indeed summoned her away? Well then, what matters it? Thy sting was taken away. What matters it that this frail tenement is returning to its kindred dust, if the redeemed soul is now before the throne of God? This we fully believe. This is our confidence and joy. Glory be to God and the Lamb for ever and ever."

A few days later a plain hearse, containing the remains of

the dear departed, left the house attended by the whole family band, consisting of father aged sixty, myself twenty-five, brother Samuel eighteen, and brother Enoch fifteen years of age. The only other person present was the conductor of the hearse. Over the hills and through the valleys of Rainow, and along the bleak moorlands of Saltersford we wound our way to Jenkyn Chapel. In that wild and solitary spot, in that ancient sanctuary, old Bible words were said with a newly-penetrative force ever to be felt by each mourner there. Returning along those weird upland roads, our words were few and sad, but our minds were full of solemn thoughts and high resolves. Strangers and pilgrims we felt ourselves that day seeking a better country, already reached by the one so inexpressibly dear to us all.

Again I copy from my diary the words written on our arrival home:—

"March 10th, 1846.—Earth to earth—ashes to ashes!—This afternoon we have taken the mortal remains of our dear departed one to the resting-place of her forefathers in the graveyard of Jenkyn Chapel. We have seen the cold and shrivelled form laid beneath the clods of the moorland and solitary valley, where it shall lie and moulder until awakened by the *first* loud blast of the Archangel's trump. 'The dead in Christ shall rise first'."

Then came the decision for father to return to the Butley Farm and for us to retain our present home, which would be more than ever dear to us. Here mother had arduously laboured, heroically suffered, and triumphantly died. Ecton hills and woods were in front, about which she had often spoken inspiring words. The Sunday School adjoined the house where we had long gone to learn and she to join in the worship of God. In the house were the books from her early mountain home, and precious heirlooms they were, begetting a love for kindred books, which we obtained as fast as our very limited means would permit. And then, was not the abode itself haunted by precious memories, and by real personal presences, may I not say, of the dear ones unseen—only by the outward eyes?

Funeral matters settled, we had to face life under new and trying conditions. The cleaning of the house, the mending of garments, the preparation of good food from plain materials, which had been so well attended to by mother before—how were these things to be managed now? Cousin Sarah Cooper did the best she could as housekeeper, and we became resigned to our lot. With long hours at work in the day and at schools and meetings at night, we spent but little time in the house, so that she had a very easy place. Religious services were sedulously attended to and helped to give comfort and rest to the mind. On the road to and from the old chapel I had often fallen in with an intelligent and good Methodist, and had pleasant converse with him. Shawcross was his name, and his house in Higher Hurdsfield. Finding he had become smitten with Mormonism, I elicited from him the following particulars. He had been reading and thinking and praying about the matter, he said, for some time, and was now about to leave Methodism and become a member of the Mormon Church. He had only read parts of the Book of Mormon, but thought it was akin to the Bible, and inspired like the Bible. Did not know where were the metal plates on which the contents of the book were inscribed, nor was he aware that any person did know where they were. Nor did Jews and Christians—he contended—know any more about the original copies of their own scriptures. Joseph Smith was a greater Moses leading the Latter Day Saints through a fiercer wilderness to a richer Goshen than the Israelites ever knew. Brigham Young was a greater Joshua who with his followers marched triumphantly through desert regions, which everywhere burst into bloom and beauty as they passed, until the glorious landscape of Utah burst upon their astonished view, and where they commenced at once to build the true city of God.

"But polygamy was in practice," we said, "both in Nauvoo and Utah." "Yes," said he, "and that shows how the revelations of Joseph Smith coincide with the revelations recorded by Moses of old. If the Bible Saints acted so, why should not Latter Day Saints do the same?" Still, there was no compulsion in the case, and he himself should never do such a thing.

A few months later, a crowd of people assembled in Plungebrook Hollow. In the midst stood a wild-looking Yankee proclaiming the new revelation of the Kingdom of Heaven. Beside a large pool of water stood Mr. Shawcross and Peter Pott, who, at the end of the speech, were plunged into the water, and from thence at once stepped into the Kingdom of Latter Day Saints. Peter Pott in his early days attended Hurdsfield School, but had never attended either Church or Chapel. Caught by the eloquence of the Prophet, he had decided that a residence in the paradise of the Saints over the sea would be far preferable to life in a coal-pit, which for long had been his unfortunate lot. But when tithes were levied on the Saints, he refused to pay, as that would take some of the money he was saving to carry him to the promised land.

Mr. Shawcross after a time slipped back again into the snug Methodist fold, and poor Peter pursued his old, hard course of life, until the end came, when we trust he found a better paradise than that he had ever dreamt of beyond the sea.

My classes at the Useful Knowledge Society had always been, and still remained, a source of strong interest and real pleasure to me. The forty or fifty youths from the age of fourteen to twenty years voluntarily attending these classes belonged to the best families of working people. For many of these youths I had strong affection, which was evidently returned. For some, I anticipated useful and successful careers, and my hopes have been fully realised.

Since then, I have often heard of Government Day School Teachers being thoroughly wearied and disgusted with the unruly children and youths under their care. There can be no wonder at that, seeing that the dull children and the bright, the degraded and the more elevated, the utterly vicious and the more virtuous, the teachable and the utterly unteachable, are forced together, pell mell, into the public schools.

A much better system of general education might be instituted in the following way: Let the Government establish unsectarian institutes for the training of teachers, both male and female. Then let them be aided in establishing unsectarian and voluntary schools throughout the kingdom. These schools would draw in all the willing and teachable children in every neighbourhood. The rest of the children should be forced into reformatory schools, and be placed under such teachers as would be likely to draw out the best possible result obtainable from such unruly natures. This system might be carried out with much better results and at less cost than the unjust and comparatively ineffective system now in vogue.

The Useful Knowledge Society had an interesting origin and a successful course extending over sixty years. It was formed by the junction of two mutual improvement classes, the one meeting in the large Sunday School, and the other in the old Fence Schoolroom. The members of this latter class formed junior classes, taught by one or other of the senior members. To one of these junior classes I belonged, and took great delight in the exercises by which we were taught. Engaged in some of the exact sciences, including mathematics, themselves, our teachers insisted upon our learning the exact meaning, spelling, pronunciation and origin of words. At the closing of the class a selected word was given to each scholar, of which he had to bring a full and elaborate account on the succeeding night.

On the formation of the Useful Knowledge Society—of which I was one of the first members—the same system of exact definition was carried out. In the grammar class taught by Thomas Kelley, one of the founders of the Society, we had not only to learn the grammatical forms and relations of words and sentences, but we had to get to the roots of words and learn their various and relative meanings. Parsing the " Elegy in a Country Churchyard " we found to be a most useful, interesting, and delightful exercise. Our exhilaration in the pursuit of Nominatives and Objectives was quite as great, I am sure, as that of the most eager hunters in the chase of hares or deer. Indeed, to follow out the comparison, we had the advantage in every way. We had no liability to get broken bones from leaping dangerous fences. Nor were we in danger of broken consciences from killing innocent creatures of the moors and woodlands. Meeting with a member of this class some forty years afterwards, the following colloquy ensued: "Have you forgotten parsing the 'Elegy'?" "No," I said, "I could not if I would, and I would not if I could." "It was a most inspiring exercise," said he. "I am glad to hear you say so, for such I have ever felt it to be," I replied. "And permanently beneficial," he remarked. "That is exactly what I have found," I remarked in return.

The teacher of the Shorthand class was John Wright, a fellow-warehouseman. He was a devout and enthusiastic worshipper of Byrom's system of Stenography as improved by Mollineux. At the same time I was taking a leading part in a class outside the Society for learning Pitman's Phonography. The relative value of these two systems was the subject of vehement dispute. In trials of speed there proved to be something like equality. But in the reading of the words written, Phonography had most decidedly the advantage. I got to write with tolerable ease some 120 or 130 words a minute. I had no particular object in view in learning Phonography, but wrote it because I liked it. In after years, when I went to college at Manchester, I found I could not have succeeded in my studies without it.

All the classes at the Useful Knowledge Society were entrusted to amateur teachers, who had peculiar methods of teaching. Luke Fox, for instance, lecturing on astronomy, fixed on a man in the middle of the assembly to represent the sun. Then, lifting up a bladder containing a large quantity of peas, he threw it in a curved line over the sun man, and hit a man at the end of the room. "This," he said, "represented centrifugal force." The man, seizing the bladder, hurled it with great force at the head of the lecturer, who exclaimed, "That is centripetal force, and that is how the planets move round the sun." Such teaching was simple and amusing, but also effective.

The earliest teacher in the Chemistry Class was William Pedley, a slim young man about middle height, with a thoughtful face, and with his head singularly bent on one side. Probably the emaciation of his body had set in during his incarceration for long days in the mill during his early years. At the instigation of the heads of the firm (Brocklehursts) he devoted much of his time in the class to the mixing of colours for dye stuffs. At the time, the firm was engaged extensively in the dying of silk for the manufacture of costly silk, and benefitted much from Pedley's experiments. Edward Davenport joined Pedley as an assistant, and together gave most interesting lectures to the students and others. Several of these lectures, which greatly interested the spectators, were on the composition of atmospheric air, with illustrations of its compressive and expansive force. On these occasions the air-pump was always in a conspicuous place, with which—after a sweating effort in exhausting the receiver—striking experiments were performed. A chip of wood and a feather would fall at equal speed; shrivelled apples and pears would expand their seemingly dead skins and look like fine fresh fruit; the air at the corner of an egg would force out the contents of the shell, and a bladder would show how the human lungs drew in and expelled atmospheric air. This latter experiment led to the consideration of the bad effect of breathing impure air and the necessity of breathing pure air. But what could we poor factory slaves do who were compelled to work in a bad atmosphere through six long days in every week? Many died in consequence within a few years of confinement. Others struggled on for many years, but with impaired constitutions and shortened lives.

Edward Davenport entered with delight into experiments showing the proportionate combination of atoms constituting gases, fluids, and solid bodies. Sometimes he would expatiate on ultimate atoms, and the effect of magnetic, galvanic, and electric forces on those atoms. In private circles, after some of these lectures, very recondite questions would arise. Amid the mighty natural forces of the universe, where did God come in, would be asked. Pedley could not see any place for such a being. Edward and myself thought these very forces proved that His place was everywhere. But the whole subject was rendered ridiculous—contended a third party—when it was claimed by an immense majority of Christians that this infinite being was ever at the beck and call of a priest, who could concentrate Him—the whole of Him—in a wafer of bread. From these premises of the priest the Indian convert's logic was correct when he affirmed that he had swallowed God in a wafer and there was no God left. If the priest should contend that the logic of the convert was false from the darkness and ignorance of his mind, it might be replied that the priest's logic was false for being founded on the irrational dogmas of an irrational church

Notwithstanding the scepticism of Pedley, he always proved himself to be an honest, intelligent, moral, and kindly man. This surprised both Edward and myself, as we had always heard preachers affirm that sceptics were ignorant, or, if not ignorant, were wilfully wicked men.

One of the first patrons of the Society was John Brocklehurst, M.P., who, from an early period, became its President and remained so for many years. His speeches at the annual meetings were fairly good, if not fluent, and read well in the newspaper reports. He had a fine and rather tall figure, and was the best dressed and smartest-looking man in the town.

Honest, bluff, sturdy, plain-spoken John Wright rendered good service for a long time to the Society. Having got a Jacquard loom fixed up in the lecture-room, he mounted it himself, on occasion, and wove away, making superior figured silk goods, stopping from time to time to explain each minute operation to the audience present. His son Joseph, when a very young man, aided the Society in many ways. I very well remember his first speech at an annual meeting, which discourse was thickly adorned with flowers and spangles of many kinds. This style of speech was in such complete contrast to his father's style that great merriment prevailed in the assembly. Many thought he would be discouraged and deterred from speaking again. But, nothing daunted, he was ever ready to speak on any subject on any occasion, and soon became and long remained one of the leading men of the town. He rendered yeoman service to the cause of Liberalism in the town until the latter part of his life, when he turned right round against it and shattered the party which he and his father had laboured so hard and so long to place and keep in executive power. It was then prognosticated that he would soon secede to the Established Church. And sure enough, he was rather often seen there, but I think he never ceased to be a member of the Congregational Church. Had he lived longer, it was conjectured, his secession would certainly have taken place. There is indeed a fascination in that direction, and an unceasing march to the Church. It is quite a familiar saying that the third generation of well-to-do Unitarians never drives its carriage to chapel but always to the Established Church. Mr. Chamberlain, the firm Unitarian dissenter and whilom denouncer of Church and State, has gone over to the Dukes and Duchesses of the Establishment—if not to the Church itself. Other dissenters are largely drawn in the same direction. Such is the great stream of tendency in the direction of that best of all possible societies for the ambitious—the English aristocracy.

The funny speaker at these meetings was James Rathbone, proprietor of spirit vaults in Mill Street. He was always invited, always attended, and always delivered the same speech. Narrating the history of the silk trade in Macclesfield, he always, at a certain point, referred to the first methods of printing bandanas. On the utterance of this last word, every one smiled and loudly whispered, " Now, then, the blackberry spot is coming " ; and then it came. " This is the way it is done," said the speaker. " You tie up a given number of loops on the face of the cloth, and then dip it into the die-tub. You then dry it, and untie the loops, when the blackberry spots, in all their beauty appear." Then invariably came loud bursts of laughter, in which he often joined himself. When spoken to about these humorous repetitions, he simply replied that the progress of the silk trade ought to be remembered, and he was determined it should not be forgotten. He was a kindly, genial, charitable man, and filled many important offices in the town. He was an earnest dissenter, a decided liberal, and a member of the Townley Street congregation through the larger part of his life.

John May rose into prominence in the town as a young man not by any ostentatious display, but by steady attention to his profession and also to public business. At our meetings his speech was never impassioned, but calm, easy, informing, and decisive. He has proved the greatest church builder in the town during the century, and, probably, of any century. He took a leading part in bringing down the Commissioners, who made such a dreadful political earthquake in the town.

For a considerable time the clergy took no notice of the U.K. Society. One of the first to discover it was Rector Stanley, of Alderley, who delivered a lecture on geology. There was some report of heresy in this discourse, and some interesting discussion on the matter. The phrase, "In the beginning," as treated by the lecturer, was not deemed satisfactory. Nor yet his extension of the six days of creation beyond twenty-four hours each; as also the extension of the seventh day. Stanley was evidently a precursor of that broadening thought in science and religion which has been going on during the last half-century with ever-increasing speed and force. Either just before or soon after the coronation of the queen, she passed, with her retinue, Monk's Heath, where a great crowd of country people were assembled to give her welcome. Conspicuous in the crowd was Rector Stanley, riding a white horse and marshalling the people. His figure arrested the attention of Victoria, who sought audience with him, when a very interesting conversation took place, which greatly gratified the Queen, the Rector, and all the people there. Some time later, by royal mandate, the Rector was made Bishop of Norwich, and proved one of the ablest, the most tolerant, and most charitable prelates in the Church. By the same royal influence, at a later time, his son was made Dean of Westminster Abbey, and became the greatest of all the distinguished clerics who had occupied that honourable post. All noble-minded and advanced thinkers he ever encouraged and aided, including the arch-heretic Colenso himself. Cheshire, and especially Alderley, should be proud of connection with the two noble Stanleys, father and son.

Rev. Dr. Burnett, Incumbent of St. George's Church, was a welcome speaker at these annual meetings. His popularity in the town was much enhanced by his lecture on the nonexistence of the first Napoleon, by his discourse on the text, "He shall be buried with the burial of an ass," and by his public declaration that a death-grasp had been, and was, and ever would be upon Unitarianism, from which it could not escape. All these discourses in their applications were inappropriate, superficial, and indefensible, and yet they hit exactly the public orthodox taste, and helped to make the author a notable public man.

In the first discourse he proceeded on an assumption, and could not literally have believed his own words, nor could his hearers have believed them, as all knew that, historically speaking, Napoleon's* existence could not fairly be questioned. He had tried to draw two straight and parallel lines when one of the lines was palpably crooked and of necessity failed. The second discourse about the burial of an ass, was quite as applicable to many a professed and prominent christian as to any leading sceptic or heretic that ever lived. The third discourse only proved what a marvellously tenacious and nobly unconquerable life Unitarianism had ever enjoyed in the past, and was destined to enjoy in the future.

A very different personage was Rev. Cruttenden Cruttenden,

* Taken from a satire by Jean Baptiste Perès, and published in 1827.

minister of the Old Church. Rather over the middle height, with a lithe body sometimes bent a little and sometimes upright, and with prominent features on the face, he had a picturesque figure. His appearance was that of a combination of a country squire, a military officer, and a church clergyman. His address to the students was substantially somewhat as follows:—Get all the useful knowledge you possibly can. But mind you honour and obey the king, and all that are put in authority under him; and submit yourselves to all your governors, teachers, spiritual pastors, and masters; and order yourselves reverently to all your betters. Nevertheless, he was a kindly, charitable man, as manifested in the utterance of these words: "Believe me, it is no gratification to me, in fulfilling the part I have undertaken this day, to be thus constrained to speak of a religion which is still the religion of many of our countrymen. But let it be all along remembered that it is not against persons but against principles that we are contending." These words were spoken at a great church Protestant demonstration in this town, when a strong attack was made against Roman Catholics, and hard hits dealt out to dissenters. This latter attack brought into public conflict another able and eminent man who frequently attended our Useful Knowledge Society meetings. Samuel Bowen was minister of Townley Street Chapel. He had a firmly-knit figure, with broad shoulders which had the scholar's stoop. He had a dark complexion, a pale thoughtful face, a rather low but clear distinct voice, and spoke with a strong Scotch (?) accent. He took up the gauntlet thrown out to Dissenters at the Protestant meeting with right good will, and dealt out thrust and parry in the most gallant style. Here are some of the blows he fearlessly struck:—"Enter their (Protestant) meetings. Open your eyes. Do you see those twin gods, the one of gold the other of iron? On the brow of one you read 'Mammon,' and on the brow of the other, 'Domination.'" "The religion of the Priest, devised by the art and craft of Priests, for their own honour, gain, or influence, is a religion of dogmas, of ceremonies, of authority, of external rites, of priestly manipulations." "Priestism or Hierarchism, I take to be the man of sin." "The clergy exclaim their church is in danger, meaning that their emoluments are endangered." "The church has often been in danger—rather, was never out of danger for many an age—and no cry has been in its effects more fatally ruinous to these realms." These stinging words roused the Dissenters of the town, and rallied them in earnest for union and self-defence. Unfortunately, apathy succeeded action here, as elsewhere, while sacerdotalism has been advancing with swinging strides, and to-day its triumphant pæans are everywhere sung aloud. But our hero Bowen had not only to cope with church platform speakers, but with newspaper assailants. In the *Macclesfield Courier* appeared numerous columns of historic dogma, muddled, confused, and made almost unintelligible. Our hero describes the writer in this fashion:— "On the verge of chaos; a dark illimitable ocean, off he goes! and through a boggy Syrtes, neither sea nor good dry land, nigh foundered, on he fares, treading the crude consistence; half on foot, half flying, over bog or steep, through strait, rough, dense, or rare, with head, hands, wings, or feet, pursues his way; and swims, or sinks, or wades, or creeps, or flies." After such a tremendous excursion as that, there can be no wonder that Bowen's assailant was heard of no more.

Sitting beside Bowen on the platform would sometimes be seen George Barrow Kidd, minister of the Roe Street Congregational Chapel. A finer and more exact representative of the puritan preacher of the commonwealth age could nowhere be found. He had a rather tall, lithe, wiry frame, crowned with a fine head and a solemn thoughtful face. His speech was earnest, emphatic, and effective. His thought was intense and deep, but moved in a narrow groove. Some of these strong thoughts were embodied and printed in a book on "The Sovereignty of God." Intensely Calvinistic, very deep, awfully solemn, and soaringly sublime were the sentiments of the book; but its sale was very limited, and I never heard of a second edition. Nor did I hear of his publishing any other book during his long ministry in this town. One experiment of that kind was sufficient for the lifetime of an author with restricted means. His reading of the Scriptures was rendered very peculiar by his leaving out all words in italics which were men's words—all the rest of the words being God's words. To make the sense clear, however, he had to supply his own words—an inconsistency I never heard him explain away. His prayers were very earnest, very importunate, and very long. On one occasion, in a full pew, I had to kneel down because all the others did; but the aching which seized my bones, during a twenty-minutes prayer, I did not get rid of for some days. It was some comfort to me to learn that others had a similar experience. His discourses were often convincingly and overwhelmingly prophetic, even when not fulfilled. "They shall flock like doves to the windows," he vehemently exclaimed on one occasion; meaning that enquirers and worshippers should regularly crowd the chapel. But they never did, but diminished in number as time went on. I think his explanation would be that the members of the congregation were not so earnest, prayerful, active, and good as they ought to be to secure so great a blessing.

Becoming weary and faint with the awful work of saving souls and keeping them saved, he suddenly began to save the bodies of men. Entering upon the homœopathic treatment, he met with wonderful success. Crowds of poor sick people besieged his house, who all received treatment, and most were cured of their diseases, and entirely without charge. Numbers of well-to-do people were cured by him, who—although he made no charge—offered remuneration, more or less. So numerous and marvellous were the cures effected that had he been a Romish priest his house would have become a holy shrine, to which in succeeding years bands of pilgrims would have journeyed, bringing offerings with them. Like a beautiful and fruitful oasis in a somewhat desert plain seemed this period of his life to lookers on. The rest of the fifty years of his ministerial warfare and pilgrimage had passed away without any visible striking events. Numbers of worldly and superficially-minded persons had carelessly thrown a glance in his direction and passed by on the other side. But who did, or could, enter into the surging depths of that man's experience? Very few knew anything about it, and fewer cared. But one or two could enter into the deep, warm gulf stream ever flowing through his soul. The wife of his early life had soon faded, and then with heart-breakings died. "Take care of my sister," was her departing bequest. Through a long series of years that parting bequest was literally and exactly kept. Through all that extended period Miss Wheelton was ably and constantly engaged in the work of the congregation—in teaching young people in the Sunday School, and in helping the sick and the poor,—and also most efficiently managed the minister's house—but she could not be his wife. But could not that iniquitous law preventing marriage with a deceased wife's sister be repealed? Alas! the most determined and oft-repeated efforts in that direction always met with defeat. In this town, as elsewhere, petitions were frequently carried round and numerously signed, the impetus, it was said, always coming from the vicinity of Roe Street Chapel: but always without the desired result. Hope deferred maketh the heart sad, and in the minister's house, for a long series of years, sadness reigned supreme. How keen, how deep, that protracted sadness, none but themselves could describe. That perennial sadness with other trying events of the passing years began to tell seriously on the lady's health. Then came experiences suggesting to the mind's eye a beckoning finger from the guardian angel who had left the house to the angel left behind. And soon the summons was obeyed. Another wrenching of earth's dearest ties, another heartbreaking farewell, and the aged minister was left alone.

His friends, beholding his deep depression and great prostration, said the dear old minister must have help and comfort and rest. The sum of £300 was subscribed and a life annuity secured, so that he might calmly and safely pass through his second dotage into the dark valley of death which was not far away. And now a marvellous thing—almost a miracle—came to pass. Another angel had entered the house, and finding the old man not dead nor dying but only sleeping, rolled away the stone from the door of the sepulchre, when straightway he awoke to fulness and vigour of life. So great was the love of the angel, and so great was the gratitude of the risen man, that they married, and became united in heart and soul and life. While men marvelled and women exclaimed, the rejuvenated pair departed hence and settled in some quiet place destined to many years of happy and useful life. "How wonderful!" said some; "How shocking!" said others. "God bless them!" said a third party, to which latter exclamation I said "Amen!"

The last but not the least, indeed, perhaps the greatest, of our platform speakers at the Useful Knowledge Society meetings I shall mention, was Samuel Greg. When he rose to address the meeting he strongly impressed his hearers, not from his stature, which was rather below the medium height, but by the far-off look in his eyes, by the low but distinct, soft tones of his voice, and by the lucid, forcible, and noble ideas he expressed. The clerical speakers remarked patronisingly on the importance of working men obtaining some degree of literary and scientific knowledge, which must never be made to clash with religion, but to harmonize with it and support it. Many of the students called this talking "shop." The business gentlemen on the platform urged the necessity of acquiring such knowledge as would help them to become superior workmen. "The profits to be mainly the masters'," impudently said some of the students. Greg would say, "Literature is good, science is good, and religion is good, but are you students becoming individually good yourselves? Are you aiming to acquire such nobility of character as will enable you to carry with you an elevating influence in the family, in the workshop, in the institute, in the Church, and in the world?" These speeches were but seldom followed by adverse remark.

CHAPTER XIV

DEBATING SOCIETY

A LIVELY debating society was carried on, I was informed, at Church Street West Schoolroom, which I was strongly urged to attend. I hesitated for a time, experience having convinced me that such societies often did little good, and some evil. To be serviceable and efficient, a debating society must have (1) an able and experienced chairman, commanding the respect and obedience of all the debaters. The speakers should (2) hold sincerely the opinions they express and defend. Sometimes mere talkers for the purposes of debate will assume opinions which they don't really hold, and defend them. This is demoralising to the intellect. Carried out to any extent, it induces an individual to hold all opinions lightly, or to have opinions not worth holding at all. Dominant speakers (3) should be kept in check; hair splitters should not be encouraged; and rambling talkers should be brought to the point of the subject under debate. All moral subjects (4) should be admitted for discussion, preference being always given to subjects of immediate and paramount interest, whether individual or public.

Eventually I joined the class, and found that the stock subjects, "Was Napoleon or Wellington the greater general?" "Was Pitt or Fox the greater statesman?" "Which was the greatest poet in England, in France, in America?" etc., etc., had been discussed and disposed of, which I was glad to have escaped. "Which is the true Church?" was the subject greatly exciting the meeting when I was introduced. Mr. B., a Roman Catholic, contended that on Peter—declared by Christ to be the rock of the Church—was the Catholic Church built. In reply it was contended that on the rock of power and plunder and massacre was that Church founded. Mr. B. claimed that the Clementine Homilies of the second century; the Donative of Constantine; the hundred letters known as the Isidorial Decretals produced in the ninth century were the immovable bulwarks of the Roman Catholic Church. Every one of these were declared by the other side to be baseless and shameful forgeries. And if, as affirmed, these documents were quoted as true by successive Popes, then their claims to infallibility was another forgery added to the lot. "But," said Mr. B., "the Romish Church rests upon the Apostolic Succession stretching in one unbroken chain from Peter to the Pontiff and Bishops of the present day." In reply it was shown that the first link in the chain was rotten. While Peter sometimes fulsomely professed adherence to Christ, he at another time denied Him with oaths and curses. "What sort of a link," it was asked, "was the Pope John XII., who made the Lateran Palace anything but a school of virtue? Or Sixtus IV., at whose death one great sigh of relief was breathed with the conviction that no successor could be so bad? Or Innocent VIII., who was pronounced even worse than Sixtus IV.? Or Leo the Sensualist, whose face, it was said, told the tale of his life? How, for shame, could any Church claim any connection with such a disgustingly rotten chain as that?

"But," continued Mr. B., "the Church, with its numerous monasteries, was the depository of nearly all the literature, and science, and useful knowledge in Christendom, through the dark ages, extending over a thousand years." "Then," it was replied, "the Church was a dark lantern which opened on one side to let in light upon itself so that it might see how to consolidate its own tyrannic power and gather into itself the wealth of the world—taking care that worse than cimerian darkness prevailed around." "But," continued Mr. B., "the blood of the martyrs has ever been the seed of the Romish Church.

During the martyrdoms of the Roman Emperors the Church grew to be a mighty power. Under the persecutions of Henry VIII. and his successors the Church grew in England, and has continued to grow, and is now stronger than ever before."

This brought the Protestant champion to the front in the person of Rev. — Meade, a rather popular Church Missionary in the town. With indignation Meade said, " The martyrs in the days of the Roman Emperors were not Roman Catholics, but disciples of Christ, as were the Protestant martyrs in the Reformation days. Ridley and Latimer were noble Protestants martyred by fierce Roman Catholic bigots. From apostolic days the pure stream of Christianity had flown along through the falsities and pollutions of the Romish ages until Reformation times, when it swelled into a mighty flood and washed out Romanism from the English Church, which had now become so strong that the Romish gates of hell would nevermore prevail against it."

The non-sectarian, rising in the meeting with determination in his look and earnestness in his voice, exclaimed, "A plague on both your houses! The world would have been much better without either. The partizan of one Church descanted about a long chain of Apostolic Succession. History shows it to have been a chain of tyranny, oppression, slavery and murderous death. The partizan of another Church spoke of the pure flow of its dogmas through the polluted stream of the darkest and foulest ages of time. The possibility of such a thing he did not and could not show. Black and thick as the Stygian lake was the stream of succession in both Churches alike. Some of the earliest Christians wanted to get fire from heaven to burn mankind. Having obtained power in later days, they made bonfires on earth and roasted men to death. Having incorporated hordes of fierce Christian bigots in his army, Constantine the Great conveniently beheld a glowing cross in the sky bearing the inscription ' Conquer in this,' an injunction literally carried out with the direst results. Over a thousand battlefields, strewn with the bones and sodden with the gore of millions of men, waved the war-flags bearing that direful injunction, 'Conquer in this.' Sweeping along the Alpine valleys and mountains, where the noble-minded Waldenses and Albigenses dwelt, the Popish armies shot, or burnt, or cut down men, women, and children, and made waste, howling wildernesses of what before had been an Eden realm: all this murderous havoc being committed with the cross of Jesus going on before. At the midnight hour of St. Bartholomew's Eve there rushed through the streets and suburbs of Paris wild hordes of Popish, armed men, who slew 20,000 Huguenots—with the cross of Jesus going on before. At the Reformation in England, and for generations later, Catholics butchered Protestants and Protestants butchered Catholics with a wonderful alternation; but always with the cross of Jesus going on before.

"In later times the same amazing alternation of murderous proceedings took place. Bruno was hunted down and burnt by Roman Catholics. Servetus was trapped and burnt by the Protestant monster Calvin. And even Dissenters in England and America instituted the hunt for witches, and burnt thousands of innocent and worthy women to ashes. And always with the cross of Jesus going on before."

During these philippics it was admitted there were always large numbers of saintly persons who had no part in these barbarous persecutions. Still it was clear the saints were not numerous enough to prevent these barbarities taking place.

"Unfortunately the spirit of proselytism and persecution amongst Christians still remains. All the Christian nations are rushing upon heathen communities to convert them to their creeds, and to steal their lands. 'While we looked up to heaven as the missionaries told us,' said the Maoris, 'the soldiers took the land under our feet.' It is generally admitted and causes no surprises that the formula of proceedings may by stated thus:—The missionaries sail to heathen lands with Bibles and tracts which they do not want, the merchants follow with clothing which does not suit and alcohol which makes the people mad, and then the soldiers follow with maxim guns to mow the natives down." After this heated discussion, the Class began to wane.

Mr. B. and the Catholic party did not like the course of the debate. Mr. Meade and the Church party saw they could not make the Class a standpoint for successful propaganda purposes of their own. The non-sectarian party seemed most satisfied with results.

Succeeding debates of literary and political subjects gradually declined until the close of the session. Not many, if any, converts of any kind were made. Still, many minds were set thinking more deeply than before on important things, the results to be seen only after many days.

CHAPTER XV

JOSEPH BARKER

AT this period Joseph Barker had a predominant influence on my thought and life. Many incidents in his career came directly home to me and influenced me greatly. Methodism fastened on him in early life as it did on me. When a lad, under conviction, he said, " The unfrequented wood, the deep, solitary valley, or the high hill, were the places selected for my meditations and prayers." This was exactly my own experience in very early life; and hence the powerful sympathy by which I was drawn to him. His reverence for Methodist preachers was greater even than my own. " I thought," he says, " they were as holy as angels, that they preached by divine inspiration from heaven, and always did what was right." Convictions of that kind give the preachers a tremendous power over the minds and destinies of their disciples. Such clerical power as this it was which enabled Wesley and Bunting to plant Methodism on so firm a foundation in the world. My own lofty estimate of ministerial endowments kept me from entering the ministry until a rather late period of life. When urged on the matter, I determinately objected. My call was not loud enough, or distinct enough, or impressive enough. I had not sufficient inspiration, or dedication, or sanctification, or education, for so high and holy an office.

I went on reading and thinking and questioning from year to year, until it became clearly apparent that if I did ever enter the ministry, it would not be that of Methodism, nor any orthodox ministry whatever.

My personal attachment to Joseph Barker—whom I had

never seen—was greatly enhanced by the reading of the following sketch by an eye-witness of the scene:—

"Conducting a meeting for Renewing the Covenant, Joseph Barker said, 'This is a solemn moment; the eye of the divine Master is upon us. Those of you who are willing to pledge yourselves to live more entirely and devotedly to the service and glory of God, stand up.' Immediately a large part of the assembly stood: when Mr. Barker, with deep solemnity and fervour, clasped his hands, and looking upward, said in tones which thrilled the congregation, 'Lord Jesus, ratify the solemn Covenant which Thy people have now made!'"

Having attended a great many Covenant Services myself, I could fully enter into the details of this graphic sketch, and could almost feel the same fervour as those who were present at the scene described.

At length the long-wished-for opportunity came when I saw and heard Joseph Barker himself. Coming from the vestry of the New Connexion Chapel, he walked up the pulpit stairs in an easy and unconcerned manner, as if nobody was near him. Having sat down, his eyes swept round the gallery and along the pews below, as if taking stock of the crowd filling the chapel. His glance was keen and piercing. His face was rather rugged-looking, but expressive of intelligence and feeling as well as strength and determination. His bearing in the pulpit was that of a man entirely independent. His movements were fitting, and in no sense ungraceful. His prayer was simple and natural, and not at all conventional. An American said he went to chapel to hear Robert Collyer have a talk with God. That was the exact impression I had of Joseph Barker's prayer that day. The reading of the chapters was made intersting by brief and pointed comments. Coming to the injunction, "Train up a child in the way he should go," he inquired who was to do it? Parents often entirely spoiled children either by petting or neglect. The day-school master taught professionally, and for the most part unwisely. The Sunday School teachers—the best of them—were the most effective trainers of the working-class children at the present day. His voice was musical and strong, but under perfect control. Sentences now and then, all through the discourse, struck and burnt like red-hot shot. The peroration on individual duty was a storm of word-bullets, when, I think, everyone in the great assembly must have been hit. I was hard hit myself, and walked home by a circuitous and solitary road, brooding over the impression made, and which has never been erased.

A most striking incident was at hand, which placed our hero amongst the great crowd of witnesses for truth and righteousness which has been persecuted by priestly tyrants through all the Christian ages. The Conference of the Methodist New Connexion of 1841 resolved itself into a miniature imitation of the Diet of Worms. A leading authority in the prosecution was Thomas Allen. The illustrious culprit was Joseph Barker. The said culprit was charged with contending that the art of writing should be taught to the children of the poor in Sunday School. This contention endeared Barker to thousands of people, who, like myself, had learnt to write in the Sunday School. Otherwise many of these would never have learnt this useful art at all, while others could not have learnt until late in life.

Another charge against the culprit was that he refused to practice Water Baptism, and wrote and spoke against it. My own conviction came to be that this should be an open question. I always announced, during my own ministry, that I would sprinkle with water, or plunge into water, or dedicate without water, according to individual desire. I never met with the least difficulty from first to last. On Barker being questioned after a lecture what he would substitute for Baptism, he said, "A good washing." An incisive and decisive way of settling the question.

Another charge was that he denied the present obligation of the Lord's Supper. Practically this ceremony is set aside by numbers of professing Christians, who never observe it.

Besides. the Friends dispense with the ceremony altogether and are not considered the worse Christians on that account. A very weak charge indeed was this.

A still further charge was that he would print and circulate books on his own account. This the authorities at the bookroom would not brook by any means. But why not? He might have proved a good auxiliary to themselves. But these matters were all brought to a point in substantially the following way:—"Will you, Joseph Barker, conform to the order and belief of the Methodist New Connexion, which are founded on the Scriptures?" "I adhere," he replied in substance, "to the Scriptures as expounded by reason." "And we," it was replied, "adhere to the Scriptures as expounded by the creeds of the Connexion." And they cast him out.

Was there ever a convocation of Divines, or any assembly dominated by Divines, which had not a conscience that would stretch to any length to secure power and pelf and stability for itself? The replies of history to this question are awful to read. The expulsion of Barker, however, was one of the mildest of ecclesiastical prosecutions. The Fly Sheet prosecution of the Wesleyan Conference, which shortly followed, was of a far more iniquitous kind. Against Everet, Dunn, and Griffiths, there was no evidence. They were expelled on suspicion. Four Fly Sheets had been written reflecting on Missionary mismanagement, and on the domineering and tyrannical behaviour of Bunting in Conference and elsewhere. Even if the Conference had been certain of the writers, there was no fair case for expulsion. It was a case for explanation and refutation, if that were possible. But it appeared impossible, and so there must be expulsion. But who must be expelled? Osborne—a minister of unenviable fame—laid a trap. He wrote on a sheet of paper the declaration, "I have not done it." A majority of the ministers slavishly signed the declaration. A very considerable minority refused to sign. Great as was the audacity of the leaders, they dared not expel the lot. But they fixed upon three victims and demanded from them a reply.

This they promised to give if allowed to state particulars and make a defence. "By no means," said the fierce prosecutors, "we demand you say 'Yes' or 'No'." But Everet, Griffiths, and Dunn, were not slaves, but free men. They were faithful amongst the faithless found. The three heroes were turned out of the Wesleyan Society, and some 30,000 members followed them into exile, and formed themselves into the Methodist Free Churches.

But the Fly Sheets—with their scathing exposures—were not stopped. No. 5 of these fiery shafts was signed by "A Methodist minister not yet expelled," and No. 6 was announced. With consternation the rulers of the Conference heard everywhere the cry that "they had shot the wrong birds." In the proceedings of this Inquisition it is notable to observe there was no charge of heresy. From first to last it was simply a case of just resistance to the tyranny of a clerical clique. And, indeed, has not that been the issue in all ecclesiastical Inquisitions? Has not that terrible word "heresy" itself been simply a bugbear used by the priests to frighten the people and rally them to the support of the tyranny by which they were being crushed?

Let us now view Joseph Barker on the highest pinnacle of influence and fame he ever attained. Incessantly assailed by preachers in the pulpits and the same preachers in the press, he threw out a challenge to meet any one of them, or any number of them in succession, in public debate. After much delay, Wm. Cooke rashly accepted the challenge, which he tried to get out of, but was not allowed. On August 19th, 1845, in Newcastle, the great theological tournament began, and was continued through ten nights. Ten distinct subjects were originally agreed upon for discussion by both committees. But at the beginning of the debate a mere summary was foisted in, which greatly confused matters.

Yielding to pressure from Cooke's committee, Cooke was allowed to have the leading speech on each occasion. This proved to be very unfavourable to Barker. After a good hearing had been obtained for Cooke, there was continual uproar for Barker, many noisily going out during his speech. Both speakers occasionally used hard words. This was sure to be the case after Cooke in his first speech had remarked, "The Christian loves the poor heretic. Though he may feel it to be a public duty to draw aside the veil from his protean form, and trace the deceiver along his slimy, sinuous course, into the secret recesses of error, yet after all he loves him." A bit of concentrated, vicious cant like that was sure to create an unfavourable state of feeling on both sides. Amongst the tremendous uproars which ran through the whole debate there was a very notable one on the sixth night, when Barker made a great crash about the Inquisition, Bartholomew Massacre, Waldensian exterminations, and other monstrous crimes which blacken the history of Christian nations.

Another scene of the kind happened on the seventh night, when, in a peroration, Cooke quoted popular passages such as "Blessing and honour, and glory and power, be unto Him who sitteth upon the throne, and unto the Lamb for ever and ever," and finished with the favourite, if hackneyed, lines:—

> "Were the whole realm of nature mine,
> That were a present far too small;
> Love so amazing, so divine,
> Demands my soul, my life, my all."

When Mr. Barker began to speak on one of the later nights his opponents—as usual—began to go out, making much noise. Barker sat down and said he would go on when the disturbers were all out. "Don't go," cried Cooke, "I have 500 tracts to give you at the end of the meeting." "You can have them to-morrow night," cried Barker, "when I shall have 1,000 tracts to give you."

On the tenth night, in a most skilful and conclusive manner, Barker closed the debate. In sixty-three propositions bearing on the whole discussion he aimed to show how utterly futile and inconclusive were the arguments of Cooke, and how completely demonstrable were his own. Although the uproar was continuous while he spoke, he went on with the greatest imperturbability to the close of his speech. Then the following amusing colloquy took place:—

Barker.—I propose to go on with the discussion through all the subjects proposed.

Grant (Cooke's chairman).—As soon as Mr. Barker shows he has kept to the terms of the discussion, he shall have as much as he pleases!

Barker.—My opponent never kept the terms in a single speech.

Cooke.—When Mr. Barker has answered one-half of the arguments I have already given him, I will meet him again.

Barker.—I will meet Mr. Cooke again, if he pleases, though he has not answered a *quarter* of my arguments.

This was the greatest theological debate of the century in this country, and made Barker immensely popular for a time. He spoke, and wrote and published books incessantly, and was wanted for lectures everywhere. The heroes he worshipped just now were Priestley, Channing, and Theodore Parker, whose works he published and circulated far and wide.

The Unitarians began to rally around him, and certain leading men helped liberally to furnish him with a printing-press. In his eagerness to aid every kind of reform he began to publish political pamphlets of an advanced kind. This, it was said, offended some of the leading men amongst the Unitarians; but one does not see why it should. Many, however, fell away from him, and he fell away from them and rushed headlong into politics. This was a most unfortunate circumstance for the advanced religious movements of the day. Hosts of semi-religious reformers were waiting to be gathered into some organised fold. The chief shepherd and his helpers, however, had gone elsewhere, and so the sheep were scattered abroad. The greatest opportunity Unitarianism ever had for collecting masses of awakened men into its churches passed away with meagre results because the great leader was not secured when he was near at hand. The fields of religious reform were white unto the harvest, but the great reaper and his zealous adherents were allowed to go and reap in less important fields of labour, so that the Unitarian garner had but few sheaves of grain to show.

In eager haste he entered upon the duties of the new life which opened before him. He sought new worlds to conquer, and found them and conquered them. He had made the rulers of Churches quake, and now he was going to frighten the rulers of the state. In the Parliamentary election at Bolton in 1848, he was elected on the nomination day by the overwhelming majority of five votes to one. The Mayor declared him duly elected as Member of Parliament for Bolton. At once he was served with a Government writ, seized by the police, and thrown into prison.

In the prison cell with Barker was a Mr. White, who was wild with excitement, while both of them were amazed and shocked with the almost continuous howls, shrieks, and curses coming from adjoining cells. In his report of the conduct of prisoners, the jail inspector said the man White was a raging fire, but Barker was as mild as a lamb. That testimony concerning Barker coincided with my own experience of the man. On hearing him preach and speak I was always impressed with his complete self-possession. On one occasion when I was preaching a special sermon for the Unitarians at Burnley, Mr. Barker was in the congregation. After the service he desired to speak to me, and I was happy to meet him. He was evidently inclined at that time to unite permanently with the Unitarians, and I earnestly urged him to do so. His whole demeanour on that occasion was that of an intelligent, well-intentioned, noble-minded, honest, and sincere man.

During his trial at Liverpool he was quiet, but also very firm, as the following colloquy will show:—

The Attorney General.—If the prisoner will plead guilty he may possibly obtain a discharge.

Barker.—Guilty? When I have not broken the law! I should then make myself guilty. Never! never!

Attorney.—Will the prisoner enter into recognizances to keep the peace?

Barker.—No! For that would imply that I had broken the peace!

The Judge.—What! does the prisoner refuse the kind offer of the prosecution? He must be a fool!

Barker.—I am as innocent as yourself, my Lord, and I wish to be equally free.

Judge.—I shall consider you so till you are proved guilty. But now, what do you want?

Barker.—I want to go home.

Judge.—And I want to go home, too.

The prisoner was acquitted, and the court closed.

As the Attorney was leaving the court, he was abruptly addressed by John West, a political prisoner from Macclesfield, who exclaimed, "And so, sir, you dare not prosecute Barker, the Bishop of Wortley." The Attorney looked daggers, but made no reply.

This was another great victory for Barker. He had previously triumphed over redoubtable Doctors of Divinity, priestly conferences, reactionary politicians, and great conservative and orthodox debaters, and now he had triumphed over the Attorney General and the Judge in a Court of Justice.

Barker was now at the zenith of his power, and crowds everywhere followed him. He wrote and spoke with his usual vigour, zeal and effect. But one great omission was fatal to his permanent success. He did not organize his disciples. Had he formed classes, bands, and love-feasts, and induced each member to pay a penny a week, a shilling a quarter, and contribute to many collections, a strong reforming society might have been firmly established. In the absence of any such arrangement his crowds of motley followers gradually forsook him and fled. Some slunk away to their old snug quarters in orthodox chapels, and were warmly welcomed back. Some made tracks to Unitarian Chapels, and found plenty of freedom, if not much warmth. The larger portion became wandering sheep without folds or shepherds, and without rest for their weary feet or peace to their troubled souls. Barker was shocked and distressed, but did not despair.

He dreamed fresh dreams, he revelled in new visions, he was inspired by glowing hopes. A new Canaan, flowing with milk and honey in the far western world opened to his view. He crossed the sea, surveyed the land of promise, made good reports, and invited his friends to enter with him this goodly land.

In the backwoods he ploughed, sowed, reaped, and earned his living by the sweat of his brow; brooded over the hardships of his lot; became heart-sick and home-sick; sailed back to England; took refuge in Primitive Methodist Chapels, and preached a mixture of dogmas, old and new, until the end came, when as he hoped, he passed on to—

"Where the wicked cease from troubling,
And the weary are at rest."

After the reading and close study of the volume containing a full report of the ten nights' discussion between Barker and Cooke, my orthodoxy—before much shaken—was now shattered into atoms.

CHAPTER XVI

MARTINEAU—PRIESTLEY

My mental conflicts throughout this important period of life were difficult to describe. Diverse influences never ceased urging me now in this direction and now that. No father-confessor—whether Catholic, or Ritualist, or Methodist—would have been satisfied with a statement of my experiences, or have refrained from a severe condemnation of the same. From being a questioning Methodist, could I go back and become an unquestioning and fervid Methodist devotee once more? Nay, that could hardly be. Not my class-leader's solemn warnings, nor the sweet influence of the departed mother could induce me to retreat. Warrenite commotions, the New Connexion's expulsions, and the Fly Sheet inquisitions and fierce persecutions had for ever barred the way of return to clerical tyranny and rule. The way in front seemed to lead directly to Unitarianism, which, until lately I had ever heard described as a desert realm, without fruitfulness or prosperity or rest of mind.

While anxiously surveying the new pathway opening before me, a friend placed in my hands two volumes, saying, " You will find there Methodistic feeling wedded to rationalistic thought." I opened the volumes, scanned their contents, and read and devoured them. Then page after page in my notebook I crowded with the impressive sentiments of this work, entitled " Endeavours after the Christian Life," by James Martineau. I had never seen Martineau; I have never seen him since: but how tenaciously his ideas have clung to me, and how powerfully they have influenced my life, it were impossible to tell. "See Wesley or Whitfield," said the author, "at sunrise on the hillside. Hear what a great heart of reality there is in that hymn that swells upon the mountain air. See the rugged hands of labour clasped, and trembling, wrestling with the unseen in prayer."

"Bless me!" was my first thought, "but that scene will not help me along the new road before me. Rather it will force me back upon the old road, where that picture had been before me and thrilled me from my early days." "Nay, not so!" was my second thought. "That picture must enter into my heavenly vision and help to cheer me in the labours and conflicts which await me." And so it did.

"It is a solemn thing," said my new guide, "when we gaze intently on the dial of our fate, and listen to the beats that number our vicissitudes, to see its index pointing distinctly to eternity." And indeed! my own fate was trembling in the balance. Audible enough were the beats of past vicissitudes. The Index? Ah! that points onward. Along this road, then, I advance towards eternity. "Continuing this soul communion," says Martineau, "the memories of childhood, how do they rush upon the heart, when we revisit the very scenes in which they had their birth! How they do blessed violence to time, and snatch us into the past!"

And how these words vivify my own blessed memories and take me to sacred places where I have often prayed and meditated, and where the dark clouds of life have parted, and let the light of heaven through!

"However strange," says the author, "the colony to us may be in which they (departed friends) dwell, if, as we cross the deep of death, their visionary forms shall crowd the shore, and people the hills of that unvisited abode, it will be to us a better country, even a heavenly."

Hardly a strange colony to me, my mentor. For have I not accompanied some of the best, the most saintly ones I have ever known to the very verge of the blest abodes? Did I not see the last triumphal signal of the dear mother at the moment she passed onto the heavenly realm? And was not the last hand-clasp of Edward, on the margin of eternity, a pledge of his outstretched hand to welcome me when I should join the sacred band beyond, according to the compact we had formed years before? And have I not heard the last adieus of Sunday School teachers and scholars as they passed to the other shore? And are not these a bright cloud of witnesses holding me in full survey, and which, in heavenly vision, I survey in return?

"Turn to the old Puritan," he continues. "Here is a man plainly living for sublime ends, beyond the baubles of the world. A man who has got pain and fear beneath his feet; who walks the earth as in the outer fringe of the beatific vision."

No wonder, I thought, these words should fall from the lips of the descendant of a refugee. The fervours of a noble ancestry glow in his own mind, and find utterance in these inspiring words.

I have never taken much trouble in searching out my own pedigrees in the past; but I have often thought that, if I could trace out any thread of connection with the Ironsides who triumphed so gloriously on the battlefields of Naseby and Marston Moor, my joy would indeed be great.

A poem entitled "The Puritan's Grave" came into my hands when a boy, which I wrote down in my copy-book at the Sunday School. Ever afterwards I was eager to learn all I could about the Puritans themselves. In our family, the names of Hampden, Pym, Milton, and Cromwell became household words. "The countenances of the heroic Puritans," said the caricaturist, "were shrouded in awful gloom." I warrant that in stern conflict, whether civil or military, there flashed from those sombre faces gleams which filled the hearts of their enemies with dismay. If these serious people did love quiet Sundays—well, and so do we. We wish there were some of that sort now with power enough to put down the rowdyism in our streets and byways which often makes it dangerous to walk to a place of worship on the Sabbath Day. If they did delight in long services of psalm-singing, preaching, and prayer, what then? It was because they were hungry for the Bread of Life. On these occasions they were feeding in green pastures and resting beside still waters, and were not eager for the feast and the rest to end. The experiences of these solemn-looking Puritans were frequently sweet and entrancing to me. The lofty and yet tender thoughts expressed in Baxter's "Saints' Rest" and "Dying Thoughts," may be taken as their prevailing experience, and may show how near they lived to heaven and to God.

As my last quotation, I give these startling words:—" The gliding heavens are less awful at midnight than the ticking clock. . . . So passes, and we cannot stay it, our only portion of opportunity. The fragments of that blessed chance, which has been travelling to us from all eternity, are quickly dropping off. Let us start up and live. Here come the moments that cannot be had again. Some few may yet be filled with imperishable good."

Ah, I thought, here we have the secret of a successful and noble life. We see how, by a vigilant and wise use of opportunity, our author became a hard student, a bold thinker, an eloquent preacher, and a literary writer of the highest class. In contemplating so striking an individuality, how one feels abashed. And yet in some remote degree I claim kindred to him. These copied notes, and heaps of manuscripts besides, remind me of numberless midnight vigils and of morning studies before sunrise on summer mornings. My arduous labours of from twelve to fourteen hours each day did not quench the ardour of my search for the highest truth. Often were the heavy burdens of the day lightened by this thought of the rich feast of knowledge enjoyed in the morning, and to be partaken of again at night. Thus he, moving along his high and honoured and extended course of life, and I in my lowly, but not unhonoured nor unuseful life, have had points of contact which, unknown to him, have been rich and sweet to me.

Joseph Priestley was another Unitarian worthy whose life and writings I became eager to study and understand. My friend Edward had often spoken to me about his many scientific attainments, and specially of his discovery of oxygen gas. I had also heard preachers denounce him as a heretic whose theological writings it was dangerous to read. I now determined to make a thorough study of the whole matter. His appearance, if not imposing, arrested attention. He was described, as seen in the streets of Birmingham, as a "quick, erect, neatly-dressed, sweetly-clean, and mildly-good old man." A person who knew him well spoke of his "gentleness, simplicity, and kindness of heart, united with great acuteness of intellect. Being brought up by his parents, and afterwards by an aunt, in Calvinistic principles, he was plunged into great distress by seeking unsuccessfully to be born again. This was my own experience, which ended, as I thought, in the process of conversion being complete. That religious struggle made him more solemnly thoughtful than otherwise he could possibly have become. And such was certainly my own case. In these throes of the new birth of the soul, strange to say, the victory is in the struggle, whether there be a positive or negative result. Ah, if a few thousand Unitarians—ministers and laymen—could only get into this mighty soul-struggle, what a glorious revolution in the churches would take place.

His relatives urged him to enter the ministry, and he was anxious to do so, but some slight development of heresy on his part barred the way. I can enter fully into his disappointment and deep sorrow on this occasion, as my own entrance into the Methodist ministry was prevented in the same way. Subsequently he found a small chapel at Needham, in Kent, where heresy was allowed, and there he became minister, with a salary of £30 a year. To eke out a living, he had to pursue some other calling. These joint pursuits placed him in exact line with Jesus and his Apostles. Paul joined on tent-making to his ministry, and Jesus must have done some joinering to get a living. Both Jesus and Paul were heretics in their day, as Priestley was in his day. With all the facts in view, we declare that Priestley was as directly in the line of Apostolic Succession as any Pope or Bishop or Priest that ever lived, and much more so than nine-tenths of such ecclesiastics as have made the claim.

A few years later we find our subject the minister of a small chapel at Nantwich, with but little, if any, increase of salary. In succeeding years I had the great gratification of preaching in this chapel on many occasions. In the pulpit, I noticed a large number of shelves, and supposed he must have had books and papers placed there for reference during his discourses.

We next find him at Warrington, where he married a most amicable and gifted lady, who proved a true helpmeet throughout his remarkable career. Again, we find him as librarian to Lord Shelburne, when his fame as a scientist spread far and wide. Sir Humphrey Davy said he was "the father of pneumatic chemistry." "The medical faculty," said Hutton, "have acknowledged that his experimental discoveries on air have preserved the lives of thousands." The Rev. Robert Hall had the frankness to say that Priestley "poured light into every department of science"; while Bishop Horsley enviously said it was a "most unfortunate thing that Priestley should have hit on such discoveries." In Chamber's "Encyclopædia," the substance of Priestley's "Philosophy" is admirably stated in the follownig concentrated terms:—"He (Priestley) partly materialises spirit and partly spiritualises matter." There, I think, we reach the *ultima thule* of the subject, and there we leave it.

With Priestley's important work on the "History of the Corruptions of Christianity," we are told, President Jefferson was so deeply interested that he read it twice over. And no wonder, for any person deeply interested in Christian history, if aware of the book, would be sure to do the same.

On the early Paganising of Christianity, Priestley quotes from Vigilantius, who says, "We see in effect a Pagan rite introduced into our churches, when heaps of wax candles are lighted up in clear sunshine. They honour the martyrs by lighting paltry candles to those whom the Lamb, in the midst of the throne, illuminates with all the lustre of His Majesty. Saint Jerome," says our author, "excuses these ceremonies by saying 'That was once done to idols, and was to be detested, but this is done to the martyrs, and is therefore received.' Gregory Thaumaturgos," continues our author, "was commended for changing the Pagan festivals into Christian holidays, allowing the same carnal indulgences, with a view to draw the heathen to the religion of Christ." Such is the tempting logic of these Christian fathers. All you Pagans, they plead, leave your old idols and feasts, and come to our images and festivals and we will provide you with better entertainments than you ever had before; only you must attend and support the church. This fascinating and alluring logic proved very successful in those early churches, as similar logic has been in all the great churches since.

Concerning the amazing influence of sacred relics in the earlier and later churches, we read that "Gregory I."—or someone of that age—"placed in a box a piece of cloth which had only touched a relic, but when cut with a pair of scissors by Pope Leo, blood came out of it." There need be no doubt as to the blood coming out of the cloth, nor about the liquefaction of the blood of Saint Januarius which takes place periodically down to the present time. The question is, how are these things done? Miracles! miracles! exclaim the believing multitudes. Tricks! tricks! exclaim the unbelieving scientists. There the uninvestigated matters rest.

"Pope Leo X.," says Priestley, "had recourse to Indulgences, in which he promised the forgiveness of all sins—past, present, and to come—which mandate was acted upon with great vigour by the Monk Tetzel, who boasted he had saved more souls from hell by Indulgences than Saint Peter had converted to Christianity by his teaching." We have frequently heard both Pope and Monk fiercely condemned by certain clerical parties for doing what, in another form, these parties were doing themselves. Both Leo and Tetzel had the genius of finance—had money on the brain—and were just such men as the Christian churches have been evolving from Apostolic times to the present day. Among the latest evolutions of the kind we have John Wesley, General Booth, and Bishop Knox.

That Protestant Churches, like Romish Churches, rest on a cash and conversion basis is seen at a glance. When, in a Salvation Army furore, the drums and trumpets have sounded an alarm, then comes the proclamation of instant pardon for all, with a call for cash down. If a convert is tempted by a strong ambition to become a captain or lieutenant, he can have the title with plenary indulgence, on the condition that he begs much money and converts many souls.

In a Methodist Revival meeting conversion is offered on the spot, but the operation must be paid for in cash. A penny a week, a shilling a quarter, and many collections must be duly paid, and then the convert may be designated a saint. In class meetings, band meetings, and love-feasts he will get easy-going indulgences on his confession of the shortcomings of his daily life.

In the Church of England, the making of saints is a most elaborate and costly affair. To an infant at the church font, baptismal regeneration is applied. In mature years the individual is confirmed, and receives the Holy Ghost. At the Lord's Supper he gets peculiar mystical influences he cannot explain. Finally, he obtains priestly absolution from sin, and his saintship is complete. For the performance of these marvellous ceremonies a vast army of priests is supported by the enormous endowments of past ages; from millions of pounds annually received from tithes; from piled-up hoards in the coffers of the Ecclesiastical Commission; and from the constant contributions of the saints.

Now, surely, none of these Churches can fairly condemn the cash transactions of Leo the Pope and Tetzel the Monk, seeing that they are all thickly tarred by the same mammonish brush.

"In the fourteenth century," says Priestly, "there were some Franciscans who maintained that neither Christ nor the apostles had any personal property. This most innocent opinion was most vehemently opposed by the Dominicans, and Pope John XXII. in 1324, pronounced it to be a pestilential, erroneous, damnable, and blasphemous doctrine, subversive of the Catholic faith. In consequence, great numbers of these poor Franciscans were apprehended by the Dominican Inquisition, and committed to the flames." Such is the record of one of those awful religious tragedies which crowd and darken the pages of historic lore.

In reference to such events, Canon H. Scott Holland makes the following remarks*:—"Religious persecutors, Roman or Puritan, did it always for the best. They obeyed rigidly the law of the highest conscience, but why did no divine instinct check their confidence?" There the Canon checks himself, and dares not answer his own question. Indeed, in face of such awful facts, a thoughtful individual must either swear or be dumb.

Again we read, "About the year 600 A.D., the tithes, from being established as a custom, became in some instances legal rights. By degrees the Clergy excluded the poor and appropriated the tithes to themselves. In the time of King John, the Pope made a law ordering that all tithes should be paid to the parish priests, and after some time they were levied by law in all parishes without exception." Here we see the iniquitous way in which the great burden of tithes was fastened on the land, and the great burden of the poor-rate was fastened on the people at large.

* From *The Literary Guide* of October 1st, 1906; quoted from *The Church Times*.

To conclude these startling quotations, we note that " In 1366, the taxes paid to the Pope were five times as much as the King's revenue; and at length the Church is said to have got possession of one-third of all the landed property in England." Just so: and the Pope and Cardinals at Rome to-day are looking complacently and encouragingly on while the Ritualist priests and fanatical laymen led by Lord Halifax are leading back the Church of England, with its mighty millions of revenue, to the Papal fold.

In view of these ominous things, we may fairly apply the judgment of Taine, and say, " Jesus Christ entered Jerusalem in triumph, riding on an ass; but now the asses are riding on the back of Jesus Christ," as they proceed to the conquest of England and the world.

CHAPTER XVII

UNITARIAN MINISTERS—METHODIST CLASS MEETING

THREE scenes in the life of Channing made me intensely desirous to become thoroughly acquainted with all his writings. In the first scene he is sitting as a boy beside his father in Church. He listens with solemn awe to the preacher, who is describing the terrible doom hanging over mankind at large. At the same time the boy is amazed at the apathy with which this solemn message is received by the members of the congregation. The picture we have seen of young Samuel listening to a divine message would, we think, exactly represent the attitude of the boy Channing on this occasion.

In the second scene, he is preaching in his own church to a distinguished congregation, many of whom are upholders of negro slavery. In clear and distinct terms he denounces the abomination. Many a gifted minister at that time hedged about this exciting question until his meaning was obscured. But Channing was true to himself in this matter and therefore, could not be false to another man, whether black or white.

The third scene was in a crowded public hall, where he was confronted by a howling mob of slavery defenders and owners. Notwithstanding continued opposition, he kept his position and continued his speech. His stirring and inspiring words were reported outside that hall, and were carried all over the States, and helped to prepare for the great emancipation by which every negro in the States was made free.

Another and even bolder and more determined opponent of American slavery I found in Theodore Parker. In crowded and excited audiences in his own church, in crowded halls amidst continual uproar he fiercely denounced all pro-slavery men. He singled out for special invective such ministers of churches as defended their pro-slavery sentiments by Bible texts. But he was not content with bold words, but proceeded to daring deeds. He helped to work the underground passages along which fugitive slaves fled to freedom in Canada. Sometimes he harboured the fugitives in his own house. At these times, while engaged in writing his letters and discourses, a revolver lay on his table fully charged. Sooner than let any slave be rescued, he determined the rescuer should be shot. But this courageous man not only assailed the upholders of body slavery, but the upholders of soul slavery, as well. He would not only have the body saved from the deep scars made by the knotted whip, but the soul saved from the deeper scars of a knotted theology. That knotted theology itself he tore to pieces, and stripped religion from the corrupt wrappages which had so long encased it. Then, rising from the dust of decaying parchment creeds, appeared to him the Absolute Religion. Cardinal Newman at one time professed to have made a similar discovery, and affirmed that he was only certain of two existences—his own soul and the infinite soul. But how startling was the contrast between these two great men in their treatment of the Absolute Religion. As if becoming uncertain of his great certainty, Newman went falteringly to ancient cathedrals hoary in virtue and crime. At their altars he bowed low and long, until his religion became overlaid with cruel creeds, false decretals, fantastic legends, corrupted histories, assumed authorities, and the nails, hairs, and bones and blood of dead men.

Parker, in confidence and joy, presented his Absolute Religion in a grander cathedral, vaulted with sunlit or starlit skies, and challenged the investigation of all sorts and conditions of men. History could not cloud it. Literature could only adorn it. Out of the alembics of science it came forth, seven times purified: while the religions of Egypt, Greece, and

Rome, of Confucius, of Buddha, Mohammed and Christ flashed their purest splendours around this Absolute Ideal, making it a glorious guide and instructor for all mankind.

During these Unitarian studies, I, of needs, visited occasionally the Old Chapel, situated in a backyard of King Edward Street. "The narrow entry forming the only approach to the chapel suggested an unanswerable argument," said an old member, "of the truth of the religion preached in the chapel. For, did not Jesus say, 'Narrow is the way that leadeth unto life and few there be that find it'?" I had previously heard Rev. (afterwards Dr.) Vance Smith preach learned sermons which I rather liked; but did not like the chilling atmosphere of the place. The present minister was the Rev. John Wright, of whose advent I had heard an amusing account. Although he must have been some thirty years of age, he had a very youthful appearance. His first text was, "Be not afraid, it is I." Even the few select, sedate, and grave persons forming the congregation could not help smiling at the preacher's appearance and words. During his seven years' ministry both School and Chapel attained to a far greater degree of prosperity than at any time before or since during the century.

Sometimes Rev. T. S. Poynting preached, whom I liked to see and hear. His sermons were full of descants on flowers and trees seas and mountains, rising and setting suns, and star-gemmed skies. The substance of these and other discourses he published in a book with the title "The Heaven that lies around us." The first part of the work was sharply criticised as being too flowery, and the second part as being too dryly scientific. He was urged to recast the work and blend the two parts into one. But, as he said to me, "he was not inclined to give another illustration of the moral of the story of the old man and the ass."

The first time I heard Rev. John Colson, I had a most agreeable surprise. His scripture lesson was the story of Jesus giving sight to the blind man. I had heard the chapter read often enough by Methodist ministers in an over-accentuated way. But here was a perfect dramatic representation. One heard the varying voices and saw the several attitudes of the Jewish rulers, the parents of the blind man, and the man himself. From this time I became dissatisfied with my own reading at Sunday School and at the Useful Knowledge Society. I also became critical of the reading and speaking of public men. I was impatient of the formal and perfunctory style of reading by the Church Clergymen. Even the unction and fervour of the Methodist minister's style of speech failed to satisfy me. Some of my own mannerisms, I think, I must have got rid of. Hence, at the Home Mission College, both Dr. Beard and Professor Gaskell said I was a natural speaker.

My interest in the class meeting had for some time been on the wane. My visits to the vestry of the Old Chapel on Sunday mornings had become few and far between. My experience, when I did happen to go, was given with reserve. The ever-repeated question, "What is the state of your mind, brother?" became monotonous to others beside myself. Hence the good Dr. Birchenall, who had perceived this, introduced a series of readings. The first book he read from was "The Spiritual Husbandman," by an old Puritan Divine. This change I liked and attended more frequently. Other books were referred to, and hence we had something like a literary class. This was a novelty, and pleased most of the young men.

Another very pleasant novelty we had during the quarterly visit to the class by Rev. P. C. Horton. Somehow, he referred to Dean Stanley's "Life of Dr. Arnold," and recommended us all to read it. Then came the acquirement of the book, the passing of it from one to another, and much expression of opinion concerning it. A report of these things got outside the class and a great fluster came about. The venerable Doctor was greatly concerned about the matter, and blamed the minister for having recommended the book. I perceived some of the heresies in it, and pointed them out. This made matters worse, and brought on a crisis, during which the book disappeared, and all discussion about it hushed up. After another period of absence from the class, I met the Doctor in Hurdsfield Road, and made some sort of unsatisfactory reply. And then, with sparkling eyes, and something like a smile on his face, he put the question, "Is there a lady in the case?" I was confused and dumb with surprise, when he grasped my hand and said, "I shall expect to see you at the class on Sunday morning next." After some time, and when I had come to myself, I decided that my answer ought to have been this: "Yes, I am courting the spotless virgin, Truth, who prevents me coming to the class." Alas! this great difficulty of finding the right answer at the right time has haunted me all through life. In writing I could always manage replies better. Later on I had a written correspondence with the Doctor carried on at considerable length.

And here before me are the carefully preserved letters written over sixty years ago. The writing indicates sharpness, smartness, and decision of character, and is more legible than the writing of most professional men. The ideas expressed show a close study of orthodox theology, and a limited knowledge of heterodoxy, and a strong antipathy to any study of it. I am astonished the dear Doctor should have found so much time to write these letters, one of them covering fifteen pages. While mistakenly deploring my supposed dangerous condition, he displays much kindly feeling, with an intense anxiety for the salvation of my soul. The line of controversy pursued may be seen in the following quotations and my replies:—

Birchenall.—" If any man will do the will of God, he shall know of the doctrine whether it be of God."

Rushton.—Yes, and part of the will of God is that we should " Prove all things, and hold fast that which is good." This is what I have been doing for some time, with much anxiety as to the ultimate result.

B.—You speak of the views of an objector, as if you were consulting a controversialist. I would much rather have to do with yourself alone.

B.—I did not like to place myself in direct antagonism to

you, and so introduced the objector. I have simply stated the result of my own investigations without reference to any living person.

B.—Such serious doubts and questionings could scarcely have happened when you were walking in the light of the Divine countenance, and when you had passed from death unto life.

R.—It was precisely then that these questions arose; and these investigations began to be pursued. It was when I was most eager to advance along "the path of the just, which shineth brighter and brighter unto the perfect day." It was when I was in ardent pursuit of a fuller, nobler life than I had yet attained, that these serious questionings arose.

B.—I find a qualified belief in Holy Scripture.

R.—Nay, but only in what is *called* Holy Scripture. Permit me to ask, respectfully, if you yourself believe the statement about the three heavenly witnesses in the First Epistle of St. John, v., 7? And if not, have you not also a qualified belief in what you term Holy Scripture?

B.—The Scriptures require a self-interpreting principle.

R.—By that statement I understand you to mean the comparing of scripture with scripture. But if some of the passages selected for comparison were proved to be spurious, how then? Suppose several very dark passages believed by credulous persons to have some remote intimation of the doctrine of the Trinity should be brought to receive light from the spurious passages about the three heavenly witnesses. A thicker darkness than before would rest on all the passages concerned. That the First Epistle of St. John, v., 7, is spurious is demonstrated by Dr. Adam Clarke, the greatest of Wesleyan scholars. Should not, therefore, a critical examination precede all other methods of testing what is commonly called the Word of God?

B.—The doctrine of the Trinity is objected to because the term itself and its cognates as defined in the creeds are not found in the Scriptures. This statement supposes either an obliquity of judgment, or of moral purpose in the objector.

R.—That is a sort of condemnation I have often heard

pronounced by the preachers. With such authority on my side I have in the past pronounced such condemnation myself. I have also heard unbelievers condemn believers on the same ground of obliquity of mental and moral vision. I am afraid this said obliquity is almost a universal failing. Surely the best way of treating an important question is to examine it from all possible points of view, and then judge in what direction the line of truth lies: and then pursue it with continuous and unabated zeal.

B.—To condemn the Bible because of certain assumed interpolations and some various readings is as unreasonable as it would be to condemn the foundation of a noble building because of some weakness of the superstructure.

R.—[My notes of reply to this point are lost, but my statements would be something like what follows]:—My contention is that the great dogmatic structures of Christendom have been built largely of unsound materials taken from the Bible. The very foundations, I contend, are laid on Scripture passages which are frauds. These unsound structures are only kept in position by the determined and continuous efforts of mighty armies of priests and their disciples with mountains of wealth at their command.

B.—I forward you a book which is held in high repute among us on the Unitarian controversy.

R.—[Minus notes I judge I must have said]:—Thanks for the volume, which I find to be the Bible rearranged. Long lists of passages are strung together pell mell, each list with one of the old assumed dogmas at the head. The many categories seem mere ropes of sand. The few arguments in the book are not nearly so cogently written as the statements in your own letters. With very great regret I must absent myself from the Sunday morning class. What I conceive to be the truth is mighty with me, and does and must prevail. With unbounded gratitude for all the instruction and comfort I have received from you for many years, I am, in the pursuit of love and truth, Yours faithfully, A. R.

B.—May Jesus, the wisdom of God, and the power of God, be the stay of your mind, the joy of your heart, and your everlasting portion.—I am, my dear brother, Truly and affectionately yours, J. BIRCHENALL.

While poring over these old letters, how distinctly has the form of the dear and worthy man come into view! Rather under the middle height, his frame was slim and wiry, his face was thin and had an intensive look, his nose was rather large and his eyes dark and sparkling, his walk was quick, with a stoop to the right and a firm tread of the right foot on the ground, his dress a black cloth suit with swallow-tailed coat and a black silk handkerchief folded twice round the neck, with not a vestige of shirt collar to be seen. I have seen him walking along Plunge Brook Hollow sometimes looking to the hill-tops, sometimes to the sky, and sometimes standing still as if enrapt in prayer or profound thought. On these occasions I have concluded that when he got to Rainow he would have a happy time with his friend Matthew Longden, telling him of the glorious visions he had seen on the way.

CHAPTER XVIII

DR. BIRCHENALL'S CLASS: SKETCHES

THE members of the class greatly regretted my departure from the class. Some of them hinted at the danger of being driven about by every wind of doctrine. They could not see that I was retreating from windy doctrines, and trying to place my faith on the everlasting rock of truth. The changes through which they themselves passed—although different from mine—were remarkable enough.

Matthew Moss was a silk weaver working quietly at home when I first knew him, diligently reading books on theology and general literature. He tried hard to get a clerkship, but his defective hand-writing barred the way. He was in a cheese warehouse some years, during which time he became a local preacher as well as visitor in the Sunday School. Then he left Methodism, and joined the Church, and was appointed Scripture-reader. In his later days his hold on the Church relaxed and some of his dogmas grew faint and thin.

Samuel Moss thought to win me back by means of written letters, but they were so wanting in pith and point that they were without effect. After deprecating my changes, he changed himself, and became a Free Methodist. In his later days his views were what he called broad, but what I called hazy and indefinite, and, as far as I could make out, quite as heretical as my own.

Mr. —— was a fine, hearty fellow, and full of religious zeal. He, too, left the class and became a Free Methodist. But, poor fellow, he had a worse change than that. Extensively engaged in the silk business, he suddenly got into difficulties and disappeared from the town. He had married a good-looking and every way excellent lady, the daughter of Joseph Brightmore, the much-loved Superintendent of Hurdsfield School. Their married life, so bright at first, became shrouded in impenetrable gloom.

John Birchenough as a bright-looking youth had been converted in a revival, and was joyfully welcomed into the class. Our good Doctor exclaimed that he was the first person to welcome him into this world, and now he had the great joy of welcoming him after his second birth, into the Kingdom of God. In a short time he fell away from the class, but continued to attend the services at Brunswick Chapel. Entering into business, he married the daughter of Mr. Taylor, and became his partner in business, and prospered notwithstanding the many ups and downs experienced in the silk business. Becoming the Mayor of the town by the aid of the Liberals, he afterwards became a Liberal-Unionist, and helped to wreck the Liberal party. He became half a Churchman, and the members of his family have become entirely so. One son married the accomplished daughter of the prosperous and generous Unitarian, Mr. Peacock, of Gorton Hall. Another son married the learned daughter of Dean Bradley, of Westminster Abbey. A daughter married Mr. Adshead, a partner in a large brewery. The whole family became Churchly, conservative and aristocratic. And now I cannot help exclaiming, "How great is the contrast between the case of John Birchenough and that of my own!" He moved away, although a professed believer, from the Doctor's class in the direction of the pomps and vanities and wealth of the world. From the same class, with the brand of unbeliever stamped upon me, I went along a lonely road, "far from the madding crowd's ignoble strife." Sometimes I fell in with a few kindred souls, when our hearts burned joyfully within us as we talked by the way of perils past and overcome and victories won. Always, too, I had the company of the saintly writers of books, who ever cast a heavenly radiance over the dark hours of my earthly lot.

Francis Follows—who was owner or manager of a boot and shoe warehouse—was a full-hearted, sincere, and devout young man. While a member of the class he married a lady of an old Methodist family with every prospect of a happy life. Alas! after a while sad domestic difficulties arose, and ever-darkening clouds of trouble gathered over their abode. Often he came to class under deep depression, and as often went away with his mind lightened of its load. The kind words of the leader and the warm sympathy and earnest prayers of all the members met together, lifted entirely, for the time, his clouds of sorrow, so that entering the class was entering into heaven. Many years afterwards I heard of his departure hence, and felt sure he had met death with a welcome word.

George Follows, a younger brother, was a bright, genial, studious and deeply-religious youth. His entrance into the class was like the coming of additional sunlight. I said from the first he would become a circuit minister, and he did, and had a very successful career. In mid-career, and after winning many souls to righteousness, he passed to his exceeding great reward.

J. D. Brocklehurst had inherited the zeal and unceasing activity of his father, Thomas Brocklehurst, so well known in Methodist circles. He, the son, was engaged with his father in a boot and shoe warehouse, and managed to get time for reading in Methodist theology and general literature. He was regular in attendance at the class, and always had some strong testimony to give. Both angels and devils constantly beset him in his daily life. He was solemn and powerful, both in supplication and thanksgiving; his prayers ranged throughout the whole of life and to the verge of death, and closed with the lines:—

> "And then clap our glad wings and tour away,
> And mingle with the blaze of day."

—— Brocklehurst, a younger brother, was of a lively

spirit. He was bright in look, quick in motion, sharp in speech, and smart in dress. I am afraid his testimony was formal as well as superficial. There were ebbs and flows in his attendance, in his moods of mind, and in his related experience. He, however, became a minister, when his religious light alternately blazed and flickered in the pulpits of a few circuits, and then suddenly went out. Only uncertain reports were heard about the closing of his ministerial work. Soon he passed into obscurity and was heard of no more. His elder brother, just mentioned, had a long and useful career as a Methodist minister, and was much honoured on his death.

Mr. Unnamed was consequential and self-confident. He tried hard to be sincere, and sometimes, no doubt, he was. He could start a tune, and was useful in that respect. He had no difficulty in giving his experience, which did not seem very deep. His several prayers were glibly given, and were very much alike. His theology was always sound, and gave him the perfect assurance that he would be saved by faith. This faith he held firmly through a long and checkered career. Unfortunately, it did not prevent him committing sin, but, as he thought, secured him God's forgiveness for the sin committed. This accommodating theology did not work out well in the man's life. Before the election commissioners at the town hall he cut a very sorry figure, the president pronouncing upon him a very severe censure. He had good natural ability, which in the early part of life was displayed with considerable effect. His life went out in darkness, and we can only hope that new light has dawned upon him elsewhere.

G. S. was a young man who had been snatched away from his worldly pleasure by a revival whirlwind, and set down in our Sunday morning class. He was a member of an old Wesleyan family, and there was great rejoicing in the family as well as in the class when he had become the subject of saving grace. He was in the silk business with his father, and afterwards on his own account. His course, for a time, was very promising and hopeful, but difficulties arose in business, when he disappeared from the class and passed into oblivion. O! that silk business! what a deep and awful gulf it has ever been, and into which untold numbers of men have sunk to rise no more!

J. B. I had long known as a scholar in the Sunday School, where he was sometimes under good impressions. I persuaded him to attend the class, and for a time he was regular in his attendance, and was sincere and earnest. But the good seed which had been sown in the School and the class had evidently fallen on stony ground where there was not much earth. The fruitage sprung up quickly, existed feebly a short time, and then withered away. Numerous sowings of seed took place by teachers and preachers, but always without permanent fruit. Many years after he had left the class, he married a Baptist lady who made him go to chapel with her, and in other respects kept him in due submission. He did a great amount of business in the way of buying and selling houses and land. He just made a living out of the profits, the greater part of which profits, like the gospel-seed, withered away. He was not a bad man, but his many attempts at being and doing good were attended with very meagre results.

H. N. was born in a rude family; worked in rough company in Kerridge stone quarries; got little education; yet went to Sunday School and wished to lead a better life than hitherto he had been able to do. I helped him to learn writing, to read in the school-books, and persuaded him to take and read a penny magazine. When he could keep clear of the evil influence of his old companions he made progress in the better life which he wished to lead. After a time I persuaded him to attend the chapel and then to attend the class. Poor fellow! he never could state his experience definitely and distinctly, and never attempted to pray. He began to feel and say he was not fit to attend class and be a society member. He would learn more at Sunday School, he said, and then try the class again. It was in vain I urged that his humble opinion of himself was proof of his fitness to attend the class. He had the unusual defect of sincere personal disparagement, and would not pretend to be what he felt he really was not. He concluded he was amongst the many called, but not amongst the few chosen. I inclined to think that his calling and election were as sure as that of many self-confident members of the visible church.

George Cox was perhaps the most steady-going and persevering member of the class. He was ever ardent, hopeful, unwavering. Most of us thought it likely he would enter the ministry. His speech was quick and nervous. Perhaps the nervous timidity hindered him in continuous speech. Perhaps application to the higher studies would not have been in his way. He was well read in Wesleyan biography and magazine literature, but drew a restricted line as to pagan learning, which some of us passed over with ease and delight. He would have no part in any qualifying opinions about the inspiration of the scriptures, nor would he have anything to do with higher criticism of any degree or kind. He was untouched by religious or philosophical doubt. Heresy he kept at an immeasurable distance. To the sermons of the preachers he was a most tolerant hearer. To him they were all good men, divinely called by God to preach the Gospel. To question, or doubt, or neglect their message was sin. Faith in God and in God's messenger was salvation, the absence of it was damnation. The latter word, however, he would never use, but he would use a paraphrase meaning the same thing. My intercourse with him was of the most cordial kind until my faintest heresy began to leak out. Then he was astonished, perplexed, and deeply grieved. I must pray—he urged—he must pray, and all the members must pray earnestly to God to set me right. When this failed of immediate effect, then it was concluded that God in His good time would bring me back. On my return home from Lancashire some thirty-five years later, I met him in the street, when he heartily welcomed me back to the old town, and would most gladly welcome me to the old class. The last time I spoke to him was just when the Rev. M. Ballard had preached a sermon in the old chapel, in which he spoke favourably of Spiritualism. Somewhat as follows was the conversation that ensued:—

R.—Did you hear Mr. Ballard's sermon?

C.—No, but I have been told about it.

R.—It was unusually pleasing to hear Spiritualism spoken favourably of in a Wesleyan Chapel.

C.—Mr. Ballard is like the men of Athens in seeking for some new thing.

R.—Those inquiring men of Athens prompted St. Paul to deliver a most eloquent discourse, which has charmed and instructed innumerable multitudes of people. Besides, all things are new at first.

C.—We must be guided by the Word of God.

R.—But Spiritualism is in the Bible as well as outside of it.

C.—We must be saved by faith in the merits of Jesus Christ.

R.—Spriitualists seek to be saved by adherence to the two commandments of love to God and love to man as enunciated by Jesus Christ.

C.—(Grasping my hand and pointing upward, he exclaimed): We shall meet in heaven!

R.—Amen!

That was our last meeting on earth. Some time afterwards came the message—"George Cox is dead!" Solemnly the announcement struck home to my soul. Of the numerous band meeting in the old chapel vestry over sixty years ago, I alone, then, remained alive on earth! I alone! The heretic, the much advised; the much reasoned with; the much sympathised with; the much prayed for; the much blamed by that band of brothers: am the only pilgrim of them all left travelling on to the eternal bourn which they have reached! But I too, shall soon arrive. Will there be bands of brothers there with music and song, and communion of soul with soul? I soon shall know. I wait in tranquillity and hope for my summons hence.

CHAPTER XIX

WESLEYAN MINISTERS I HAVE KNOWN

With these mementos of my class-mates may be fittingly joined brief sketches of ministers who greatly influenced both them and myself. In the record of conversation with my mother I have already given some account of ministers I greatly revered in my very early years. My mother thought them all saints, inspired by God and full of the Holy Ghost. My own thoughts were just the same, and I never approached a minister without a feeling of overpowering awe. This feeling continued until the time I came under the influence of the Rev. Alexander Strachan. Thence my critical and reasoning faculties awoke, and I began to form independent judgments of men and things.

The following sketches of ministers were formulated in my mind at the time I heard them preach. Bernard Slater, broad set, flabby-cheeked, cheerful-faced, charitable of disposition, genial of speech, and fond of preaching from hopeful texts in the Book of Psalms—was a colleague of Mr. Strachan. So, also, was Israel Holgate, a little man of pleasant speech, with a bright face and a curly-haired head, which, however, did not seem to contain much depth of thought.

A third colleague was George Greenwood, an earnest, bustling young man, with no great force of character, but who was a great favourite with the females of the congregation.

No Methodist preacher, except Mr. Strachan, influenced me so deeply as Jacob Sidney Smith. In every respect he was a remarkably superior man. He was tall and slender in form, had an intellectual face, with bright, piercing eyes, and had a lofty head crowned with light-coloured hair. His voice was low, soft, clear, distinct, and sometimes piercing. His first sermon in the old chapel was based on the text, "Get wisdom, get understanding," and was altogether out of the line of ordinary Methodist discourse. It was instructive, elevating, inspiring. Instead of doctrinal commonplaces, it contained literary gems; and instead of maudlin sentiments, came promptings to high and holy endeavours. This sermon was the keynote of all his discourses. Nothing of the kind had been heard in Methodist pulpits or in any other pulpits in the town. Some of his hearers felt mystified; some were dumbfounded; others denounced such worldly-mindedness; whilst a few, mostly young men, were edified and delighted. He remained his term of three years, but had little peace. Some of the elders were always complaining, and then others followed suit. Now and again he broke out into torrents of eloquent invective against the crying evils of the day, which startled everybody within hearing, and which crowded the chapels on succeeding Sundays. Then, as if despising popularity, he fell into quiet trains of noble thoughts and expressions until the excitement was over. Some years after leaving Macclesfield, there came reports that he had been found drowned, and other accounts that he had gone abroad. The truth about the matter I never learnt; but his ennobling influence over me from my seventeenth to the twentieth year of my age I have never ceased to feel.

From my twentieth to my thirtieth year I continued to be influenced by Methodist ministers, but in a less degree than before. At the beginning of this period, William Bird appeared in Macclesfield. He was singular in look, in gesture, and in speech. The shrugs of his shoulders, the nods of his head, and the winks of his eyes, were things not soon to be forgotten. During a sermon in the old chapel, he quoted these lines from Pope:—

"For modes of faith let graceless zealots fight,
He can't be wrong whose life is in the right."

Those lines—said he—contained an abominable falsehood; every word being emphasized by shrug, and nod, and wink. He then proceeded elaborately to prove his statement. Some thought he succeeded in his task, while I thought he utterly failed. On another occasion he undertook to demolish Dr. Adam Clarke's views of the Eternal Sonship of Jesus Christ. His whole argument against the Doctor he clinched by the affirmation, " That as there could not be a son without a father, so neither could there be a father until there was a son." Many thought the argument unanswerable. I was puzzled rather than convinced, and years afterwards saw that the so-called argument was only a juggle of words. He left the town at the end of two years on account of some difference with the officials of the Society. On his departure he said Providence would find him a place somewhere, even if it were on an island in the Hebrides. The peculiar reasonings of this peculiar—but well-meaning—man, were apt to lead to conclusions the very opposite of those he wished one to reach.

John Lambert was the very opposite kind of man to Mr. Bird. He was less original, but more plausible; had less shrewdness, but more unction; and to some was very impressive. His discourses were certainly very eloquent sometimes; but were delivered too much like the recitations of a school-boy. At times I doubted if the discourses were his own, but at length doubted no longer. I had bought from the bookroom a very highly-recommended volume of discourses by a number of Scotch ministers, and which I had carefully read. Just then, on a certain Sunday morning at the old chapel, Mr. Lambert preached, or rather recited, one of these same discourses, almost word by word. Thus the secret of his eloquence was out, at least, to myself, and I took care to say nothing about the matter, not wishing to hinder the man in the work he was doing. It is certain he would have preached much worse sermons had he made them himself. But what a fine memory he must have had, and what pains he must have taken in preparing discourses in this arduous way. If nine-tenths of ministers could be compelled to preach first-rate discourses in this way, I am sure it would be more educative to the preachers themselves and much more edifying to the hearers than the methods then and now in vogue.

Joseph Roberts, who was appointed to the circuit for one year only, was a returned missionary, and quite familiar with the manners and customs of Jews, Turks, and Arabs. From scenes he had witnessed he illustrated scripture narratives in a most striking way. The events in the story of Isaac and Rebecca—he said—were being repeated from day to day at the present time, and had been re-enacted from age to age, and from century to century. Eastern customs—he said—seemed to be immutable, and the history of the patriarchs was the history of Bedouin life in the deserts of Arabia at the present time. The whole circuit felt a great loss when Mr. Roberts left the town to resume his missionary labours in the east.

Robert Jackson was strong, burly, rugged-looking, and had retained his marked Yorkshire accent. He was earnest, sincere, industrious, and sharp-tempered. He was strongly attached to old Methodism, thinking there was nothing else so good in all the world. Hence he wrote and published certain strongly-worded pamphlets in its defence against aspersions by certain clergymen in the neighbourhood. He could tolerate no criticism on society administration; hence his sharp quarrel with Matthew Longden of Rainow, who advocated some slight alteration in certain methods of missionary procedure. According to his character and ability he did his work here and went his way, leaving no special mark behind.

Thomas Hardy was a rather small, active man, with his head on one side, and his mouth inclining to the other side. His speech was plain and rugged, and without containing any humour, produced humorous effect. A favourite text of his was, "Be not unequally yoked together," his great object being to secure safe marriages for Methodist people. To marry individuals of other religious views might prove detrimental to the Society, and must not be tolerated. This doctrine pleased elderly Methodists, but some younger ones kicked wilfully against it.

Joseph Mood was a good-hearted young man who looked and spoke like a farmer. His favourite text was, "Feed my lambs." A friend who had heard him preach from these words in different chapels on several occasions, said, "Mr. Mood, I am afraid your lambs will never grow into sheep." "O yes, they will," Mr. Mood replied, "if you will feed them well enough and long enough." With very moderate ability he did good work in the Sunday Schools, and amongst young people generally.

A very different young man was Frederick Wooley, who was scholarly and eloquent. But being very modest, shy, and retiring, did not obtain much popularity. On being called upon to speak at a certain missionary meeting, he made a short apologetic address and sat down; whereupon Mr. Harris (superintendent) harshly insisted he should speak longer, saying, "Little birds that can sing and won't sing, must be made to sing." For a few minutes he again spoke, and then sat down. I felt very great sympathy for him, for, evidently, he was not in a condition to speak, and should have been let alone.

Thomas Harris had the look of a smart country squire, and was dictatorial, like one. At a revival meeting in Brunswick Chapel, Henry Newton rose up and pleaded for the meeting to be lengthened, that more souls might be converted. "No, it must not," exclaimed Mr. Harris. "I have the conduct of this meeting, and know how to manage it without advice." "Aye, yo' dun, mon! Amen," replied Henry Newton, and the meeting was closed. Discipline was of more importance to Thomas Harris than even the saving of souls, as many thought and said.

Now and again, distinguished ministers came to preach special sermons in one or other of the chapels, some of whom left strong and distinctive impressions on my mind.

Dr. Bunting—whom I saw and heard only once—was rather over middle height, of stout build, of commanding attitude, with an easily flowing voice expressing sentiments in an affirmative and very positive way. He has often been termed the Pope of Methodism, but a better and more comprehensive designation would be that he was the greatest of the Methodist Popes. "Adapt your principles to your exigencies," was the rule he laid down, and he was faithful to it throughout his long career. The way he applied it was seen when, after uniformly advocating neutrality in politics, he wrote to the "Standard" in favour of the Tory candidate for Finsbury, and appeared on the hustings to advocate his cause. He has been called the Sandow (strong man) of the Conference, because, whoever might be the President, Bunting was the Prime Minister who never went out of office. He was only consistent in his intolerance. "We cannot be friendly to Dissent," he said, "for the genius of Methodism is not the genius of democracy." With reference to teetotalism, he said, "Two things must be insisted upon: first, the use of *bona-fide* wine in the Lord's Supper; second, the not allowing of teetotal meetings in our chapels."

When he was chairman at a certain election for President of Conference, two of the candidates had equal numbers of votes. "Will either of the two withdraw?" asked Bunting. "Yes," I will," said Mr. Slugg. "Then I give the casting vote for Mr. Slugg," said Bunting, and Mr. Slugg became President. Was that an illustration of Bunting's craft, or shrewdness, or wit, or what? For forty years, Bunting's almighty domineering force held sway over the great Methodist Society. One result as seen in Mr. Fowler's "Notes of Conferences," was the great disruption of 1849. In reference to that event, it has been said that, "If on one of the occasions when Dr. Bunting threatened to resign his office, the Conference had taken John Wesley's advice in another case, and reached him his hat, the hats of 50,000 seceding Methodists would have remained at rest on their pegs." Another result was that spirit of reactionary conservatism which has so largely prevailed in the Wesleyan body ever since.

Dr. Robert Newton I once saw and heard preach at Brunswick Chapel, and have a distinct recollection of his fine appearance and impressive discourse. "He had the dignity of a noble Roman," said some one, and I daresay the description was correct. "His voice" was said to be "like an organ peal, alternately loud, and soft, and sweet," and I think the comparison was fit and true. So thrillingly did he read a poem by Montgomery, that the poet, who was present, became quite entranced. The proud Lord Wharncliffe, who was chairman at a Bible Society meeting at Barnsley, wept freely all the time that Newton was speaking. The melting power of his speech was felt by persons of all classes, and especially by thoughtful young men, many of whom—including John Rattenbury—were thus induced to become Methodist ministers. And yet, at the beginning of his preaching career he despaired of success. To a friend he exclaimed, "I must go home; I can't stand it. I have got through all my sermons, and have no time to study." This was a very unusual display of modesty and frankness on the part of a young minister. If the majority of young ministers were as unconceited as was Newton, the cry of home-going would fill the air in the neighbourhood of churches and chapels. Earnest persuasion induced him to stick to the ministry. Some young ministers need no persuasion. They fasten like leeches on the churches, and draw the life-blood from them, until, in many cases, they become collections of galvanized corpses.

Our subject married a gifted, somewhat wealthy, and every way eligible young lady. He would have been very imprudent to have married a less worthy person, seeing the splendid choice afforded in the numerous circles of Methodist ladies. Such circumstances, indeed, are not peculiar to Methodist Societies, for in the Established Churches curates are said to be raided by bevies of accomplished women. Still, Methodism is the most promising of happy hunting-grounds for young preachers, and both numerous and valuable are the prizes gained. I have known a young man leave the shop counter, and within three years enter the Methodist ministry and marry a lady with an income of £500 a year.

After a great missionary meeting, at which Newton and several other leading ministers had spoken, the following colloquy took place just outside the chapel:—(First critic): I like William Dawson best, he is so humorous. (Second critic): But Newton is by far the finest orator. (Third critic): Richard Watson is the man for deep thought and beauty of expression. (Fourth critic): As to Dr. Clarke, any old wife can follow and understand him. "I think that the very highest compliment that could possibly have been paid me," said Dr. Clarke when he heard the statement.

With my mother and all the Cooper family, Dr. Clarke was the greatest favourite amongst all the preachers they ever knew. The great esteem in which my uncle, Adam Cooper, held the learned Doctor was shown in having one of his sons christened Adam Clarke. I loved him for the Commentary which he wrote and published. It cost me a large sum of hard-earned money, but in its perusal I found my exceeding great reward. I thought him then, and I think him still, by far the ablest commentator that Methodism has ever produced.

William Morley Punshon I heard preach and lecture on several occasions, and always regretted I had not the opportunity of hearing him more frequently. He was of middle size, of stout build, with a broad, intellectual face. His voice was not soft nor sweet, but it had great momentum, which steadily increased as he proceeded in his discourse. A sermon was a series of pictures. The life of Christ, on one occasion, he made into a panorama. The angels singing—the suspended star at Bethlehem—the flight into Egypt—the disputation with the doctors in the temple—the temptation in the wilderness—the sermon on the mount, with picturesque groups of hearers—the boat on the tossing waves of the sea of Galilee—Zaccheus on the tree-top—the woman at the Well of Samaria—disputations with Pharisees and Saducees—the raising of Lazarus—the last supper—the judgment-hall of Pilate—the crucifixion, with its awful glooms—the resurrection, with its glowing splendours, were all made to pass like a magnificent vision before the hearers' view, the whole culminating with the Ascension—described with overwhelming force in the following words:—" Lift up your heads, O ye gates; and be ye lift up, ye everlasting doors; and the King of Glory shall come in. Who is this King of Glory? The Lord strong and mighty, the Lord mighty in battle—He is the King of Glory!"

Popular as a preacher, he was much more so as a lecturer. "The Pilgrim Fathers," "The Prophet of Horeb," and "John Bunyan," were amongst the subjects of these lectures. Historic facts, poetic allusions, and artistic gems, crowded and adorned these discourses. "He worships reverently," says one, "at the shrine of beauty, and gazes profoundly in the halls of classic grandeur; he treads softly in the groves of Arcadia, and stands proudly on the brow of Olympus. To him flowers and thunderbolts are alike familiar; songs of happiness and sentences of earnest appeal are similarly suited. The chaplet of beauty and the wreaths of majesty appear equally adapted to his ability."

William (commonly called Billy) Dawson was one of Methodism's eccentric preachers. I was but young when I heard him preach in Brunswick Chapel, but I never forgot the appearance and manner of the man, nor the substance of his discourse. After reading the text, "Thou art weighed in the balances and found wanting," he divided the crowded congregation into several classes. Then he pretended to place a pair of scales with weights on one side of the pulpit. The requirements of the gospel were the weights in one end of the scales. On the other end he placed a man who was an outsider attending no church or chapel. Lifting the scale, the man rose in the air for want of due weight. "But," replied the man, "I believe in God and the Bible, and say my prayers, and work to keep my family." "But," said the preacher, "you want the weight of saving faith." Lifting the scales again, the man's end jerked into the air and pitched the man into the pit beneath the pulpit, indicating that was the way he would be pitched into hell if he did not repent.

A backslider was placed in the scale, and proved an awfully light weight. "But I had good reason," said the man, "for leaving the Society. I found some of the leading saints were great sinners." "Then," said the preacher, "you should have stayed and shamed them by your own good example," and out of the balance he fell into the pit below. Another backslider (always numerous in Methodist chapels) appeared very repentant, very believing, and very good in intention. He quivered much in the balance, but escaped the pit beneath. Next came a sceptic, and boldly stepped into the scale. He had been adopting the principles of Tom Paine and Voltaire, and thought he had weight enough to pass the scales. But alas! the scales jerked him to the ceiling, from where he fell with a great thud into the pit beneath. A life-long member, who had done much work for the Society and given much money to it, and who had always had unbounded faith in the blood of the Lamb as applied to himself, was of full weight, with much to spare. A crown of glory and a palm of victory—the preacher declared—would be his at any moment when he should be summoned to heaven.

Another of the eccentrics was Peter McKenzie, whom I always liked to see and hear. He was a coal-miner in the early part of his life, with no opportunity for education except a little self-education. Having become converted, he developed a wonderful power of racy speech. His services as a local preacher were numerous and very successful. Wherever he went to preach large crowds assembled, and big collections were made. Conference authorities, hearing of these things, were greatly delighted, and determined to have this rough diamond polished, and rendered still more effective in the Master's work. To college he was told he must go, and to college he went. Not making sufficient progress in grammatical studies, he was called to account, when he simply replied that he had read his grammar-book through, and had not once met with the name of the Lord Jesus Christ, and had therefore given the whole thing up. On another occasion he was called into the presence of several grave and reverend Seniors, who complained of the crudeness and abruptness of his speech in preaching. They advised he should devote more time and trouble in properly clothing his ideas. "But," said Peter, "my ideas come and go at so great a speed that I cannot get any clothing on them, not even their shirts." A marvellous relaxation then took place in the faces of all present, and thenceforth Peter was left to his own shirtless speech. My own opinion was that Peter's naked truth-speaking was far more interesting, instructive, rousing, and every way effective than the fashionably-dressed speaking of most Methodist preachers. The poor man was kept continually at work, and preached himself to a premature death.

Hugh Price Hughes may, I think, be fairly placed in the category of eccentrics. True, he had been privileged with a much more fashionable education than either of the last two preachers I have named. But he was erratic and abrupt of speech like them, and much more audacious than either of them. When I was at St. James' Hall—now many years ago—he commenced his sermon by a sharp criticism of the prayer which had just been offered by another minister on the platform. "The prayer," said Mr. Hughes, "had been marked by a very serious omission. Earnest petitions had been offered for the conversion of poor and degraded and wicked dwellers in the slum regions: but not one petition had been offered for the conversion of wealthy wicked sinners dwelling in palatial regions." On this theme were made some pungent remarks which seemingly pleased the large congregation.

Preaching in Trinity Chapel, Macclesfield, a short while before his death, on the subject of Faith, he mentioned the case of a woman of very great faith whom he knew. "Is your faith strong enough to enable you to go through a crack in a great wall if God wished you to do it?" said Mr. Hughes to the woman. "I would try," said the woman. I looked round at the large audience, but did not see a sceptical look on a single face. If I had seen my own face, I could not have made this declaration.

During the last forty years, I have taken every opportunity to see and hear Charles Garret, the prince of Methodist preachers. His orthodoxy does not trouble me in the least, which, indeed, he does not obtrude unnecessarily. When he describes the temptations, and sorrows, and woes of life, and how to overcome them, I feel helped and strengthened. When he tells of the joys, triumphs, and serenities of life, and how to attain them, I feel uplifted to, at least, the third heaven. When he depicts the crises of a soul, and its glorious deliverance therefrom, I am pierced through and through, and want to get behind a screen to hide my tears, which will not cease to flow.

On one occasion I went to Sunderland Street Chapel long before the time of service in order to get an out-of-the-way seat, but found the place full. A gentleman, seeing me, took me along the gallery and deposited me in the corner of a front pew, only a few yards from the pulpit. I did not like my position, but braced myself up to be resigned to it. Describing the path of the just, Mr. Garret said it might be rough and rugged and thorny, but it was always bright. It might be steep and hard to climb, but with every step came a more extended view. Dark clouds might gather around it, and fierce storms break over it, but, emerging from it, the traveller found the light to be brighter than ever before. Even the dark valley of death itself, to such an one, was ablaze with light, and then beyond was the light of perfect day. Then, turning towards me, and looking me full in the face, he exclaimed with a smile, "Is not that not so, brother?" I smiled and nodded, and then he smiled again, and the light and inspiration of that smile I never lost. Such was the nearest approach I ever had to intercourse with this gifted, noble, and venerable man.

These sketches of Methodist ministers I have known, and whose influence I have strongly felt, must be concluded by a notice of one I consider the greatest and noblest of Wesleyan revivalists.

James Caughey, who came from America on a preaching mission, was over the middle height, with a thin, wiry body, and pale, mobile face. Solemnity, pathos, love, terror, hope, joy, and rapture, seemed to chase each other with marvellous rapidity over his fine features as he spoke. His voice was low and soft, clear and penetrating, and sometimes piercing. His first appearance in Brunswick Chapel on a Sunday morning has been a gracious and enduring memory to me. His prayer was pointed, pathetic, touching, and short. His lessons were read with brief comments, which threw vivid flashes of light on the words. His text was, "Rejoice evermore, pray without ceasing, in everything give thanks." "Yes," said he, " let us rejoice that we have met in this sacred place to-day; that we have felt the blessedness of sacred song; that we have felt the mighty power of prayer; that we have felt the beginning of an overwhelming shower of divine grace, which is falling, falling upon every one of us, flowing, flowing into every heart, sweeping away indifference, doubt, and fear, and sin. Yes, pray without ceasing that the glorious spiritual impetus of this sacred hour may ever remain with you, bearing you along triumphantly amid the rocks, and shoals, and whirlpools of the sea of time. Yes, in everything give thanks, especially that so many souls—in the gallery and under the gallery there—are being born again, and that all present are having a new consecration by the holy spirit of God."

Although absorbed in the thrilling discourse, I could not help glancing at the serried ranks of faces crowding the great gallery of the chapel. When the preacher smiled in rapture, nearly every face caught the smile. When a shade of pathos passed over his features, the cloud was on all faces. When he melted into subduing tenderness, the tears flowed from almost every eye. Sunshine, clouds, and showers followed each other in quick succession to the close of the discourse. Orthodox doctrines, at this time, had lost their dominion over me, but the personality of this man completely ruled me for the time. Since then I have often thought that if this inspiring personal force could be applied to Unitarianism, it would become a mighty power in the world. I fear this will never be, and yet I know not why.

In the same chapel, and on the evening of the same day, the text was, "This year thou shalt die," and the discourse was awful in the extreme. In the morning the congregation had been lifted to the verge of heaven, but in the evening the congregation was conveyed irresistibly to the very confines of hell. The sight of the lurid regions caused many to shriek aloud in fear, and the penitent forms were crowded with agonizing souls. As a result of Mr. Caughey's preaching, some hundreds of converts were enrolled, and there was great rejoicing in Methodist circles. Great care and watchfulness was exercised over the new converts, and yet, they would slip away. Within a few months, three-quarters of these mushroom Methodists had backslidden into their old ways. The most signal trophies of the revival had vanished away. One of these was John Dakin, of Hurdsfield, whom I knew well, and whom I counselled to persevere in his better life. He attended Hurdsfield Sunday School regularly a while, as also the chapel and class meeting, but finally broke away from all these connections, and what became of him afterwards I never knew. Nearly all the converts who remained true to their new calling were the younger members of Methodist families, or such young persons as had been taught by earnest and devout teachers in Sunday Schools.

CHAPTER XX

MARRIAGE — TRADE — REFUGEE MISSION

I HAVE a strong impression that in the several particulars of this particular revival we find an epitome of the history of most Methodist revivals everywhere. If dogmatically I had broken away from Methodism, I was still held by association. My brothers both attended Brunswick Chapel, and I felt bound to attend with them. Uncle Adam was the leader of the singers, and Cousin Adam played the organ, and we all loved the music and liked our relations with whom we often met, and so a strong tie bound me to the chapel in this way. And now another and a stronger bond was beginning to be felt. My mother's picture of three angels was having a second realization. In a front pew in the gallery were regularly seen on the Sunday three good-looking ladies. When there was no attraction in the pulpit, there was always attraction in that pew. The preacher's influence was often nil, but the influence of the angelic ones became strong and constant.

Pious platitudes fell flat in presence of this new inspiration. The most fervid appeals lost all force with this other force at work. Certain extra saints have become so entirely absorbed in the love of God, that no room or capacity was left for sexual love, but they have been few and far between. A large number of individuals, indeed, have been shut up in religious houses professedly absorbed in the divine life, but concerning some of them sad revelations have been made. The best of saints are such as manage to have a due blending of divine and human love, and such was the kind of blending I was now endeavouring to secure.

Careful investigation showed that this interesting trio of ladies had spent their early days in the country, had come to the town later on and joined together in a business which had proved successful, were members of the Wesleyan Society, and were of good character in every respect. To the central one of the group as they sat in the pew, I paid court from time to time with definite and favourable result. Mutual affection was developed and grew stronger and stronger as the days went on, while the question of ways and means developed at the same time.

Principles, practices, and habits, past, present and future, were fully discussed. I had long practised Teetotalism, she not entirely, but nearly so, and therefore abstinence was to be the rule of the house. That I was no longer a member of the Wesleyan Society was a disappointment; that I intended still to go to chapel was satisfactory. My heresy was fully explained but not easily understood: still, tolerance was to be the rule. This rule acted well until intolerant friends intervened, when trouble arose. Her friends, in politics, were conservative, and so, therefore, was she. My radicalism in all things was a disturbing force. A fair amount of harmony was, however, maintained. The fateful time arrived when we were united at the old church, and thence proceeded to Beaumaris in North Wales. There we read poetry, history, and romance, and talked moonshine as we walked under the shadow of the mountains and along the shores of the sea. The time passed much too quickly, and soon we had to return to the work-a-day scenes of our old town.

Living at the house in Chester Road, where the business was carried on by Mrs. R. and her two cousins, I was one-and-a-half miles from the warehouse in Hurdsfield where I was engaged from six o'clock in the morning until eight o'clock at night. At noon I had to walk three miles and get dinner in just an hour. Formerly, when I went to dinner in Higher Hurdsfield, I had the sight and smell of green fields and trees, and felt the refreshing breezes from Ecton hills or widespread vales. But now I had to pass through crowds of people in ugly and ill-smelling streets. Depression seized me, and my indigestion increased in force. Evening meetings were constant and lasted until late in the night. In twelve months' time my health entirely broke down, when I was warned that my life was in serious danger and I must give up all my engagements at once.

During a whole month I lived at Red Wharf Bay, in the Isle of Anglesea. The sea, the air, and a little mountain-climbing, began to revive my health and strength. This was improved by intercourse with a Welsh curate in charge of a lonely church. The acquaintance seemed to do him good as well as myself. In our conversation we were literary, scientific, historic, religious, and romantic in a limited way. Many things we had nearly forgotten were revived, while new stores of knowledge were gained in each case. The discourse went on the following lines:—

Rushton.—Why should your language be disfigured by so many double letters?

Welshman.—Those letters add to the beauty and glory of the language, and make it the most perfect of all languages. Besides, the English contains many double letters, not placed there by method, but thrown in by accident. Such, indeed, is the case with your irregular verbs and other abounding irregularities of the language.

R.—I admit all you say about the imperfections of English, but that contains no justification for the imperfections of the Welsh language.

W.—What do you propose for reform in either case?

R.—Phonetic spelling in both cases. Increase the letters of the alphabet until there is one letter for one sound and only one sound, and then the present bewildering combination of letters and sounds would cease to exist, and then the form of written language would be beautiful to see and easy to learn and read.

W.—An utterly impossible scheme!

R.—Both possible and easily practicable but for educational vested interests and established forms in schools and churches, with inveterate preujdice to boot.

R.—How wild, weird, and plaintive Welsh music is.

W.—Ah! you have not heard much of it yet, or you would know that our music is solemn, deep, sublime, and rapturous, as well as plaintive and serene. As may be observed at the Eisteddfod, our music enters into all things. It enters into art, science, history, literature and religion, and carries them into the minds and hearts of men, thrilling them with rapture.

R.—About fifteen years ago I was present at a great open-air meeting of Welsh Methodists at Carnarvon. Some 10,000 people were present, who all seemed earnestly to join in the singing of the hymns, producing such a mighty mass of overwhelmingly impressive sound as I had never before heard. There might, indeed, have been sublimity and rapture in the song, but one long, low, soft, sweet, melting wail was the pervading sound. The same subduing, magnetic, penetrating wail was heard in the voices of all the preachers, some three or four of whom were speaking at the same time from different platforms in the wide fields. Although I could not understand a word of the language uttered, I felt strongly the mighty spiritual force which pervaded the place. The effect on the people was overwhelming. Great numbers fell on their knees in fervent prayer; some lifted their arms in ecstasy towards the skies; some fell prostrate in anguish; while nearly all seemed uttering exclamations.

W.—If you had only understood the language, you would have been in anguish or ecstasy yourself.

R.—But I might have been restrained by theological dissent.

W.—Ah! there might have been something in that. Welsh Methodists are Calvinistic for the most part, and wonder at the Arminianism of English Methodists, and also a small minority in Wales. But the Calvinists have the best of the argument, for all nature moves and exists by predestined force.

R.—Then Nature's laws are inviolate?

W.—Nay! hardly so. Certain events may be produced by, to us, unknown laws which seem to contravene such laws of nature as we understand.

R.—To what events do you refer?

W.—Biblical miracles.

R.—But what about Roman Catholic miracles?

W.—They cannot be true, as miracles ended with the Apostolic age.

R.—But the evidence for Roman Catholic miracles is nearer and clearer and stronger than the Biblical evidence for miracles. Besides, miracles are claimed as indisputable evidence in favour of all the great religions, whether Pagan, Mohammedan, or Christian.

W.—If the divine authority of the Bible be set aside, all certainty as to the true religion is lost.

R.—Such authority is already set aside by the higher criticism of the day, and yet nothing is lost from the book except falsehood, fraud, and mistake.

In these conversations the curate manifested more patience and toleration than is common wtih clericals in his position. The most hearty good-wishes were expressed by both of us when the time of my departure came.

A few months later I was induced to go to the Water Cure Establishment at Alderly Edge, where I remained four or five weeks. Only cold water was applied, and in severe forms. Entering, stripped, into a sort of sentry box perforated all over with holes, through which rushed streams of water, I was nearly frozen, almost choked, and entirely stunned. The doctor decided it must not in my case be repeated. Wrapped in a wet sheet, around which a heap of blankets was rolled, I should have sweat copiously, but I could not get sufficiently warm to sweat at all, and so that treatment was discontinued. Ultimately, I was ordered only one ordinary bath a day, and then my health began to improve a little.

There were so many visitors, that some had to be lodged at neighbouring houses. All met together, however, at meal times, when the conversation was remarkably varied and interesting. The most rapid speakers were two young American merchants. They were about the middle height, thin, wiry, nervous, and quick of movement. Their talk was chiefly about merchandise, and the great fortunes made thereby. Dollars! dollars! was their unceasing theme. They seemed to have no object in life but to accumulate dollars. I tried to draw from them descriptions of natural scenery in their own country. In reply they said they had the biggest cataracts, the longest and broadest rivers, the highest mountains, the most extensive forests, and the most sea-like lakes in all the world. Everything was big which arrested their attention, the lesser beauties of nature being of little account. They would have me to walk with them in the woods, but their speed exhausted me, and I had to walk with others at a moderate speed. Several Quakers were in the company, who were very orthodox in their religion. One lady had detected heresy in some of my remarks, and was very much concerned about it. Several conversations ensued, the substance of which was somewhat as follows:—

Quakeress.—I fear thou hast not sufficient reverence for the word of God.

Rushton.—I not only reverence, but try to obey any true word of God.

Q.—But dost thou accept the Bible as the Word of God?

R.—I accept the Bible as the word of God, the word of the devil, and as the word of man.

Q.—That seems a shocking statement, but explain thy meaning.

R.—Certainly, in the words of the Bible itself: "I am that I am," "I am a jealous God," "Thou shalt have no other gods before me." Those are a few of God's words, not very tolerant words, certainly.

Q.—Oh!

R.—Now we quote a few of the Devil's words. Satan, in

a conversation with God about Job, said, "Touch his bone and his flesh, and he will curse Thee to Thy face." So effective were these words that God said, "He is in thine hands." As the result of this compact between Satan and God, the most terrible afflictions and losses were heaped upon righteous Job. Another notable quotation of the Devil's words we give from a conversation with Jesus Christ: From the top of an exceeding high mountain the Devil showed to Christ all the kingdoms of the world, and the glory of them, and said, "All these things will I give Thee if Thou wilt fall down and worship me." These tempting conditions were rejected with disdain by Jesus Christ; but have been eagerly accepted by His disciples, and hence the kingdoms of the world are rapidly becoming their own.

Q.—Oh dear! Oh dear! If thou had'st but the Inner Light how very different these things would appear.

R.—But, as you contend that that light enlighteneth every man that cometh into the world, I must have some share of that light.

Q.—Jesus Christ said, "Ye must be born again." Dost thou practically understand that?

R.—As Methodists understand it, I went through the operation of conversion.

Q.—Ah! then, thou hast backslidden.

R.—No! No! I have forward slidden, and am pressing forward to the prize of my high calling, consisting of the everlasting revelation of truth. But let me now point out certain words in the Bible spoken by men. "What doth the Lord require of thee (O man) but to do justly, and to love mercy, and to walk humbly with thy God." Such are the words of Micah. "Whatsoever ye would that men should do to you, do ye even so to them." Such are the words of Jesus. These words, it will be admitted, are amongst the very best in the book.

Q.—Then thou considerest the Saviour to be a mere man?

R.—In converse with His persecutors, He says, "Ye seek to kill me, a man that hath told you the truth."

Q.—But He says, "I and the Father are one."

R.—He also says, "The Father is greater than I."

Q.—May not men wrest the Scriptures to their own destruction?

R.—Well, even you "Friends" wrest Baptism and the Lord's Supper from the Scriptures, somehow. The great Church of England decides from the Scriptures that those two ceremonies are necessary to salvation. How then can the Friends be saved? Had we not better adopt the dictum of Paul, that the greatest and most saving thing is charity, and act up to it?

As these conversations went on the Friends looked very serious. Others smiled, and commended the good temper displayed by both disputants. A lesson of tolerance would be learned, I think, by all concerned in the dispute.

When I was a few months over thirty years of age, I wrote in my diary thus:—"For ever farewell to the silk mill. The crushing slavery of twenty-one years is ended; simply because physical endurance utterly fails. But I must have a pursuit of some kind and must secure subsistence so long as I am alive. Mrs. R. continues her business with fair results. I continue my teaching at the Useful Knowledge Society, and other teaching with a limited income. Work at a loan society with the management of several small investments brings in a small additional remuneration. In this way, income meets expenditure, and leaves something over, thus securing an honest and independent course of life."

Could my health have improved, prospects would soon have been bright and hopeful, but my strength began to fail, and I seemed to be sinking fast. In alarm, several friends urged I should consult Dr. James Bardsley, of Manchester. The fee was large, but life was at stake. At the first interview, which lasted about a quarter of an hour, the following colloquy took place:—

Doctor.—You are a teetotaller?

Rushton.—Yes.

Dr.—You are a very abstemious eater?

R.—Yes, for I have no appetite for food.

Dr.—Your employment is, and has long been, sedentary?

R.—Yes, for over twenty years.

Dr.—How many hours a day are you, or have you been, engaged in mental labour?

R.—Fifteen or sixteen hours a day, until lately.

Dr.—The wonder is that you are alive. Any attempt to resume that course of life, and your time will be short. Less mental effort and more physical labour, of an easy kind, and in the open air, is what you need. I shall prescribe you a very simple medicine, which will be of no use if you neglect to follow the advice given, and not very much then, for a considerable time.

After a few more visits the doctor said, "It is no use your coming to me, I cannot take your money any longer. You have no organic disease, but your nervous and muscular forces are reduced to a very low point. By a thorough change of circumstances, you may gradually recover lost strength, and live many years."

For several months I followed as far as possible the advice given, but remained in a very weak condition, and was anxious and depressed about many things. Friends were anxious about me also, and some of them urged me to consult the Rev. George Barrow Kidd, who was treating great numbers of persons with homœopathic medicines with much success. Calling at the house, I found the waiting-room full of patients, and was taken into the library to wait. That was just what I liked, and only wished to be left alone for some time. The books were numerous, and, from a theological point of view, of a superior kind. The saints of all past ages were there. The great Puritan preachers and writers were in great force. The classics, in original languages and translations, were in full array. His own work on "The Sovereignty of God," a most terrific and decisive treatise, was in a promient place. The most sweeping and uncompromising Calvinism I knew was there. From all eternity the doom of every human being was fixed; the few being destined to an eternal heaven, and the many to the fiery torments of an eternal hell, said this awful book.

On the table lay a book which arrested my attention. I had heard a little about "Festus," by Philip James Bailey, and here it was. I dipped into it, reading here and there, and wished to devour the whole. Among the lines that fastened on me were these:—

> "We live in deeds, not years ; in thoughts, not breaths ;
> In feelings, not in figures on a dial.
> We should count time by heart throbs. He most lives
> Who thinks most, feels the noblest, acts the best."

"I see you are absorbed in 'Festus'," said Mr. Kidd, as he entered the room. "It is a noble poem, and will live, and its author will prove to be a leading poet of the age."

Having stated my case, he said, "Certainly, homœopathic treatment will do you good, but will not cure you all at once; your vitality has been waning too long for a speedy restoration to health. You suffer, no doubt, from depression of mind common in lingering afflictions." "Yes, to some extent, but only from a sense of my inability to realize the ideals I have cherished throughout my life." "But you may realize them, to some extent, yet. I shall be glad to aid you in that direction to the utmost of my ability." He prepared me two kinds of medicine to be taken alternately.

Some slight improvement in my health became apparent soon. In about a month I felt an important change. My feet, which for years had been constantly cold and rigid, began to tingle. The same pricking sensation was felt in the hands. Then the unpleasant stinging was all over me, and made me very restless. In a while a genial warmth succeeded, and I knew a great improvement had come.

With improved health came the desire for improved income. Looking around me, I found two gentlemen who proposed with myself as manager to form a company for manufacturing silk. The whole capital raised by all three of us when put together was a very small amount for such an undertaking. A garret in Pickford Street was secured, large enough to hold twenty looms. With constant thinking, much scheming, and hard working, the end of the first year showed fair profits made. The two partners being eager for extension, two rooms were taken in Buxton Road Mill, and Pickford Street room given up. Besides weaving,—winding, spinning, and throwing machinery was bought and got to work. Increased care and labour were required, and also more capital. Mr. Alcock, a silk dealer, advised payment for silk by three months' bills. One bill for £105 was secured. But oh! the horror of it! It took away all peace, robbed me of much sleep, and injured my health for the whole three months. By dint of terrific energy the money was secured, and paid just in time, but I never took another bill. The two partners, being both silent and inactive, the business rested on me with crushing weight. Having selected and bought the silk required, I had keenly to watch the winding, spinning, doubling, throwing, dyeing, and weaving of it. In my absence something certainly went wrong. A few of the hands used the silk carefully, but the greater number wasted it in the most shocking manner if I were not present. One man should have acted as caretaker in my absence, but nobody cared for him, and he was of little use. A weaver whom I thought I could trust, I sent to get change for a sovereign, but he never returned, and I never saw him again, but heard that he got drunk and remained so until the sovereign was all spent.

With certain local silk brokers I had some trying experience. Mr. ——, a town councillor, bought some silk which he was to pay for at the time; but when he had got hold of the parcel he found out he had no money with him. He would, however, take the silk to a customer he had for it, and would bring the money that day. He did not call again, nor send the cash. In a fortnight I called at his house, and he promised to send the money forthwith. For some weeks I called upon him every day, except Sundays, until at length one day he came to the door in a towering passion and dashed a handful of money on the ground, gold, silver and copper, exclaiming, "Damn you, pick it up." I did so, and found it was not the whole amount; but I was glad to get away, as he was swearing all the time.

Another broker, Mr. ——, got a parcel of silk, for which he would pay cash down, but, seizing the parcel, he rushed to the door, shot down the steps, and could not be overtaken. No amount of dunning would induce him to pay. In the most unconcerned way he said I might sue him in the county court, but all the expenses would fall on me, as he had nothing with which to pay. To distrain on the furniture in the house would be serious to me, as it did not belong to him; he had long since made it over to another party. He was never excited, whatever I said to him, but was astonishingly civil. When and wherever he saw me he was profusely polite, but he would never pay for the silk. He lived in a very easy way, securing all the necessities of life, and many luxuries as well.

Agents on commission I found much difficulty with. With Mr. ——, of Manchester, I had a connection for several months. The first few parcels of goods he sold quickly and with little reduction of price. Succeeding goods he did not seem as if he would sell at all. Going to his office, I found the goods packed just as I had sent them. He had made no effort to sell. With many apologies he requested me to wait, and away he went with some of the goods to certain of his customers. Shortly returning, he said he could sell at a certain reduction of price. I knew that the price would not meet cost of production, and would only sell a part of the goods for which he deducted his commission, and paid me the money. If I would send a large parcel of the same sort of goods slightly altered in weight of dye, he could sell at once with a good profit. I made a great effort, and completed the order in the time specified. During several weeks he only sold part of the goods, and at a reduced price. On my remonstrating, he offered to supply cash before sale of articles. I began to suspect a trick, which I had learnt was often used by agents, by which a claim was made for money advanced, a sale of goods was forced, a profit secured for the agent and buyer, and a serious loss for the manufacturer. On the instant I went to Manchester, found some of the goods sold, requested payments on sales due, paid commission, and brought away the goods and escaped a serious disaster experienced by other parties of whom I heard.

Then I changed the plan of sale by going with large parcels of goods direct to the buyers in the large wholesale houses in Manchester. For a time I found these gentlemen attentive and ready to purchase goods which suited them. Soon, however, each in turn shied off from buying in a very curious way. I was perplexed, and consulted an old trader whom I could trust. "What personal terms had you with each of the buyers," he asked. "What do you mean?" I asked in turn. "Secret commission," was the reply. I could only say, "I would not do such a thing, and besides, I sold at too low a price to afford such a payment." "But," said he, "you might increase the price and more than cover the commission." I did not do it, and would not, although, as I found, it was the general custom.

John Webb, of London, proved to be an honest man, and so I consigned all goods to him, who did fairly well in all sales until the close of the business, which had continued from three to four years.

To the keen anxieties of trade at this period was added the still keener anxieties caused by unpleasant proceedings at the Sunday School. When Rev. John Wright was minister all affairs went on in a pleasant, orderly, and successful way. A band of gardeners was formed, plots of land secured, and cultivated with pleasure and profit. Week evening classes were formed for the study of science, literature, and religion, and free debates thereon. By these means many scholars and teachers were drawn to the school. Unfortunately, Mr. Wright had to leave the town, which caused much fear and regret. But by following his advice and carrying on his plans, matters went on as successfully as before. Shortly, however, came the advent of Rev. ——, when trouble began. He disapproved of our studies, our methods of procedure, and of everything in connection with the school. Especially obejctionable was our favourable treatment of the writings of Joseph Barker, Theodore Parker, and Francis William Newman. A mild protest by six teachers led to their instant dismissal from the school. An interview with one of the proprietors of the school building was of no avail. On the following Sunday there was a strike of the scholars, who would not go on with their lessons without their old teachers. A pressing message from a very influential party came to me, desiring I would detach myself from the dismissed party and conduct the school. This undertaking I declined on the instant, saying we must be all restored, or none. The revolting teachers and scholars who appealed to us we advised to attend the school as before. We could not engage other rooms, as desired, being all poor men without any influential friends.

At this period of perplexity and acute mental pain, we imitated devout Catholics, and went into solitary retreat. On each Sunday morning we wended our way to the woodlands, hills, and dells of Ecton range. Here were our sacred fanes, where we had read, studied, recited, and debated at intervals during many years. The woodlands were our Parnassus, the quarry gorge our Delphi, and a lovely dell carpeted with long grass and wild flowers, and fenced round with bushes of gorse—so beautifully green in summer and so gloriously golden in autumn—our Conventicle, which we had dedicated to the noble army of heretics of all climes and ages. On a suggestion being made that this fine circular dell should have the additional name of "The Pantheon," the following debate ensued:—

1. That means that we should honour the gods of all peoples and ages.

2. But some of those gods are very queer and objectionable beings.

3. According to many judgments, the gods are all queer and very shy about making themselves clearly known.

4. But each one of the gods has secured extensive homage, and should have our attention and regard.

5. Of course we must include in our regard Jupiter, Jehovah, Buddha, and Christ.

6. Yes, and all the rest.

7. Are the goddesses to be admitted, also?

8. Certainly; Juno, Minerva, Venus, and the Virgin Mary, with all their kindred royalties.

9. Seeing, then, that these great personages have secured the reverence and worship of vast numbers of mankind, they ought, at least, to have our toleration and respect.

10. Agreed, by all.

These Sunday exercises, so exhilarating and improving, were interrupted in consequence of a visit paid by several of us to Mr. Samuel Greg, at his request. He had heard, he said, that the King Edward Street Sunday School had become a wreck; that four fifths of the teachers and scholars had left the School, and were becoming waifs and strays. With much earnestness he urged us to collect the scattered flock into some meeting-room, when monetary help should be found. In a short time we had collected some 150 teachers and scholars inside a long garret stretching over several houses in Commercial Road. Classes were formed and conducted in the forenoon and afternoon of each Sunday. An evening service was largely attended by all sorts and conditions of men and women, the preaching devolving on me during more than a year. While thus doing our duty as best we could we got much abuse. The orthodox Christians said we trampled on the blood of the Covenant, which we never did. The Unitarians said we were infidels, while we were no more infidels than themselves. The Gallios and worldlings laughed and scorned, which, without retaliation, we patiently bore.

Notwithstanding much opposition and abuse we were a happy and united band of brothers eager to find the truth of things, and as eager to impart it to others. Our devoted circle included Michael Simpson, James Wood, Job Walker, John Lea, Joseph Birchenough, and Enoch Rushton; all now passed to higher spheres of duty except myself. At the same time I had evening classes at the Useful Knowledge Society, containing some 50 youths, to whom I was much attached and who showed strong attachment in return. I had thus, in addition to long and severe daily labour, the arduous but joyous work of preaching and teaching on Sundays and at week-night meetings.

CHAPTER XXI

UNITARIAN COLLEGE, MANCHESTER

But just now, when I was not thinking of any further change, a great change came. I was thirty-three years of age when the greatest crisis of my life arrived. A new college had lately been opened at Manchester, and, to my great surprise, I was invited to enter it and prepare myself for the Unitarian ministry.

Ten years before I had an invitation to enter the Methodist ministry, but I was then confronted with the dilemma of John Milton. Could he so stretch his conscience as to be able to accept and preach Christian doctrines in a non-natural sense? He could not, and so was unable to enter the ministry of the Church. For exactly the same reason I could not enter the ministry of the Methodist Church, and so the question of entering the ministry at all was dismissed, as I thought, for ever from my mind. But now I was assured that a belief in— and a life in accordance with—the doctrine of the Fatherhood of God and the Brotherhood of Man constituted the only test required on entering the ministry of the Unitarian Church. So far there was no difficulty in my way. But without time for special preparation, should I be able to pass the examination required before entering the college? And if I passed, would not my health break down under the strain of hard and constant study? However, under the influence of a strong ideal, I decided to face the examination and enter the college if I could. On the day of examination, therefore, I proceeded to Manchester, and found myself one of fifteen candidates, all in nervous excitement in view of the ordeal at hand. Very shortly we were requested to take places on each side of a long table on which were placed pens, ink, and sheets of foolscap paper. Then, the examining professors having entered the room, the Rev. Dr. Beard informed us that one hour would be allowed for each one of us to write a sermon from the text, " Come unto Me all ye that labour and are heavy laden and I will give you rest. Take my yoke upon you."

Very peculiar and rather amusing was the scene which then presented itself to the professors who were walking about the room conversing with each other, and slyly watching our proceedings. For a short space our pens were idle and our hands trembling. Some were looking at the ceiling, as if anxiously expecting inspiration from above. Some were looking towards the window, as if expecting some illumination to come from that direction. Some looked at each other and smiled a ghastly sort of smile, and some again looked beseechingly at the professors as if they were very much inclined to exclaim, " Dear masters, have pity upon us, and let us out of the room." The professors all the time looked as relentless as fate. By-and-bye a few pens began to scratch on the paper, then more and still more. The speed of the pens was as variable as the parties who wrote. Some pens went quickly, some slowly, and some made many full stops.

In some twenty minutes several had got to a second sheet of paper, in forty minutes to a third sheet, and in sixty minutes were driving hard on a fourth sheet, when a halt was called, and we were marched out of the room, leaving all the written papers to be scrutinized by the professors. Whatever they thought of these productions, we felt ashamed of them, as most of us confessed. No yoke had ever been placed upon us so suddenly before, nor any burden more trying to bear. Tea was provided for us, but our appetites were not keen, some hardly eating anything at all. After tea came a *viva voce* examination of each one of us on theology and literature in general. This was done singly, and we could not tell how each other fared in the ordeal, but the general feeling amongst us was that we had done anything but well.

But this was not all: another and more overfacing trial was at hand. Singly we were ushered into the presence of the Committee. On my entrance, some twenty gentlemen were present, including Mr. Ivie Mackie and Mr. Grundy, who both became Mayors of Manchester, and also Mr. Harry Rawson, who was solicited to be Mayor, but refused. The questions and answers were such as these:—

Q.—Have you been connected with Sunday Schools, and how long?

A.—From five years of age until the present time, as scholar, teacher and manager.

Q.—Have you attended week-evening classes, and how long?

A.—About the same length of time, and for fourteen years was an evening teacher at the Useful Knowledge Society.

Q.—How long have you been a lay preacher?

A.—During the last twelve months regularly, and frequently for years before.

Q.—Will you particularise your theological studies?

A.—I have read the whole works of John Wesley, and closely studied some of them. The Commentary of Dr. Adam Clarke I have largely read and studied. More lately I have read the writings of Joseph Barker, Henry Ware, Channing, Martineau, and Beard.

Q.—To what extent have you gone into history, ancient and modern?

A.—I have read Goldsmith's "History of Greece and Rome," and Rollin's "Ancient History" (surprise and questions), Hume's and Macaulay's History of England.

Q.—What have you done in general literature?

A.—Read Carlyle, Emerson, and Macaulay in particular.

Q.—In poetry?

A.—Thomson, Cowper, Pope, Milton, Longfellow, and Shakespeare in particular.

Q.—Anything in science?

A.—Yes: in Priestley, Combe, Sir H. Davy, and Joyce's "Scientific Dialogues."

Many questions were asked, and pleasant remarks were made by most of the gentlemen present, and satisfaction seemed to have been given; and thus ended the most searching examination which up to then I had known.

The examinations ended, the verdicts were soon pronounced. Seven parties were called out of the room in which we were all met, and told by Mr. Armstrong that they had failed to pass. Sorrowfully they parted from the rest of us and went their way. The remaining eight of us waited a few minutes in painful suspense, and then I was called out of the room and informed I had passed with much satisfaction. Then my yoke seemed easy and my burden light.

But how great my change of life which was at hand! I had always escaped from worrying cares in green fields and mountain tops, but now I must labour where fields and mountains could not be seen. Occasional crowds in Macclesfield had troubled me, but how should I live in the greater crowds of Manchester?

In a few weeks I had to say farewell to home, school, congregation, educational societies, old veterans and companions in many a hard battle, and dear brother Samuel, who never failed me in need, and pursue my course in strange places and amongst strange people for the rest of my life. During the three years of my studentship, my wife would carry on her business in the old home, after which we must again take up our abode we knew not where.

In due course the summons from the secretary of the U.H.M Board arrived, when Henry Eachus and myself proceeded to Manchester to begin our studies. Very uncomfortable were the lodgings we at first obtained, and my health began to fail. But shortly, Henry decided to bring his family to Lower Broughton, where he took a house, and I became his lodger and remained with him the whole of the term of three years.

Our studies commenced in Dr. Beard's house, which was some half mile from where we lived. Here the old and new students—fifteen in all—were united in study. The Doctor's lectures on John Milton I liked well, as, I think, did all the students. The "Origin of Shemitism (or Semitism)" I liked in parts. It was a literary and religious history of the Shemite family, taken largely from German sources. My own feeling was that these discourses would have been as instructive and more interesting if the matter had been condensed into about half the number of words used. Elaboration, no doubt, is the great art of the learned, and certainly Dr. Beard was a very learned man. My opinion, therefore, would have no weight with the erudite.

The "Biblical Exegesis" course was not so fully appreciated by a number of the students as it ought to have been. The expositions were keen, and subtle, and deep; but we felt we could not follow that method in preaching to ordinary congregations. The aim of the tutor, nevertheless, was unquestionably good. Revelling with great satisfaction in the practice of the fine art of Biblical discrimination, he earnestly tried to make us partakers of his joy.

But what could be said about a course of lectures on "The Greek Article"? Surely, some of us thought, such a screwing and twisting of a few Greek letters never took place under the sun before now. But that only manifested our want of experience. As we afterwards learnt, the same sort of presentment of wire-drawn Greek letters had appeared in worse form by very erudite scribes.

The Doctor's course of lectures on "The Sinlessness of Jesus Christ," I entered into with great zest. I earnestly wished he would be able to refute Professor Newman's views on that subject. I had been much moved by the keen battle over the matter between the Professor and Martineau. This left me in a state of indecision, and I wished the Doctor to strengthen the position of Martineau. In the end my decision was against my earnest desire. Very regretfully I had to conclude that neither Dr. Beard nor Dr. Martineau had been able to move the position of Professor Newman as described in the following passage:—" In the *British Quarterly* is the following sentence concerning Madame Roland: 'To say that she was without fault would be to say that she was not human.' This so entirely expresses and concludes all that I (Newman) have to say, that I feel surprised at my needing at all to write such a chapter as the present."—" Phases of Faith."

Our studies with Mr. Gaskell were carried on at his house in Plymouth Grove, over three miles from where I lived. One hour in going, and one hour in returning, with from three to four hours' study, greatly exhausted me. But Mr. Gaskell's instructive matter and pleasant method of teaching helped me to bear the strain. Even Latham's Grammar he made an interesting study. I had previously gone carefully through Lennie's and Cobbet's Grammars, but I now found I had much to learn as to the origin, structure, and use of our English tongue.

The reading of " Paradise Lost," with his comments and questions, was an inspiration. With ancient history I was tolerably familiar, but I was glad of the new light thrown upon it. English literature had always been to me a favourite study, and I thought I had a fairly wide acquaintance with it, but I now found how narrow were the bounds in which I had moved. Greek and Roman literature I had much delighted in, but now saw a new and brighter lustre thrown around it. Of the Greek language I had known but little, but now had great pleasure in learning and understanding the language in which the New Testament was written.

To hear Mr. Gaskell read and pronounce Greek was a delicious pleasure. At one meeting each week we delivered short extempore addresses, during which he made notes and afterwards read them out. On one occasion he said to a student, " Have you any idea how many times you have repeated the phrase, 'As it were'?" " No," said the student. " I only once remember saying it, and that was when I was explaining, as it were, a certain idea." "Ah! there you have it again," said Mr. Gaskell (laughter), "and let me tell you that you have uttered that phrase twenty times in twelve minutes" (much laughter). Very nice was this sort of amusement for all of us, except the one feeling the lash.

On another occasion I had, by arrangement with the students, to deliver *memoriter* one of my own written sermons. As I proceeded, I saw him writing notes during half of my discourse, when he stopped writing and fixed his eyes steadily upon me until I had finished, when he threw his notes into the fire and said, "That will do." On the next occasion Mr. Street went through a discourse like myself, without a halt or break. One or two other students tried, but failed, and the rest would not attempt. Mr. Gaskell said several great French preachers memorized their sermons, which were few and far between. The method took up much time, and caused a great strain on the nerves, and so he could not recommend it.

The last examination of my college course concluded on the day of the Annual Meeting held in the Manchester Town Hall. As Senior retiring student, it was my duty to address the meeting, but I was so tired and ill I told Dr. Beard I could not get through even a short speech. There must be no excuse, said the Doctor: I must make the attempt, even if I failed. I ascended the steps to the platform with the greatest difficulty from bodily weakness. The Hall was crowded, and contained the *elite* of the Unitarians of Manchester. I had not a word to say, but stammered out a sentence or two in description of my past career. I had been warned by influential friends, I said, against Unitarianism, which they defined as the half-way house to infidelity. That was, I replied, exactly what I had found it, and very glad I was to have discovered such a refuge from the storm-winds of false dogma and such a safe haven of rational repose.

Perceiving my statements were well received, I woke up, and felt some incoming strength. Reviewing my three years' course at the college, I said, some of the studies had charmed, inspired, and elevated me, and, I hoped, prepared me for a future useful career. Theology of many varieties I had studied under the direction of Dr. Beard, and learned many noble things which I hoped to retain and faithfully use. Some other matters I thought, I might forget, and, indeed, might confess had already forgotten (laughter). The reason was I supposed, my inaptitude for taking in bewildering technicalities. Of course these learned puzzles had to be reproduced in the examinations whether understood and appreciated or not. France Germany, and Dutchland, as also Egypt, Greece, Rome and Judea had furnished erudite and perplexing definitions and phrases to which I could not become easily attached, and from whose company, I might say, I am not unwilling to break away (laughter).

These statements slipped out unintentionally and spontaneously, and surprised no one more than myself. Continuing my unpremeditated speech, I said, with Mr. Gaskell I had had a very delightful experience. In his company I had visited the seers and sages of Greece and Rome; had become familiar with the great statesmen, warriors, and scholars of ancient times; had made close acquaintance with the persons and writings of England's greatest literary men; had passed from the times of Merlin, the enchanter, to the times of Caedmon and Chaucer; on to the days of Shakespeare and Milton, and down to the distinguished scholars of present times. Through the whole of that glorious region I hoped, I said, to pass in happy pilgrimage again and again, not forgetting my venerable guide who had pointed out the best roads along which to proceed. The methods of examination, I continued, followed by our professors had been of a peculiar and trying kind. Sometimes it happened that when with great pains we had dressed up our literary heroes in the most attractive way, we were greatly disappointed to find that they were not required to appear on the stage. In this very week's examination I myself had prepared quite a host of the most distinguished Scottish literary worthies for presentation: and, "Would you believe it, Mr. Chairman (Mr. Ivie Mackie, a Scotchman), not a single Scotchman was allowed to appear." Rising from his chair in excited amusement, Mr. Mackie turned round to Mr. Gaskell, exclaiming, "Is that true, sir?" "Quite true," said Mr. Gaskell. The whole audience enjoyed the fun immensely. Mrs. Gaskell, who sat on a front form, was intensely amused. This scene, she said to a friend, was the most interesting event of the meeting.

During the three years now closing I had not only had the training of the eminent scholars, Dr. Beard and Mr. Gaskell, but the valuable guidance of the missionary tutors, Rev. W. Hutton and Mr. Curtis. Mr. Hutton was a most genial and kindly man. My intercourse with him was pleasant and profitable from first to last. Mr. Curtis was a solid, sedate solemn-looking man. For a Unitarian, he had a remarkably devout spirit and manner, which I think he must have acquired by early Methodist training. I was introduced by him to the back slums of Deansgate, which I had regularly to visit and report results. To make the acquaintance of back-settlement populations consisting largely of drunkards, thieves, and prostitutes, is appalling enough at first. When one has got to know these people and they have got to know their visitor, intercourse is tolerable. What they want to know is whether you have any connection with the police, or whether you are an agent of capitalists, or again, whether you are a charity crank with plenty of money to spare. Very effusive is their welcome to the crank: they will believe anything he wishes them to believe; no creed is amiss if there be cash with it. Personal reform amongst these people is a very rare thing. But mixed up with them is a more hopeful class of persons. Many of them have drifted down from better conditions, and would like to rise again to a better and happier state of life. Here lies the benevolent visitor's chance. If drink has brought a man down, and yet has not entirely enslaved him, you may get him to sign the temperance pledge, and by watchful visits help him to keep it, and thus lay the foundation of deliverance and salvation for both him and his family. Want of care in the use of money, inability to save money, with entire want of thrift in all the arrangements of the home have dragged down innumerable families into the slums. Some of these, by the earnest and continuous efforts of the visitor, may be induced to place small and then larger sums of money in savings banks. In this way, a spirit of independence is created, and then a determined effort is made to get into better and happier conditions of existence. If now such parties can be got into mission-rooms and schools and induced to like them, and regularly attend them, then their redemption is at hand.

Happily, some of these cases of reformation I have known, and great is the joy of the mission-worker when such cases occur.

The two mission tutors were succeeded by the Rev. Francis Bishop, a pleasant, genial, and easy-going gentleman, with whom I worked in a most friendly way. He mapped out districts for visiting in the vicinity of Rochdale Road Domestic Mission Chapel. We had here a better class of working-men's houses to visit than such as we had visited off Deansgate. I soon got on good terms with most of my people, some of whom were induced to sign the pledge, to place money in the bank, send their children to the Sunday School, and occasionally attend chapel themselves.

Having to preach almost every Sunday during my student years, I had a curious experience of the attitude of many and various congregations. In Methodism, as I had learned, the fervour of the congregation gave fervour to the preacher; but I could not perceive that Unitarian congregations had much fervour to supply, and concluded that if their preachers must get much of that fine quality, it must be derived from some other source.

On the first Sunday after my arrival at Manchester, I was appointed to preach at Ainsworth, situated on the high moorlands some three miles from Bolton. The village contained twenty to thirty scattered houses, with the quaint old chapel in the midst of them. Inside the chapel I found about fifty people sitting in perfect repose in large, comfortable pews. In the gallery there was a good organ, which was well played, and a choir of fairly good singers. The services were quiet, orderly, and edifying, if not demonstrative. Half-a-mile's walk through country lanes and fields brought me to the Parsonage, a large, ancient-looking house with gardens and fields around it. In a large, comfortably-aranged room in the house I found the aged and venerable Mr. Whitehead, the minister of the chapel, but prevented preaching by temporary illness. My intercourse with him was very interesting. He was an Arian in theology, and argued with great ingenuity in favour of his views. I had got through that phase of faith and advanced far beyond it, as I gently hinted. I would not disconcert the worthy man by controverting his opinions, but led the way to other important subjects on which we perfectly harmonized, and so spent a very happy Sunday afternoon in the ancient Parsonage. More than forty years he had been minister of the chapel, and dwelt in the quiet moorland Parsonage, and must have had a Unitarian minister's ideal life.

At Rochdale I found two chapels—one for the rich, and one for a poorer class. At the former chapel I preached two written discourses without feeling I was producing any good effect. I dined with a rich banker's family, and went through to me, unusual ceremonies and customs with a fair amount of composure. All seemed kindly and courteous, but I was out of my usual element, and was glad when I got away. Amongst the working-class congregation at the other chapel I needed no written sermons, having full freedom of extempore speech. Nearly all my hearers were teachers and scholars, and to such parties I could always speak with ease and effect.

On such congregations the success and, indeed, the life of Unitarianism depends. If Unitarian families of all classes would regularly attend and support existing Sunday Schools, and earnestly aid in forming new ones, Unitarianism would acquire an impetus onward such as it—except in isolated cases—has never known.

At Mossley was a large congregation and a large school, where I preached several times, and always with freedom and, apparently, with good effect. The labours of Joseph Barker and Joseph Cooke in this town had been attended with amazing results, including the formation of the Unitarian School and congregation. Rationalism and emotionalism were happily blended in Mr. Barker, as also in his very numerous disciples. If a blend of these two fine qualities could be introduced into all Unitarian congregations, it would supply the uplifting force they so greatly need. It will be long, I fear, before it comes. There has been only one Joseph Barker and one Joseph Cooke during the present (nineteenth) century, and their reforming influence is now on the wane. Ministers still come from Methodism into Unitarianism, but they do not convert their congregations and bring them into their new fold. Even the personal fervour which these new ministers introduce into Unitarian circles soon cools down, and is often quite frozen out, and hence their congregations remain on the same dead level as before.

Sometimes I was appointed to preach in more distant parts of the country, giving opportunity for new experience. At Lydgate I was pleased with the situation and look of the moderate-sized chapel, as also with the parsonage adjoining, both being almost surrounded with an extensive garden. Here, outwardly viewed, was an ideal position, but, sad to say, the inward appearance was anything but ideal. After I had entered the chapel, the people gradually assembled until some forty were present. The greater part of them seemed to be in a free and easy way, and without any very definite notions as to why they were there. When I was reading the lessons, I noticed a smart, good-looking young man reading a book in a pew near the pulpit. When I began to preach he placed himself in an easy position, opened his book, and settled down for a good spell of reading. Shortly, I made a pause, when he looked up in wonder, and I fixed my eyes straight on his face, when he ceased reading for the time, but was soon at it again. Again I paused, when he gave me a searching look which indicated that I must go on with my business while he went on with his; and so I preached my sermon and he read his book to nearly the end of the service. Quite a large number observed what was going on between me and the young man, and were thereby induced to pay more attention to the sermon than otherwise they would have done.

I was entertained by a very nice elderly gentleman, a retired doctor, who was strongly attached to the chapel, and was familiar with its whole history. Long ago, Oliver Heywood, he said, had preached there to large congregations with mighty effect, and he hoped for the advent of some prophet who would create a revival in the district. I joined him in good desires, but I had only a very forlorn hope. The condition of things at Lydgate must become very different before any reforming prophet appears there.

I had a memorable visit to Sheffield to preach at the chapel where Rev. Brooke Herford was minister, but who was then from home. Leaving Manchester by a very early train on the Sunday morning, I got late to Sheffield, rushed from the station, and into the pulpit, and commenced the service. From two to two-hundred-and-fifty sedate, orderly, and intelligent-looking people formed the congregation. To every part of the service they paid interested attention. On my arrival at the chapel, the officials seemed to have considerable curiosity about myself personally, and after the service the same feeling was manifested by many members of the congregation. All this was explained to me by a gentleman, who said Dr. Beard had been advertised to preach, and that a number of persons had been expressing their pleasure at seeing Dr. Beard that morning; their gratification with his discourse; and their surprise on finding he was so young a man.

With the close of the year 1858 came the close of these perambulatory preachings, and of my studies at the U. H. M. Board. Of the several applications by various congregations for my regular services, I was persuaded by Dr. Beard and Professor Gaskell to accept the one from Padiham.

CHAPTER XXII

MINISTRY AT PADIHAM

ONE of the most momentous days of my life was the 20th of February, 1859, when I became an ordained Unitarian minister. I had been a Sunday School teacher from my thirteenth year; had conducted large week-evening classes at Hurdsfield School soon afterwards; soon again I gave addresses from the pulpit on Sunday afternoons; for fourteen years I was an evening teacher at the Macclesfield Useful Knowledge Society; and for twelve months the almost sole preacher on Sunday evenings at the Garret School in Commercial Road.

These labours were incessant, arduous, sometimes breaking down my health, but always successful, and always full of inspiration, satisfaction, and great joy. All this time I was engaged in factory labour from an early hour in the morning until late at night. But now my commercial life was over, my amateurish teaching and preaching were ended, and I had entered on an important profession. From a survey of the past, my present position seemed greatly surprising. The revelations of Joseph Barker concerning the Methodist ministry, with extensive reading in ecclesiastical records, had been driving me towards the conclusion that the Christian priesthoods constituted a great confederacy for extinguishing civil and religious liberty all over the world. And yet, it has come to this, that I am entering a priesthood myself. True, I had been assured by abundant testimony, both written and oral, that Unitarianism presented the freest Church in all the world. But I knew something of the treatment of Emerson which was not encouraging, and of the experiences of Theodore Parker, which were disquieting. My verdict now, as I approach the end of my life is that the Unitarian Church is one of the two freest Churches in Christendom: the other being the Spiritualist Church, now making headway in the world.

This 20th day of February, 1859, was memorable to the Padiham congregation as well as to myself. It was my first Dedication as minister, and it was the first Ordination that had taken place in the Padiham Unitarian Chapel.

The Rev. Dr. Beard preached in the morning on the duties of the minister, which seemed to me to be the imposing of a burden exceedingly heavy to bear. In the afternoon, Rev. Wm. Gaskell preached on the duties of each member of a congregation, which seemed formidable enough, as some declared. Mr. Thos. Holland gave me the right hand of fellowship and in the name of the congregation welcomed me as minister of the chapel. Both Dr. Beard and Mr. Gaskell in affecting terms welcomed me into the Unitarian ministry. The chapel had been crowded all the day, and the services exciting and impressive, and at the conclusion I was quite spent out.

Immediately I had to leave my native town, with its beautiful surroundings, and take up my abode in the wilds of east Lancashire. On a dark, raw, and gusty day, I and my wife left Macclesfield and proceeded some fifty miles by railway to Padiham. From Rose Grove Station we walked along bad roads through a wild, bleak, barren-looking, moorland country to a cottage just outside the town, which was to be our home for the time being. On one side of the little town rose Hambledon Hill, associated with many past deeds of romance. On another side rose to a great height the more notable and more romantic range of Pendle Hills. In front of our cottage, some half-mile distant, was an ancient mansion associated with weird tales of the past, and inhabited by Sir James Kay Shuttleworth, who was living there apart from his wife, through marriage with whom he had come into possession of the Hall and surrounding estates. A mile away, on the other side of the town, was situated Huntroyd Hall, the ancient home of the Starkie family. These two families largely controlled the destinies of the town. The Starkies being strongly Tory, and Sir James Kay Shuttleworth strongly Liberal, the neighbourhood was now and then stirred with a little political, religious, and educational life.

The three principal mill-owners were Mr. Thompson, Churchman and Tory; Mr. Hull, Freethinker and Liberal; and Mr. Webster, Wesleyan, and otherwise neutral. From these parties arose disturbing influences from time to time, leading to strikes and lockouts and much volubility of speech, but not attended by any disastrous results.

The population, some 5,000 in number, was rude, bold, daring, outspoken, industrious, and over the average in honesty and truth. The church and chapel-goers were pretty evenly divided amongst Episcopalians, Wesleyans, Baptists, and Unitarians; the latter being, however, the smallest number in the lot. The most wealthy people went, of course, to the Church. The next in monetary grade were Wesleyan, who here, as elsewhere, were increasing in wealth. The Baptists were rather poor in circumstances: but the Unitarians were the poorest of all.

My salary was fixed at £100 a year, but the congregation could not possibly raise more than half that amount. Hence the Manchester Committee, including Dr. Beard and Mr. Gaskell, somehow raised a fund and placed it in the hands of Rev. S. A. Steinthal, who made annual grants to the congregation in a very prudential way. Each year the grant was somewhat reduced, which made it necessary for the people to increase their contributions—which was easily managed when they found it had to be done.

From the first I studied hard and systematically, and whatever was suitable went into my sermons, which I delivered extempore with great freedom and joy to myself, and with effect on the people. They had been accustomed to theological controversy, and so had I, but I determined to adopt that method only on special occasions. I preferred, ordinarily, to deliver illustrated and emotional discourses, which never failed to arrest and fix attention. Wellington's reported exclamation, " Up, Guards, and at them!" not only emphasised some personal duty, but led to the reading of English history; while the words, "Aim at the heart," uttered at the battle of Bunker's Hill, led some to the reading of American history. A course of lectures on the Scottish Covenanters awakened much interest and greatly intensified their feeling of antagonism to tyranny, as also their love of civil and religious liberty. These impressions were kept alive by frequent allusions to the Commonwealth days, with mention of Cromwell, Milton, Richard Baxter, and John Biddle.

Such as could not enter fully into historic episodes were enlivened and greatly interested by references to the various trades and callings in which they were engaged. The weaver's shuttle suggested the rapid flight of time; the mason chiselling stones, to the individual shaping of human character; and the building of a house to the building up of a noble life. Local traditions, weird narratives associated with the neighbouring hills, valleys, rivers, towns and villages, furnished illustrations which always riveted attention. But the most attractive of all illustrations were such as were taken from local events and daily conversation. Any reference to what was going on in the mills, in the streets, or in the houses, related with a touch of humour, was intensely exciting. After service, both old and young would form in groups and discuss the sermon. Where did he get that story? Was that a good argument? Who did he hear make that remark last week? What shop has he been at? Which of you has he been lately watching? Did you ever hear that story about old Pendle Hill before? Such were the questions discussed from Sunday to Sunday and from year to year. Often one of the best talkers would be appointed to tackle me on various matters, when I should be kept in a crowded house until midnight on Sunday evenings, and until I was so exhausted I could hardly get home.

In this way I got to the minds and hearts of the people,

and it seemed as if I could play on their intellects and emotions as a musician plays on the strings of a harp or the keys of an organ. The beneficial effect of these exercises was marked by all. Many of the young were prompted to read and study valuable books. Both young and old were stimulated to attend closely to their religious duties, and many were induced to lead better and more useful lives. The good impressions of the Sunday services were kept alive through the week by evening meetings. The Bible Class was carried on in the following way: the meeting was opened with the singing of a hymn given out by a female, often a factory girl, who also started the tune. A prayer would follow by a factory youth. The reading of a scripture lesson succeeded, with comments by a young or elder member of the class. An address with allusions and applications to local circumstances was always expected from myself.

The Mutual Improvement Class was mutual indeed, nearly every member taking some part in the proceedings. For several months we dramatised the story of "Agnes of Sorrento," by Mrs. Beecher Stowe, which was appearing in the "Cornhill Magazine." A youthful female was chosen to represent Agnes, the heroine of the story, repeating the words and assuming the attitude of the represented party. An elder female in the same way represented the worldly-wise dame Elsie, the grandmother of the heroine. Theresa, the devout Abbess, was represented by one of our most serious-looking women. A determined and solemn-looking man had to represent Father Francesco, who, said Mrs. Stowe, "had a gulf as deep as hell between himself and all women," his terrible state of mind having been caused by the fickleness and falsity of a lady he had once known. A lively youth had to be the Gay Cavalier—whose attention was forcibly arrested by the lovely Agnes when with her grandmother selling oranges in the street. The one character we had most difficulty in getting represented was Jocunda, an ugly and very wily old lady, who was an attendant on Sister Theresa at the Abbey. It was easier to find a sedate young man to represent Antonio, a worthy and altogether unsophisticated countryman, who was in love with the heroine of the story.

Many members of the congregation, and other parties, hearing what was going on, crowded into the room, and were greatly interested in the proceedings. On special occasions, dramas were common enough there as elsewhere, but this went on continuously for many months, and was educational all through.

At the earnest request of some dozen young men, I had to form a class for the pursuit of biblical, scientific, and classical studies, including New Testament Greek. The progress made by a few of them in Greek greatly surprised me, as I had thought it beyond their capacity to learn. Daniel Berry made such extraordinary progress in all his studies, that I began to prepare him for entrance as a student into the Unitarian Home Mission Board. Having entered the College and gone successfully through the prescribed three years' study, he settled with the congregation at Mossley, and was labouring hard, with much acceptance, when a sad accident closed his career. In response to his dying request I preached his funeral sermon, but in a very feeble fashion, being overpowered with strong emotion.

Joseph Pollard and Joseph Anderton were members of this class and other classes, the former subsequently becoming a successful missionary in London for eighteen years, and the latter a missionary in Liverpool for a longer period.

Much excitement was awakened by the large number of scholars, teachers, and friends which formed our processions on Annual Sermon Sundays, as also on the Wakes week days. The ministers of different denominations seemed to be alarmed, and commenced a vigorous opposition. Rev. Mr. Adamson, of the Established Church, was leader of the crusade. He had moved somewhat in this direction before my arrival as minister at Padiham. On hearing that the Unitarians were about to have a settled minister, he at once announced a meeting in the

Public Hall to warn the people against the danger of Unitarian doctrine. On the day of the meeting, a telegram reached Dr. Beard, who sent me to Padiham by next train. The meeting had been going on for some time when I arrived, and the Hall was so densely crowded it seemed impossible for me to get in. By dint of hard pushing and pointed elbowing, a dozen of our friends clove a way for me to the middle of the room and helped me on to a form, where I faced Mr. Adamson, his curate, and other clergymen on the platform. After a few minutes spent in obtaining silence, a clergyman spoke at length in defence of the orthodox doctrine of the Atonement. Many of the ancient fathers, with numerous doctors of divinity both ancient and modern, were quoted to support the views he was defending. In numberless volumes written at different periods throughout the Christian ages this doctrine had been most learnedly, eloquently, logically, and conclusively proved. In reply I admitted that mighty piles of books had been produced on the subject underneath which the plain and simple statements in the New Testament were buried almost out of sight. I admitted the learning and eloquence of the fathers and doctors referred to, and marvelled at the way they had of refuting each other, leaving their disciples in bewilderment as to what and where the truth might be.

I then took up the parable of the Prodigal Son and pointed out Christ's method of showing how God the Father saves a sinner and forgives the sin. For some quarter of an hour I spoke freely on this point, showing the difference between the creeds of the Churches and the teaching of Christ. Nothing effective was said in reply, and the meeting shortly closed. There was good temper displayed both inside the Hall as also in the streets, where the matter was discussed until late in the night.

But now Mr. Adamson pursued another course. Beginning at one end of the township, he called at every house, warning the people not to come to our chapel nor send their children to the Sunday School. On the second day of his visitation, I started where he had started, and followed closely on his track, calling at every house, not, however, with a message of warning, but of conciliation. This method was evidently more successful than the method of the vicar; for while I advanced from street to street with but little dissent, he provoked strong opposition—sometimes expressed in strong words.

This double visitation continued for some weeks, carried on in the afternoon of nearly each day. Amongst the people there was much excitement, which passed into a pleasant, daily diversion. Groups of men and women formed at street ends, amusingly speculating and chaffing about the contest of the parsons, and as to what would be the result. Having gone over three-quarters of the township, the vicar evidently decided that discretion was the better part of valor, and gave up the tramp, and I, of course, ceased where he left off. A spirit of toleration, it was generally contended, had arisen from this parsonic rivalry, and the conviction spread that one tale is good until another is told, and that it is best to hear both sides of all important questions. The street corner remarks were somewhat thus:—" Na, then, which is best mon?" "Tha're both on 'em sharp enough after th' main point." "What's that?" "Th' brass, mon—that's it." " Unitarian chap's a good un' at that, they say." "Ah, tha're gettin' more brass at chapel than tha' ever did afore." " But then it's what they given theirselves, or what is given to them by others in an honest way." "Well, and Church does same, doesn't it?" " Now, thay Churchmen robbed Catholics of a lot a brass many years ago, and are living on it na." "Ah, an' tha'n got tithes fro' th' land, a good part o' which should go to poor rates, but which goes into their own pockets." "But Catholics would get th' tithes if they could." "Ah, and so would Chapel folks do same." " Na, na!" " Ya, ya!"

The next clerical attack on the Unitarians came from Rev. Mr. Taylor, a Wesleyan minister who knew both Mrs. Rushton and myself many years before when we were Methodists at Macclesfield. He wrote a very earnest and warning letter to Mrs. Rushton, regretting to hear she was losing the true faith and was in danger of losing her soul. Mrs. Rushton wrote in reply, stating she was happy to say her faith was now a rational faith, and her soul was safer than ever before, and that if he had anything more to say on the matter he had better write to me: which, however, he never did. From the Wesleyan pulpit he declared he had never known or heard of a town so entirely infested by the dreadful heresy of Unitarianism as was Padiham at the time. He went to such length in his denunciations that his own friends wished him to desist, as he was inducing numbers to go to our chapel to hear my replies. After that he settled quietly down to his own work, and we heard but little more about him.

Very soon, however, a newly-appointed curate appeared in the town, who seemed to think that he, too, had a divine mission to put down the prevailing and shocking heresy of Unitarianism. Going from house to house in the usual way, he on one occasion came in contact with my class of young men at study in a private house. At once they accepted his challenge to a theological combat, and kept him hard at work for some hours and until he was glad to make his escape in quite a sweating condition. The advent of a new curate was always an interesting occasion to our people, both old and young. "Look out!" they would exclaim, "the new broom is at work, and every house is to be swept clean."

One of these called on old John Bertwistle and made some disparaging remark about the Unitarian faith. Never loath for a tussle, John went headlong into the conflict. The curate was astonished and defended himself for awhile, when he seemed to be getting tired, and moved towards the door, saying he would call again. "Be sure you do," said John, "for I shall look out for you." Having passed the house several times without paying his promised visit, John rushed out on him in the street, and said, "Here, I want you very particularly." The curate very reluctantly entered the house, and after making some excuse moved towards the door. On the instant John slipped behind him, locked the door, and put the key in his pocket, and said, "Now, let us have the matter fairly out." Helter-skelter, tooth and tongue, they went at it, hurling Bible passages at each other with extraordinary force and for a long time, until the curate was fain to crave release from his durance vile, and was then, in an awful sweat, let out at the door.

It was a gratifying novelty to find so many in the congregation, both young and old, able to understand, explain, and defend the religious views they held. With the exception of the congregation in the garret rooms in Hurdsfield, I have known no other assembly to equal Padiham in these respects.

These incidents we only notice by the way, our main object being of a practical kind. It was found quite necessary for the congregation to raise more money than ever before. In the first place, Mrs. Rushton formed and regularly conducted a Sewing Class, which produced articles for a bazaar which was held at the end of the first year and produced £30. The two bazaars of the two succeeding years produced £70, making £100 raised in the three yearly Sales of Work. Then an auxiliary fund was formed, to which I subscribed £5, which induced nineteen other members to do the same, and thus a second £100 was secured. A third £100 was raised by the rest of the congregation. The whole £300 was placed in the bank, and remained there until the opportunity came to purchase the plot of land on which the new chapel now stands.

The purchase of this land—which took place after I had left—was a very clever piece of work. A friend of the congregation, living at Colne, was employed to buy the land and then make it over to the trustees of the congregation. Up to that time it had been impossible to get land for a Unitarian Chapel at any price, every attempt to do so being treated with scorn. When, therefore, it became known that a whole field was actually in the possession of the Unitarians, the anger and disgust of the great land-owners, as also of all orthodox neighbours, knew no bounds. Nothing daunted, our friends hoisted a flag on the top of the old chapel, which floated in the breeze for many a day, none daring to take it down.

Although forty-five years have passed since my labours in Padiham ceased, I could easily give the names and describe the personal appearance of nearly all the members of the congregation. Just a few I must point out as they appeared to me from my position in the pulpit. In front of the organ in the gallery was always seen Thomas Holland, the leader of the choir. His serious and intelligent-looking face was frequently so fixed on the preacher that he forgot to have the tune ready for the following hymn, when a hasty rummaging of music-books ensued. His religious impressions were of the durable kind, and influenced his daily life and the lives of his family, all the members of which grew up to be steady, studious, musical, useful in business, and in the school and chapel.

Just to the right of the singers, in a three-cornered pew, was always seen the large and fine head and face of elderly John Bertwistle. Nothing of moment in the sermon did he overlook or forget, nor did he fail to have the subject discussed in the family. Even his daughters were led to enter into these matters with as much zest as himself. One of the daughters became the wife of Joseph Pollard and aided him in a very successful mission in London.

On the other side of the gallery, near the singers, sat Eli Whitehead, a joiner and builder who was often employed by Sir J. K. Shuttleworth, who esteemed him highly. He was a peaceable, good-living, hard-working man, and musical withal; as were his daughters, one of whom became an efficient player on the piano. His wife was a sturdy, sharp-spoken, sound-hearted, good-managing woman. Altogether, the Whiteheads presented a specimen of a first-rate Lancashire working-class family.

Also near the singers was always seen Henry Holland, another quiet, gentle, and generous man. It was said that he and his wife were too easy and indulgent in the treatment of their son and daughter, but both turned out well and did good service in school and chapel long after their parents had passed away.

Near Mr. Holland sat a still quieter man than he, at least when at chapel, for there he always fell asleep; and as no amount of nudging and pinching could keep him awake, he was allowed to indulge his slumberous soul in peace. The mother made up for the father's somnolence by her wide-awakeness. The sons and daughters were always alive and awake like the mother, and all got into good trades, doing well for themselves and for the chapel and the various useful societies of the town.

Amongst the singers was Jabez Robinson, one of the very oldest members of the congregation, to which through much persecution he had staunchly adhered. His aged face was always pleasant to see, and his words pleasant to hear.

From the singing gallery and its vicinity I turn to the corner front pew on the right-hand side of the preacher. In that pew was pretty regularly seen a lady with the face and form of an angel, and whose character corresponded with her appearance, for she was intelligent, genial and good. This lady, whose name was Esther Becker, was occasionally accompanied to the chapel by her eldest sister Lydia, who afterwards became greatly distinguished in many ways. Endless paradoxes, social, literary, scientific, and religious, incessantly evolved from her mind, with innumerable schemes for the regeneration of mankind. Happily, in her long and active connection with the Manchester School Board, and with many other societies, she did much to realize the dreams of her early days.

In the next pew to the front, sat regularly another excellent female—Alice Kershaw—but of a very different stamp from the Beckers. She had more physical force and much stronger passions; her emotion during service oftentimes being difficult to control. Although her early education had been very limited, she was fond of reading and study in both religion and general literature. Robert Burns was a great favourite, and she had great pleasure in pointing to and descanting upon certain pictures on the house walls representing Scottish scenes and characters, including Highland Mary.

In the gallery behind the Becker and Kershaw pews were a cluster of pews filled with lads and young men. Amongst these were the Pollards, Wilkinsons, Waddingtons, Andertons, and Lancasters: three of whom became Unitarian ministers. A stranger observing these youths during service might have thought them rude, but they were nothing of the kind: their smiles and whispers and nudges were simply mutual recognitions of statements which strongly impressed them.

On the left-hand side of the gallery were regularly seen at service a large number of big girls and young women, amongst whom were Bertwistles, Whiteheads, Harrisons, Hollands, Andertons and Hulls. Here, again, might have been observed smiles and whispers, and often tears. Most strongly were these young men and women attached to the chapel and school, and also to the minister, as he was, also, attached to them. Amongst a considerable number of quiet, undemonstrative attendants in the gallery were the Dodgsons, Bridges, Briggses, Ainsworths, and Laycocks; all of whom were liberal supporters, according to their means, of chapel and school.

I must not pass from the gallery without reference to two women sitting in a front pew near the singers. They were sisters; alike large and burly in form and feature; were sturdy-looking; had strong feelings; were plain-spoken and withal deeply religious. They were always attentive to the service; thought much and spoke much about the sermons, from which they derived much edification and comfort. One of these estimable women was Mrs. Kershaw and the other was Mrs. Harrison. Both were so strongly attached to the chapel that they would not tolerate the least depreciation of either it or the minister. In reply to some spoken words slightly unfavourable, "I tell you," said Mrs. Kershaw, "that he is a true prophet of the Lord, and if you had right feelings you would know that." To this warm appeal, of course, there was no reply.

Leaving sight of the gallery and surveying the body of the chapel, there might always be seen, near the entrance door, David Harrison, one of the strong pillars of the church. He was over the middle height, was strongly built, and had a large, florid, and honest-looking face. In chapel business he was firm and decided, but always conciliatory. When consulted on any new plan, his first question was, "What does Thomas Holland say about it?" In like manner, when consulted, Thomas Holland would ask, "What does David Harrison say?" When both concurred, it was pretty clear the plan was sound and feasible and likely to be carried out, or that the plan was of doubtful kind, and must await further consideration or be set aside. David Harrison's sons and daughters followed in his footsteps and became worthy men and women, and all active in the school and chapel.

Near by was Robert Kershaw, a strong-looking, ruddy-faced man who loved debate, but was not a good debater; was stronger in assertion than in proof; had been headstrong—as he admitted—in his youth, when he joined the Lancashire mobs in breaking cotton-weaving machines in the mills.

In the same group was seen Noah Briggs who, with his family, had gradually come over to us from, I think, the Wesleyans. He was a carter, working hard, and bringing up his family in an admirable way. One son entered the Manchester College, passing successfully through his studies and afterwards settling down as a Unitarian minister. Subsequently, however, he quitted the ministry and became a prosperous tradesman at Crewe. Twice he was made Mayor of the Borough, and filled many other important offices on the corporation. A brother of his became a successful tradesman in a Yorkshire town, and, as I learnt from him in a correspondence many years after leaving Padiham, he was a leading Spiritualist there. Miss Briggs, the eldest sister, who was very active in the Sunday School and much loved there, suddenly died. The shock in the family and the School was very great. I visited her constantly through her brief illness, and observed the hard clutching at life and then the calm resignation to death which was brightened by the hope of immortality beyond.

In the group of sedate, elderly parties described, might have been seen James Pate, the smartest-looking and smoothest-spoken man in the congregation, and strange to say, his parents were the quietest, most unassuming, and most silent people in the chapel.

But where is this sketch to end? Only a small part of the picture, as it exists in the mind, have I painted. Just as I looked on the well-known faces in the old chapel more than forty-five years ago, so I seem to see them now. How vivid and moving is the picture still. But is it only a picture that moves one so? Or is it an inspiration also? Or still further, is there with the picture a communication? Nearly all I have named are departed hence; but may not their spiritual forms haunt the old places and visit lovingly and suggestively old and dear friends? Even Dr. Joseph Parker, in his story in "Great Thoughts," makes his hero, Curfew Jessel, into a Spiritualist holding communication with his deceased mother. And why not? And have not I through a medium communicated with my own mother in the same way? Was not her attitude, gesture, tone of voice, and exact look of the face, all there? I could not doubt it. In the same way, have not many other dear ones approached with messages of hope and love and courage? And may not, therefore, at least sometimes, a cloud of spiritual witnesses hold me, as others, in full survey? I am sure there was sympathy enough and affinity enough between myself and many members of the Padiham congregation to bind us together spiritually for time and eternity. Any way, the memory is there in the form of pictures fixed in the mind, to remain there as long as the mind itself endures.

Continued efforts after intellectual, moral, and spiritual reform inside the Church led to efforts of reform outside the Church. A preaching room was secured at Lower House, where, besides myself, Daniel Berry, Joseph Pollard, and, I think, Nicholas Pollard preached. The latter of these was an earnest temperance reformer, and often created amusement when giving a discourse by constant reference to written notes on strips of paper folded round his fingers, which he gradually unfolded as he went along in his speech.

Besides cottage services held in the vicinity, we helped to organize and carry on services in other towns, where Unitarianism had not secured a foothold. At Accrington I joined with other ministers in giving a course of lectures, which created much excitement. When Dr. Beard lectured, an organized opposition attempted to break up the meeting, which crowded the Public Hall. Amidst great noise I was appointed to take the chair, when I pleaded for order and fair play, promising free discussion at the end of the lecture. The Doctor's discourse was interrupted by shouts of " Infidelity," " Unbelief," " Against the Bible," met by shouts of " No, no," from our Padiham people. At the end of the discourse, up rose the Rev. Charles Williams, and proceeded with a slashing and denunciatory attack on the several subjects treated by the Doctor, which was very loudly applauded by a large band of the disciples of Mr. Williams. When the Doctor attempted to reply, the clamour was so loud he could not go on. As soon as I could get in a few words I appealed to Mr. Williams, throwing the onus of the unfair proceedings on him, and saying he could secure order amongst his supporters if he would. This rather nettled him, but soon he and his friends subsided, when a brief reply by the lecturer was given, at the end of which I moved a vote of thanks to Dr. Beard for his lecture, when, to the surprise of everyone, Mr. Williams seconded the motion with a few conciliatory words. The meeting broke up with a better feeling on the part of all present than would otherwise have been the case without Mr. Williams' closing words.

A society was shortly established at Accrington, the names of the leading members being Salter, Mills, and Taylor. On preaching there from time to time, I was glad to find sure, if slow, progress being made.

Our Padiham congregation took a leading part in forming a society in Burnley. A small room over a stable was the only building that could be secured at first, and there I frequently preached, while the singing was greatly helped by Padiham friends.

CHAPTER XXIII

LEAVING PADIHAM—REVIEW

From my diary of February and March, 1862—a painfully perplexing time—I copy the following words:—" Amongst these rugged, energetic, intelligent, and for the most part very excellent people, three years of my life have been spent. It has been a period of hard labour, much anxiety, not a little gratification, and large success. So firmly established in the affections of the people are both myself and my wife that it seems as if our whole lifetime might be satisfactorily spent in connection with the Padiham congregation." But just now it seems as if this connection were coming suddenly to a close, caused by a missive from Rev. Dr. Beard, in which he says, " You have done your duty at Padiham as I and your Manchester friends said you would. Your success is beyond our expectation. The congregation is fairly established and on its way to independence and self-support. Your services are now wanted at Manchester. Rev. J. C. Street is conducting a Mission here, and you are desired to become his colleague, your head-quarters to be at Blackley and his at Platt in Rusholme. Your old tutor, Mr. Gaskell, joins me in urging you to join the Mission, as do members of the Committee, most of whom are your old friends."

Such was then the problem before me. What would be its solution? For a considerable time I could not see my way. I pondered over the matter by day and by night, in solitary walks, and in the privacy of my study. I seemed to hear Manchester friends saying, " Come over and help us," and to hear the members of my congregation saying, " Stay with us, and we will do everything possible to help and encourage you in your work."

I mentioned the matter first to my wife. "Manchester friends," she said, "urged us to come here and we came, they now urge us to come back and we must return." Our house was soon besieged by the members of the congregation and the young people of the Sunday School. All begged and prayed we would stay at Padiham. When we did not promise, some became angry and said we were just like other parsons and their wives—influenced by respectability, honour, and pelf. They had thought we were quite exceptional in these respects, but found we were just like all the rest; and declared they never again would have any confidence in parsons and their wives.

While I was hesitating, time was passing, and Dr. Beard was pressing for a reply. At length I wrote—not without a qualm—stating that we had agreed to leave Padiham and come to Manchester as soon as arrangements could be made. Then the storm rose to its height, and we felt anxious to get out of its reach. Deputations from the congregation waited on Dr. Beard and other Manchester friends to get them to induce us to stay in Padiham. These efforts being in vain, it appeared inevitable that we must depart, and the excitement began to subside. At length the time of our departure came, when we parted in perfect peace with many presents, with unanimous manifestations of respect and love, and with very strongly expressed hopes that we should return to the congregation at Padiham and labour there to the end of our days.

Between the time of the announcement of our leaving Padiham and the time of our actual departure an event happened which very nearly induced us to stay. A letter from Dr. Beard informed me that a meeting of the newly-gathered congregation at Platt Chapel was about to be held, at which I was requested to be present and speak. Arriving at the Rusholme Town Hall at the time appointed, I was amazed to behold a large and brilliant assembly of the leading Unitarian families of Manchester.

Newly-gathered Mission congregation indeed! Had these ladies and gentlemen forsaken their several chapels and all gathered together at Platt Chapel? However, there these accomplished and well-to-do people were, and not the working-class converts I had expected to see. The chairman (a German) said, "See what has happened at Platt! Only twelve months ago there was little of a congregation at Platt, and now behold the sight before me!" This seeming joke caused the faces of the hearers to beam with bright but peculiar smiles very amusing to see. Rev. J. C. Street spoke fluently and glowingly of the Mission's success.

Rev. S. A. Steinthal, in his ever-genial and gracious manner, said he had expected to see a gathering of working-people, instead of which he recognized friends from all the Manchester congregations and from Liverpool, all of whom he was glad to find encouraging the Mission. When called on to speak, I said I rejoiced to hear of the success of the Mission at Platt, but regretted that no Sunday School had been formed, without which the future of the congregation was not secure. I spoke with but little spirit or force, but evidently with useful effect.

Mr. John Reynolds said that although the question of a Sunday School was not on the programme of proceedings he would, now that it had been introduced, commence a subscription by giving £5, and would also promise that members of his family should help in forming and carrying on the School. Immediately afterwards it was announced that a lady present had subscribed £20 for the same purpose. Here, then, was my one consolation during, to me, this depressing night. About my coming to the Mission not a word was said to me, and then, of course, I said nothing about it myself. Indeed, I was beginning to think I had better not come to the Mission, but remain with my Padiham congregation.

Very much tired, I got to my lodgings and went to bed, but not to sleep. The following contrast took possession of my mind and held it through the night. Here in Manchester tumult, confusion, and ceaseless noise: there in Padiham steady plodding work, with rest and peace. Here, glitter, pride, pomp and show: there, ruggedness, perhaps, but nature, honest, unpretentious, and unadorned. Here, cold propriety: there, active sympathy and genial warmth. Then farewell Manchester, and welcome Padiham. But I must first of all in the morning see Dr. Beard and tell him the story of my experiences at the meeting last night.

"All trifles light as air," said the Doctor, after hearing my account. "I can well understand what happened at the meeting," he continued, "but feel certain there was nothing personal to you." "The main point in the matter," he said, "is this. You were unanimously invited by the Committee to join the Mission. I conveyed to you the invitation, as did also the Secretary, in a formal way. You replied, accepting the appointment. Your business now is to wind up your affairs at Padiham, and settle yourself down to the work of the Mission here in Manchester. Should you not be inclined to operate in one section of the Mission, you will be under no obligation to do so. There will be plenty of work for you at Blackley and Middleton and adjoining places."

These statements of Dr. Beard cleared my way, helped me to a decision in favour of the Mission, and set my mind at rest.

In packing my books and papers I could not but linger over the numerous notes of sermons, lectures, and debates which had engaged the attention of the Padiham congregation during the three years now coming to a close. Most of the subjects were chosen or suggested by the members of the congregation or Sunday School. In one case strong interest had arisen both inside and outside the chapel in the writings of Macaulay, when I was induced to lecture on the first volume of the "History of England." With the strikingly-stated facts and superbly-painted figures of this panoramic volume we were charmed and informed. The "Essays" were treated on another occasion, when we dwelt on the clear, concise, and ornate style in which they were written.

With most of the author's vivid characterizations we generally agreed. But in one notable case we almost unanimously disagreed. With Hepworth Dixon we thought he was seriously wrong in his treatment of the eminent Quaker, William Penn. Both Dixon and Macaulay were vehement in their statements of the case, and hurled the facts about in a marvellous fashion. But out of the controversy it came out clear that Penn was the most just and honourable colonizer the world had known. In acquiring the territory of Pennsylvania he entered into peaceable negotiation with the Indian tribes, and without threat or show of arms honestly paid down a fair price for land, and about the bargain no dispute ever arose, nor was the peace between Penn and the Indians ever broken. The discourse on Macaulay led to a discourse on the historic writings of Froude.

In clearness of statement, picturesqueness of description and splendour of style we thought Froude equal to Macaulay himself. But what came most closely home to us was Froude's own personal experience as revealed in his remarkable work, "The Nemesis of Faith." What solemnity and sadness there is in that book, and yet what tenderness and hope! How strikingly he anticipates the dark fate before him, and how grandly he fortifies his soul against the ills that were sure to come.

In noticing this book we could not avoid reference to another and kindred book entitled, "Phases of Faith." For writing that heretical book, Francis William Newman was banished to the wilderness of Free Thought, where, with a few loving disciples, he spent his life; while his brother, John Henry Newman, for being a gourmand of credulous faiths, was despatched to the hoary, wealthy, and mighty Church of Rome, where, amid crowds of adoring saints, he donned a Cardinal's hat.

The Oxford Essays and Reviews furnished subjects of discourse and mutual discussion such as our Padiham friends delighted in, and such as I had pleasure in enlarging upon. At the outset our attention was arrested by the curious and stinging epithets applied to the essayists by many of their clerical brethren. The Bishop of Hereford said the writers were undermining Christianity. This, we thought, was the old cry of the

Church in danger, which, being interpreted, means that more grist is demanded for the clerical mills. The bulwarks of the great Churches, we contended, were vested interests—against which neither the gates of hell nor the gates of heaven could prevail; for Churches supported by innumerable pillars of gold and silver and brass could set at defiance all the powers that be.

The Bishop of Durham said the hearts of the faithful should burn with indignation against the authors of this book. That we thought unnecessary advice, seeing that the great Churches had always contained an immense storage of indignation ready at any moment to burst out in scorching flames. Hence the fiery saints, at command, could rush in mighty hosts to slaughter Saracens at Jerusalem—Waldenses in their mountain homes—Huguenots in Paris at the dead of night—Catholics against Protestants—Protestants against Catholics—until innumerable battle-grounds were heaped with the bodies of the slain.

Another Church authority said the essayists were " Seven Clerical burglars,"* without, however, being able to show what had been stolen, and from whom. Lifting obscuring clouds from the creeds was adding to their light; removing falsities from the Bible was making clearer its truth. But, as ever, the new light-bringer was assailed with opprobrious words and persecuting deeds. Prometheus, to be sure, had stolen fire from heaven. With the greatest skill and most noble daring he had scaled the battlements of the divine abodes, and seized and borne away the sacred fire to warm and illuminate the dark and starving earth. The great gods, selfishly basking in the heavenly splendours, were enraged at Prometheus and chained him to the Caucasian rock. And so now, the great clerical dignities sitting in heavenly places in these realms, were chaining the essayists to the rock of religious prejudice, and invoking upon them the scorn and contempt of the world.

In trying to discover precisely the terrible things the essayists had done, we found that the shells of the popular creeds had

* Six clergymen and one layman.

been slightly cracked—that Greek fire had been made to pale Jewish illumination—that the Cosmogony of Moses had been tickled with the wand of science—and that there had been sharp and irritating controversy as to the exact difference between tweedledum and tweedledee.

Our difficulty was to find anything serious in the case. To us the Essays could be best likened to a mixture of milk and water, neither fluid being very clear. The prosecution of two of the essayists utterly failed. The attempt to fasten on heresy was like grasping at smoke. The chase after the writers' own opinions was like the chase of the will-o'-th'-wisp: the faster the pursuit, the faster the retreat. The writers were found to be historians and nothing more. If heresy were in the case, it belonged to other parties, certainly not to them. They were simply showing what eminent writers and critics had said. If there were really any heresy lurking in the writers' words, it was of so illusive a kind that it could not be seized, and so the alleged culprits escaped from the labyrinths of the law.

Dr. Lushington did, indeed, suspend the two culprits from office for one year. But on appeal Lord Westbury quashed this verdict and ruled that eternal punishment was an open question, and so " Hell was dismissed with costs."

Several of the more popular sciences I was easily persuaded by earnest friends to introduce into Sunday sermons and week-night discourses. These discourses proved interesting and educative to the speaker and hearers. Lyell breaking down the Genesis narrative by his daring researches into the antiquity of man—Owen reconstructing from old bones raked from the bowels of the earth strange creatures which had lived and died long aeons before the period assigned by the Mosaic narrative for the creation of animal life on the earth—Herschell and son searching for and finding numbers of double suns in the heavens, with the elder Herschell's sister discovering so many of those marvellous things termed comets—all furnished subjects of conversation in the chapel and school, in homes and workshops, and on the highways.

In the same way the characters of high-class novels came before us for judgment and debate. Adam Bede was admired as a fine specimen of an honest-minded working man. Dinah Morris was adored as a saint adorning the lower walks of life.

Silas Marner received some rebuke, but more sympathy in his quarrel with the Little Bethel, in his solitary life, and in his salvation by means of an outcast child which he took into his lonely home, which was lonely no more. Others of George Eliot's characters appeared in succession, and were welcomed with much delight.

Mrs. Gaskell's " Mary Barton " made a profound impression on our factory girls, who watched her career with thrilling hopes and fears, and in the end pronounced condemnation on Mary's betrayer in no faint or feeble words.

Dickens, of needs, appeared amongst our distinguished guests, and his words were much enjoyed. I preferred the writings of Thackeray. Proceeding to get hold of the facts and scenes of " Pendennis " and " Vanity Fair," I soon found they were getting hold of me. A quaint and subtle humour seemed to steal over my mind as I read from page to page. Fuller, richer and bolder, however, than anything in his novels were the wit and humour of his extraordinary work, " The Four Georges." Treating matters jauntingly, as it seemed, at first, it suddenly appeared he had struck a deep mine of tender pathos, or of deep passion, or of solemn awe in the human breast.

Describing an Auto-Da-Fe, he tells, as if he enjoyed the telling, how Torquemada and the Priests feasted and gloated on the sight of heretics writhing in excruciating agonies amid devouring flames. Then the narrative goes on easily and airily as before, until at length comes the startling announcement that the most awful cruelties, the most horrid murders, that have shocked the world have been done by the most religious and most orthodox Christians that have ever lived on earth.

In delivering biographical discourses I was sowing seed on good ground. Such was the veneration of many of my hearers for past and present worthies that they gave their names in baptism to their own children. Hence the names, Telemachus, Hypatia, Servetus, Garibaldi and Mazzinni were familiar in school and chapel. For the moods of mind as well as noble deeds of great men there was always sympathy, strong and deep.

Standing with Carlyle beneath the midnight sky and listening to his ominous mutterings anent the stars shining overhead, the sorrows and sins darkening the abodes of men, and the graves in the earth beneath swallowing all human forms, we partook largely of his awful glooms.

While walking with Emerson beside Walden Lake and in the woodlands around, and listening to his glowing words, we could joyously imagine with him that spiritual beings walk the earth both when we sleep and when we wake; and also believe with him that if men toiling hard amid care, strife, fraud, tyranny, and war would yoke their market-waggons to the stars, all would in the end come right.

CHAPTER XXIV

MANCHESTER DISTRICT UNITARIAN MISSION

DURING the first week of April, 1862, we were very busy in removing our furniture from Padiham and placing it in a house in Harpurhey, about a mile from Blackley. I was very glad the head-quarters of my Mission had been fixed at the ancient, quaint-looking, ivy-covered chapel, where I had frequently preached in my student days and where I had well-nigh been settled as minister.

Near the close of my term at college, Mr. Peter Eckersley and a Danish gentleman forming a deputation waited on me and urged me to become minister of the Blackley Chapel. I accompanied the latter gentleman home, and found him to be a genial, highly-cultured and worthy man. On my leaving, he pointed out to me the words " Copenhagen House," painted over the doorway, saying I could not mistake his abode, where I should have a hearty welcome whenever I pleased to come. Sometime afterwards a most distressful message came to that same house, in which it was stated that the gentleman with his newly-wedded wife was sailing from Denmark when the vessel was wrecked in a storm and both were drowned in the sea. Most of the passengers escaped in boats, but owing to the delay caused by the severe illness of the wife, she could not be removed before the ship went down, and so they perished together. This sad event caused a deep pang of grief in many hearts, including my own.

On Easter Sunday, services were held in connection with the

opening of the new Sunday School. Rev. Wm. Gaskell gave a most eloquent discourse in the chapel in the forenoon. I conducted a scholars' service in the School in the afternoon, and preached in the chapel in the evening. All the services were well attended, the collection amounting to £24.

On the Monday afternoon following, a Social Party was held in the School with a full attendance. Rev. J. C. Street (in the chair) in his genial and fluent way gave me a hearty welcome as his colleague in the Manchester District Unitarian Mission. Mr. James Bennett, wonderfully vigorous and sprightly for his years, spoke as a very old member of the congregation, comparing former things to present things, much to the advantage of the latter. Mr. John Johnson, another old member, spoke genially and pleasantly of his past experience in connection with the venerable old chapel where he had so long worshipped.

Mr. Thomas Cooke (chapel-keeper) old, tall, gaunt, and picturesque-looking, related quaint incidents concerning Rev. Mr. Harrison, who had been minister of the chapel more than fifty years. On one occasion, after a lecture on astronomy, a youth impertinetly asked what became of all the old moons. Mr. Harrison replied that they were chopped up and made into stars. That saying was transmitted far and wide. Almost everyone in the neighbourhood heard of it, and repeated it with much gusto. Not in all his fifty years' ministry had he said anything so well remembered as that queer statement about the moon and stars.

Another of the older members present was Thomas Whittaker, a quiet, honest-minded, well-disposed man. He was too retiring for much active service in the chapel, but he had a numerous family who all became most devoted and efficient workers in both School and Chapel.

Mr. Lamming, a stout-set, pleasant-looking, earnest man, gave a most interesting account of his first connection with the chapel several years ago. Hearing the clergyman at the church he attended several times strongly denounce the Unitarians, he became disirous to know who and what they were. Finding there was a congregation of these dangerous heretics, as he had heard them called, at Blackley, he visited the chapel to have a look at them and investigate matters for himself. He was so far favourably impressed that he went to the chapel again and again, and had regularly continued going to the present time. After my settlement I always found him ready for any good word or work. Having a fine musical taste, he became bent upon an improvement of the choir, which was greatly needed. In the first place, a subscription must be made for a new organ, which was shortly obtained. In the meantime, I had found in Crab Lane Village a Mr. Hilton and his son, who were both musical, and a Mr. Taylor, who, with his son, was also musical.

Reporting these cases to Mr. Lamming, he speedily made their acquaintance, got them all into the choir, got the youth Taylor into his warehouse, helped to train him in music, and finally got him to play the organ in the chapel for several years. A society with such workers as Mr. Lamming could not fail of success.

Amongst the new members was Joseph Norbury, who was engaged in the office of his uncle, a prosperous estate agent. Having seen him in the chapel at one or two lectures, I got his address and called at his house. Although reticent at first, he ultimately admitted that he had become dissatisfied with the creeds and ceremonies of the Established Church, in which he had been trained. He liked the simple method of service at our old chapel, but all our doctrines he did not understand at present. His attendance at the chapel became more frequent, but neither he nor I could induce his wife to attend a single service. But a sad event happened in the family which wrought a great change in her mind. A fine boy of ten years became ill and likely to die. During the few weeks he lingered on the verge of death she was in utter distraction. I frequently spoke, read, and prayed in the house, and she was very grateful for the soothing influence she felt on these occasions. Nothing could save the dear lad's life: his remains were buried in our graveyard. Thenceforth the whole family joined School and Chapel, and proved a most valuable acquisition to the congregation. Relatives and friends of the family did not like this change, and complained that there was no good in drawing people from one church to join another. But then, in this case Mr. Norbury had really drawn away from the Church, and his family might, probably, have done the same. The harmony and happiness of the family were, therefore, secured with no loss to the Church, and a gain to us.

The adherence of the Collenge family was quite a surprise. The mother was a sturdy-looking, strong-minded woman, and had been quite prominent amongst the Primitive Methodists. How she had been induced to attend the chapel on one or two occasions I do not know; but at the close of a Sunday evening service she desired an interview with me in the chapel. She liked the services, she said, to a certain extent, but she never heard anything said about the forgiveness of sin through the Blood of the Lamb. We seemed, she continued, too easy about the punishment of the impenitent, both in the present life and the future life. The Bible was very clear on such matters and we did not seem to make much account of them, in fact, she said, we had no hell fire. I was both interested and amused, but I saw she was in earnest, and so I spent some time in explaining these matters. I quoted passages of Scripture, and she quoted other passages, and it appeared we could not get to any satisfactory conclusion on that occasion. I had to promise to call at her house the following week, when she would have more Scripture passages ready for my consideration. I called, and a most formidable number of passages I had to face. The time was gone before I had examined a fourth of the texts. Again and again I had to call and controvert and explain. The result was that some of her doctrines were modified and hell fire nearly put out. With hell went many of her fears, so that she could attend chapel with an easy conscience, and the family attended with her.

An interesting character was the village blacksmith, who fitted in exactly the description of Longfellow where he says:—

> "The smith a mighty man is he,
> With large and sinewy hands;
> And the muscles of his brawny arms
> Are strong as iron bands."

To step into the smithy on a rainy and gusty day and warm myself at the glowing fire and have a talk with the strong, sensible man was a privilege I often enjoyed. Dogmatic religion interested him but little, but justice, right doing between man and man, he thought, was what the world needed most of all. His gratification in the Sunday services at chapel is explained by our poet when he says:—

> "He hears the parson pray and preach,
> He hears his daughter's voice,
> Singing in the village choir,
> And it makes his heart rejoice."

Yes, there was the daughter in our village choir, and a fine, tall, comely, well-behaved maiden she was. And not far from her in the choir might be seen a good-looking, steady, clever young man, whose name was John Joseph Brown. This youth and maiden singing together to make harmony in the congregation, at least made harmony in their own souls, which led to their union in marriage and the beginning of happy and useful lives. And thus, in our village, and partly in our sanctuary, was enacted the sort of love-drama which is being enacted all over the world, brightening everywhere the pathways of life.

Another interesting drama was frequently going on in the singing class taught by Mrs. Griffiths, a lady of fine disposition, rich gifts, gentle manners, and withal an enthusiastic Tonic Sol-Fa-ist. The class was so large and the blunders made so numerous and amusing, that the hilarity sometimes got beyond control. After much persuasion and some contriving I managed to attend the class, when better order ensued. Much more progress was made, and, strange to say, I unconsciously learned to sing from the new notation. In drilling each pupil singly

I had to go through the same operation, and found for the first time I could sing from notes a tune alone. This new acquisition brought great joy to me. Tunes were daily surging through my mind, and often loud vocal sounds were produced in my study to the surprise of the household and visitors present.

A harmonium having been procured, I soon found I could both play and sing, which further increased my joy. Then came to hand a rich and sweet-toned organ, since which great accession singing and playing have been an inspiration rising sometimes to ecstasy. My feeling of obligation to the most worthy woman—now gone to practise her noble gifts in a higher sphere—is too strong for expression in words.

The Mutual Improvement Class included a number of Freethinkers, who greatly helped to make the debates real, earnest, lively and instructive. The names of the three leaders of this party were Hall, Plant, and Ramsbottom. The first of these I met with in Boggart-Hole-Clough, when a long and interesting conversation took place, ending with a promise on his part to visit us at Blackley Chapel and see what we were like. He came and saw, and came again, and continued to come and brought with him his two friends and others. Any attempt at indoctrinating such men would have been futile, and so we found them something to do. And very active indeed they became, taking leading parts in dramas, recitations, and entertainments of various kinds, and to some extent assisted in the Sunday School.

In theological debates they never failed to be hard on the Bible. Seizing the facts and figures of Colenso and turning them into sledge-hammers, they smote heavily on the books of Moses. The incidents of the Exodus were smashed to atoms. Not only were the Egyptians buried in the Red Sea, but the Israelites themselves were engulphed in an ocean of myth, mystery, mistake, and untruth. The account of the killing of 150,000 lambs by three priests in twenty-four hours, and the sprinkling of the blood of 50,000 lambs in two hours by the same three priests was a hugely bloody picture of an impossible transaction, filling the mind with disgust. Then the picture of the three priests eating 150 pigeons in one day could only produce a sarcastic guffaw! The consideration, again, of the great numbers of returning Israelites, and the vast increase since their departure into Egypt, with the startling cause of that increase as stated by Bishop Patrick produced an outburst of hilariousness which hindered the further proceedings of the night.

That there should be much wrangling over words and phrases in a debating class was inevitable. Defending Christianity, a speaker presented a long array of names of great thinkers who were powerful authorities on his side of the question. A speaker on the other side said great thinkers were often great fools and were of no authority at all in the matter. A third speaker said the little-thinking fools, although vast in numbers, were of less authority still. In face of the fact stated by Carlyle that there were in these islands over thirty millions of us mostly fools, where could any satisfactory authority be found?

In the melee which ensued it was contended that the authority of the Pope of Rome was fallible, like himself; that the authority of the Bible was based on irreconcilable statements, and therefore largely unreliable: and that the Churches were built on dogmas partly true but largely false. In the last resort, it was contended, true authority must be based on reason, and that the aim of all education should be to make the intellect strong, the conscience clear, and the heart pure.

Beside preaching, teaching, and visiting, quite other work had to be done at Blackley. The great cotton famine coming on and all the mills in the neighbourhood being closed, it was decided by the Chapel Committee to open Sewing Classes in the new School. Without any distinction of sect or party, females were admitted, and soon crowded the rooms. Then came a long time of hard drudgery for the managers of the classes. Constantly I had to be in Manchester visiting warehouses, begging money and goods. Constantly Mrs. Rushton and Mrs. Whittaker had to be cutting out materials to be made into garments; Mrs. Bourne and Miss Bennett also rendering valuable service in many ways. As money did not come in fast enough, the drudgery of the managers was intensified by the Committee getting up a Bazaar, which produced with subscriptions £220. The workers received weekly wages according to their time in attendance, just as they had been paid in the mills. In this way many families in Blackley were saved from privation and distress. The people of the township formed a much more favourable opinion of us than they had held before, some outsiders remarking that Unitarians not only preached good works, but did them.

If, after these severe and protracted exertions, any of us were thinking of a little rest from our labours, the dream was rudely and suddenly dispelled. A challenge thrown out to me by Peter Eckersley was to the effect that if I would commence preparations for another Bazaar and raise money enough to clear the heavy debt from the new School, he would renovate the interior of the old chapel at his own cost. Operations were immediately going on. As before, I was diving into Manchester offices searching for money or goods; the same ladies were cutting out garments; many of the previous sewers were at work; all parties it was possible to get hold of were kept in constant service up to the time of the Bazaar, which produced £320 and cleared the School of debt.

This business ended, the undertaking of Mr. Eckersley at once began. The decayed woodwork in the interior was entirely cleared out, and the graves under the rotten flooring—from which awful smells had come—were securely closed, and serious injury to the health of worshippers prevented. Then followed the complete refurnishing of the chapel, making it safe, comfortable, and pleasant to see.

CHAPTER XXV

MIDDLETON — OTHER MISSIONS

My Mission Station No. 2 was at Middleton, where both Congregation and School met in the Temperance Hall. On my first visit to the Hall I was surprised to meet with Samuel Lawton, who, thirty years before, had been a companion schoolfellow in the old Sunday School of Hurdsfield, our native village. "Do you," I asked, "live in Middleton?" "Yes, certainly," he replied, "and have done a many years." "Do you attend the congregation here?" "Yes, and have done from its beginning some twelve months ago." "How did you become a Unitarian?" "Muchwhat as, I suppose, you did, by reading and thinking." "I am very glad to find you here." "Not more glad than I am to find you here," he replied.

Three days a week I visited Middleton, preaching, attending classes, visiting the sick, and looking after absentee members and scholars. When tired out with tramping the streets, it was always delightfully refreshing to get tea with my old friend and indulge in reminiscences of our doings in former days. It was a pleasant surprise to me to find a large number of houses with silklooms and quillwheels at work in them. My knowledge of the silk business gave me a welcome to almost every weaver's house. Mutual talk about warp and shute, entering and twisting in, plain work and figured work, heavy dyes and light dyes, fast colours and fading colours, established a permanent friendship between myself and many of the weavers. Some of them had large quantities of herbs which they had gathered, dried, and classified, and made ready for use. Their use in curing various diseases was a most interesting theme of conversation. Others were eloquent in their descriptions of moths and butterflies which they had caught and preserved in glass cases. In a few houses I found cases of geological specimens, which led to interesting discussions on the bearings of science on religion and the Bible, when they were often greatly surprised to find that I was quite as heretical on the book of Genesis as themselves.

Owing mainly to these visitations, regularly continued, the attendance at both School and congregation greatly increased. At the Mission Committee Meeting held in March, 1863, Rev. G. H. Wells reported that instead of twelve or fifteen persons being present at the services as formerly, the chapel was now nearly filled. In the Sunday School the attendance had arisen to 170. At the Christmas Day Party and Procession of the same year, more than 300 persons were present, which caused considerable astonishment in the township. I was neither so surprised nor so optimistic as many friends both in and outside the township. I knew how the movement had arisen, and I knew that reaction would follow. In the two following years there came a decline in the silk trade, many weavers having to migrate, including some who had joined us. Others could not get decent clothing, and stayed away. Still, there were large gains from the revival movement, which, it was hoped, would be followed by like movements and like gains. A very good effect was produced by the regular carrying on of a week-night Mutual Improvement Class. Amongst those attending besides myself were T. B. Wood, S. Lawton, John Hilton, E. Brookes, Clegg, and Keene. These were also our best workers and supporters. Having a generous disposition and an excellent purse, Mr. Wood had been a good supporter from the founding of the Society.

One of the subjects which long engaged the attention of the Class was "Theodore Parker and the Absolute Religion," the time being well spent in the investigation of so important a theme.

With the Swedenborgian minister I had frequent and very pleasant intercourse, as also with his gifted wife, who was the daughter of the eminent Joseph Hume, M.P.

The genial editor of the Liberal local paper always welcomed any communication from our Society, and printed at full length, with commendation, two of my lectures, the one on John Bright, and the other on Richard Cobden.

My journeys along the highways to Middleton were pleasant enough in summer-time, but in stormy, wintry weather I often got roughly used. Coming home late on dark nights was not without danger. Tramps would often make demands with threats and sometimes with blows. When late and in the dark, I walked in the middle of the wide road, keeping a keen outlook on the hedges on either side. On one occasion I saw a man crashing through the hedge in my direction, but he being entangled in the thorns, I got a dozen yards' start of him in what proved to be a half-mile race. Approaching the lights of Blackley, the man stopped, and then I stopped, completely exhausted and out of breath, and it was a long time before I was able to get home.

To my great gratification, I discovered a field-road from the northern end of Middleton, leading through Boggart-Hole-Clough to Harpurhey. Several cosy nooks afforded me pleasant rest and disposed the mind to meditation, aspiration, and prayer. It was with regret I visited these peaceful haunts for the last time.

My first Mission Service at **Miles Platting** was held on a Sunday evening in a room over a stable. The smell and noise from the horses below were anything but inspiring to the assembled worshippers. On the same day I had preached twice at Swinton, and then been conveyed five miles in an open shandry on a stormy day, so that my service was of necessity short. I got home at night in a very feeble condition and lay in bed some days in a weak and feverish state. Subsequently a new building was raised in Varley Street, in which both School and congregation assembled. Under the management of an excellent band of men and women workers both institutions made good progress.

Mr. Bibby was indefatigable at all points and whenever needed. Mr. Coleman was devoted to the training of singers, and so raised an excellent choir, which he kept engaged both on Sundays and at week-night parties. Mr. Fielding had a large family, and all attended School and congregational services. I was pleasingly surprised by the parents requesting me to baptize by sprinkling six of the children who had not undergone a religious dedication of any kind. The ceremony in the chapel attracted a large congregation, and proved to be of an edifying kind. There the six boys and girls stood in a row, their ages being from three to fourteen years, all of them looking well and behaving well, although two or three of them could not avoid laughing a little when I sprinkled water on their faces. After one of my services at Hindley in June, 1900, a woman came to me and said she was one of the six thus baptized, and that the event had always been a pleasant memory to her. It had made her feel, she continued, that she had a tie to the Unitarian Society whether at home or in other towns. This testimony seems to me a very important one, and worthy of attention by all parents and preachers in the denomination.

The Barnes family and the Burgess family aided largely in the founding of the society, and were active in carrying it on for a number of years.

For some years during my mission, the family of Mr. Birch did good service in the School and congregation, but Mr. Birch could never be induced to hold any official position. In early days he had been indoctrinated into the popular theology, but the study of historic Christianity had set his mind against all priesthoods, and alienated him from all churches. His chief study was practical science, although theoretical science had for him much charm. The facts of Darwin united to the magnificent speculations of Herbert Spencer, he contended, formed the direct way to the highest truths known to mankind.

He lived in a quaint old building which had formerly been a manor house, with extensive fields and woodlands around. But Manchester was approaching, and had so far closed upon it that only a few small fields and a small garden were left to it. Still, he very much loved the limited seclusion he found in the old house, and loved to have genial friends visiting him there. I could not accept half his invitations, but when I could pay a visit I had always a pleasant and profitable time. The latest important books on science and literature in general would be sure to come into view. But the man's own genial, quaint, and inseeing criticisms were more interesting than his quotations from books. He held an important position in certain large ironworks, where he produced many important inventions. I was informed by another party that Birch was the first to discover the method of making Bessemer steel, but that Bessemer, having more capital and more influence than Birch, secured the patent by which millionaires have been made. I became very much attached to this admirable and interesting man, and the sentiment was evidently returned.

THE SALFORD MISSION

Unfortunately for the Committee of the District Mission and for myself in particular, my colleague, Rev. J. C. Street, left Manchester and became the minister of the Unitarian Chapel at Newcastle-on-Tyne. Henceforth, for several years I had to manage six or seven mission stations as best I could. The first of the additional stations I visited was that at Ford Street Chapel, Salford. Almost at once it was decided to build a Sunday School on the land adjoining the chapel, and to make extensive improvements in the chapel itself.

Once more I was on the warpath in a begging expedition. If all parties had been as easy to vanquish as Mr. Ivie Mackie, I should have had a free and triumphant course. Entering his office on this occasion, the following colloquy ensued:—

Mackie.—Well, what are you after this time?

Rushton.—We are building a new School at Ford Street.

M.—It is fortunate for you that I know you so well, or you might have shared the fate of the Wigan man the other day.

R.—Indeed! Nothing serious happened, I hope.

M.—I sent for a policeman, who walked him off for begging on false pretences.

Then, pitching me a £5 note, he said, "Now flee for thy life." But seldom was money got so easily as in that case. Often from six or eight places I visited I got little or nothing. But with much labour the needed money was obtained, and both School and Chapel cleared of debt.

The burden of the Mission here was greatly lightened by a band of men and women able and willing to help wherever there was need. There was Mr. Bowes (afterwards Alderman), quiet, steadfast, and always helpful. Horrocks, Jackson, Milne and Hough were the names of parties ever active, vigorous, and successful in whatever they undertook.

The accession of two families (Phillips and Yates) contributed largely to the success of both School and Chapel. The young people of these two families had a double incentive to regular attendance and earnest work. They became not only deeply interested in the Mission cause, but they became personally interested in each other. Ultimately two members of the one family were married to two members of the other family. All the members of the two families were musical, and used this noble gift for the good of the congregation, one or other playing the organ, and the rest engaging in the choir. My connection with the Ford Street Mission was always as happy as laborious from first to last.

WHITFIELD STREET, ARDWICK

The Ardwick Society came under the control of the District Mission in the year 1866. The congregation had lately been formed chiefly by families originally connected with the Unitarian Chapel, Mossley. Amongst the leaders with whom I became most acquainted were Mr. Crabtree, who was musical, and presented a harmonium to the Society; John Heys, a lay preacher, who delivered weighty, instructive, and forcible discourses; and Edward Layton, a sharp business man, as I found from the prompt way in which he presented demand notes for subscriptions and donations promised. From the gratifying success observed at this Mission as at other Missions, I make with confidence the following statement:—Let a few intelligent and earnest Unitarian families unite together; take a room in the centre of a considerable population; form a congregation and society; get preachers supplied by a Missionary society or otherwise; advertise the services well: and then people will attend, and success will be secured. Of course, complete independence will be a matter of time. Very often the remark is made that orthodox societies can succeed in this way, but that Unitarian societies cannot. I maintain, on the contrary, that any religious society whatever will be successful if the conditions already laid down are rigidly followed out.

The kingdom of heaven suffereth violence and violent men take it by force. Ecclesiastical history is crowded with illustrations in proof: as also of the fact that the kingdom of hell suffereth violence, and that violent men established hell by force all over the earth, holding states and churches in their invincible grip. "Divided empire with heaven's King I hold," said Milton's satan. And that firm decision has ever been unflinchingly observed. And who can say which division of that empire wields the mightier force to-day?

Platt Chapel

It was early in the year 1864 I undertook missionary work in connection with this ancient sanctuary. I met with a pleasant welcome from a limited congregation of very excellent people. Mr. John Reynolds, an old friend, I found actively engaged, as also several members of his family.

William Smith was a convert, and full of fine enthusiasms. Several of his favourite poets he would exalt over several favourites of my own, which led to much pleasant and improving conversation. He was deep in Ruskin's "Modern Painters," with which I had some acquaintance. We cared not for art criticisms, but fastened on the author's fine moral and religious suggestions, which we found informing and ennobling.

Thomas Brittain was scientific, and gave lectures on natural objects. Taking one into the garden amongst his ferns, he would expatiate at length on the variety and beauty of these favourite plants. If one appeared at all dull of apprehension, he would hastily pluck off a slip here and a slip there, and then rushing one into the house and placing the fronds under the microscope, exclaim, " Now look there, and you will see all the beautiful distinctions I have been pointing out."

Even a still greater treat I had on entering the extensive and perfectly-kept gardens and conservatories of Mr. Broome, another member of the congregation. The trees and flowers impressed me by their variety, beauty, quantity and quality. Pointing on one occasion to a large, vase-shaped, white flower, Mr. Broome said, " Just look inside there." And sure enough, I saw a number of large insects wriggling and struggling in vain to free themselves from the terrible jaws of that fine but murderous flower. "Nature is red in tooth and claw," said Professor Clifford, and even that flower had instruments sharp enough to draw the life-blood of its victims. That fair and majestic flower was as savagely carnivorous as a lion, a tiger, or a bear.

Amongst the excellent and earnest female workers were Mrs. and Miss Gordon, Miss Whitelegge, Miss Gawthorpe, and Mrs. Breuising. With all its excellencies, the congregation had two serious deficiencies. It contained but very few members of the working class, and hardly any of the poor people of the neighbourhood. And again, although most earnest efforts had been made to establish a Sunday School, the results were disappointing. From my own visitations in the district, I found that all the best working-class children had become attached to orthodox schools. Only strays and runaways and loafing children were in any sense available for a new school, and when obtained were almost or altogether unmanageable. Now, if the well-to-do members of a congregation could in such a case induce their own young people to form themselves into mutual improvement classes meeting on Sundays and weekday evenings, they might lay the foundation of a Sunday School, and thus establish a successful institution. Before the end of the year my mission connected with Platt Chapel came to a close. The Rev. S. A. Steinthal had the courage and self-sacrifice needed to become the minister of the chapel, and the congregation had the great good-fortune of securing so able and in every way excellent a minister.

Dob Lane, Failsworth

In the year 1865, the old chapel with the new Sunday School came under the care of the Mission, and remained so about two years. The congregation consisted of the best sort of working-class people, who sent their children to School on Sunday and on certain evenings of the week days, and who managed and taught them well when there. Amongst the managers of the chapel and the school with some 220 scholars, were the Allens, Partingtons, Pollitts, Wildes and Hibberts. My time with these worthy people was very limited, but it was pleasant to be amongst them and aid in ever so small a way. Some of them were weavers with looms in their own houses, which secured labour for one or two or more members of each family. Ruskin earnestly contended that remunerative work in the home was most favourable to both intelligence and good morals: and this I found to be the case at Macclesfield, Middleton, and Failsworth. But now people are massed together in factories, mines, warehouses, and financial exchanges, with serious deterioration of body, mind, and soul. Hence our jingo outrages, hooligan rowdyisms, and Mafeking orgies.

True, in Chartist days there were outbreaks in the populace, but they arose for the most part from the interference of police and soldiers with what would have been peaceable meetings to advocate reforms. But now, ruling politicians, with soldiers, parsons, lawyers, financiers, and with three-fourths of the people, including the very lowest classes, seem ready on the least excitement to raise a wild war-whoop and rush into any warpath that opens before them.

Amongst the many historic accounts related about the old chapel at Dob Lane, was the familiar story of Unitarian families who, having become wealthy, straightway drove their carriages on Sundays to the rich, fashionable, and powerful Established Church.

SWINTON

On my first visit to the congregation at this place in my early student days, the meetings were held in a room formed out of two or three old cottages. The pulpit was so peculiarly situated that whoever preached in it went through a curious experience. The room was so low that a square hole had to be cut through the ceiling just over the pulpit, to make room for the preacher's head and chest. Through this hole, when the stove was heated, there came a mighty rushing wind, equal, I think, to that felt by the apostles on the Day of Pentecost. And, happily, not without similar results, for the cause grew and the congregation multiplied.

My first visit as a District Missionary was on the day of the opening of a new chapel, when I conducted one service and the Rev. J. C. Street another, good congregations being present on both occasions. Just as I had got into the pulpit, I noticed a quiet-looking, thoughtful, observant man enter the chapel and take a back seat. After the service he waited to speak to me, when I found he was Mr. Silas Leigh, of Monton, one of the most liberal contributors to the funds raised for the building of the chapel. Many were the regrets heard expressed from time to time that Mr. Leigh and the Misses Leigh did not marry and have families to carry on the benevolent and useful work in which they had always been engaged.

After the death of the lamented Mr. Boardman, the preachers were entertained by Mr. Collier, a gardener, and Mr. Jackson, a coal carter, both being hard workers in the congregation and teachers in the School.

CHAPTER XXVI

CLOSE OF MISSION — BLACKLEY MINISTRY

FOR five years ending in May, 1867, I had been connected with the Manchester District Unitarian Mission. During three to four years of that time I was sole Superintendent Missionary of six stations extending from Miles Platting in the north to Swinton in the south, and from Middleton in the west to Longsight in the east. All along I had liked the work, arduous as it was; but at length both the bodily and mental strain proved too much for continuation. The spirit was willing to go on, but the flesh was too weak, and my mission work, of necessity, came to a close. Crushing as the labour had been, I would not have been without the rich experience of that period on any account.

Tested by results, each of the Mission Stations could present substantial results. Much ground had been gained, and little, if any, lost. With all classes connected with the Mission I was on pleasant terms. The Committee, including Revs. Wm. Gaskell, Dr. Beard, T. E. Poynting, and S. A. Steinthal, and such laymen as E. C. Harding and B. Heape, were always kind, considerate, encouraging, and helpful.

Some of the poorest people drawn into the Missions became strongly attached to School and Chapel services, as well as to myself. A factory youth at Blackley, having been persuaded to join the Mission, could never be kept away from any service in either School or Chapel. When I removed to Hindley, he removed also, and worked at a coal-pit there, until, being taken ill, he went home to die. With young men and women in better circumstances and with better education than this youth the Mission work was successfully carried on. In this class I sought out and found teachers, secretaries, and hard workers in many ways. Securing enow of this class and getting them heartily to work, missions become invincible and victorious.

With some of the more wealthy Unitarians I frequently came into contact during my begging expeditions. I found them, for the most part, agreeable and charitable. If the cause were good and also successful, they would support it. Clear-headed, energetic in movement, successful in business, these men are sometimes severe in judgment. Applying to one of these gentlemen to get a situation for a student who was leaving the college, "Ah!" he exclaimed, with sharpness, "then he has proved a lame horse, and you recommended him." And yet that same student afterwards was a successful missionary, and now is the minister of a successful and important church.

On a few occasions during my Mission expeditions I became acquainted with several millionaires. Preaching in a certain chapel in east Lancashire at the time of the American War, my subject was largely illustrated by exciting scenes on the battle-fields, with commendatory remarks on General Stonewall Jackson's exploits. At the close of the service, three wealthy gentlemen with a number of ladies congratulated me highly on my discourse, and invited me to dine at a certain Hall. On the way we visited some splendidly-built stables, when the wonderful qualities of several horses were explained to me. One was a first-rate hunter. Another was a fine-paced hackney. Two others were magnificent carriage horses. All this time I was most concerned about their prancing feet, and apprehensively speculating as to how far they could send out their heels in my direction. Perceiving this, the gentlemen were much amused, and assured me I should escape with a whole skin, which happily I did. At dinner another trial awaited me. Being a vegetarian, I could not partake of two or three of the earlier courses served on the table. The younger members of the family were highly amused at this extraordinary thing, and the elder ones expressed their sympathy. It seemed to all of them an incredible thing that I could live without eating fleshmeat. I assured them I was much better in many ways since I had ceased eating it, but they could not be persuaded. However, I had a good and sufficient dinner from the farinaceous and fruit courses which came in due order. After dinner the other two gentlemen called at the house, and an interesting conversation ensued on the American War.

Two smaller confederacies, they considered, would be better than one great confederacy, which might become a standing menace to other nations. As to the negro question, that would settle itself in any case. Their freedom would at length be secured under any form of government. At the same time, doubts were expressed as to whether the negro could be so far educated and elevated as to become fit for freedom in any measurable time. These questions have since been answered to some extent by the rapid advance in education by some portion of the negroes, and by their entrance into many, if not all, the leading professions.

Subsequently the minister wrote, urging me to preach special discourses in the same chapel, saying the aforesaid gentlemen and the congregation generally would very much like to see me again. I wrote an excuse, and never went to the place afterwards. My habits, thoughts, tastes, and feelings were entirely averse to those of wealthy and fashionable people, and the aversion could not be subdued. No doubt I was greatly deficient in accommodation, diplomacy, and tact. But I was myself, and how could I have acted otherwise than I did?

At the close of my five years' Mission, I became minister of Blackley Chapel alone. At the welcome meeting, a financial statement was made showing the extra sums of money raised during the past five years. To pay the debt on the new School, £320; for the Cotton Famine Sewers in the School, £220; for a new organ, £40. At the same time it was shown that Mr. Eckersley had renovated the Chapel at his own cost, and that the congregation had improved in number and good works.

On my new settlement, it was anticipated, of course, that past achievements would be surpassed. And, indeed, such was the case to a considerable extent. But endless meetings and incessant visitings began to break down my health.

Then it was agreed that to save me so many long journeys between Blackley and my house in Harpurhey, a new Parsonage should be built near the Chapel. Then I entered on another begging expedition in Manchester and elsewhere, while Mrs. Rushton and other ladies were hard at work in preparation for another bazaar. After about a year's incessant labour, it was found that the bazaar and subscriptions had produced over £300.

Ground was selected, plans drawn, and the Parsonage built. But just as we were about to enter the new house, there came an unexpected and sudden change. Preaching on a certain Sunday at Hindley, I was urged to become the minister of the Chapel. At once I declined, but at the request of the Committee I promised to preach again in a short time. In two weeks after the second visit, I engaged to become the minister of the Hindley Unitarian Chapel. At the very same time, some of my oldest and best friends in Manchester—including Mr. E. C. Harding and Revs. S. A. Steinthal, W. Gaskell and Dr. Beard—had decided to invite me to take charge of the Rochdale Road Mission Chapel. This invitation was a great trouble to me, as my engagement at Hindley was a surprise and trouble to them.

Mr. Harding urged I should get a release from the engagement. Mr. Steinthal did the same, saying that Manchester was such a fine field of labour that I should settle there. Dr. Beard said they had killed one minister at Hindley, and would kill me, and serve me right for burying myself in such an out-of-the-way and beggarly and barren place.

Peter Eckersley, junr., visited Hindley to discover what was my great attraction there. In his report to Blackley friends, he said he found, in a forbidding-looking back settlement a tumbledown old schoolroom adjoining a dingy old chapel;

an old straw-thatched, decaying cottage near the chapel with a sty in which pigs were grunting, and close by a small graveyard, in which some fowls were scratching, clucking, and crowing. He was disgusted, he said, at what he saw, and with me for going to settle in such a repulsive place.

I was not surprised nor offended at Mr. Eckersley's report, nor did I think that any other graphic report would be more favourable than his. What, then, was my inducement to settle at Hindley? Well, there was a salary of £100 from endowments and £5 a year from the congregation, with an old decrepit Parsonage to live in. But where, then, was the bare possibility of a successful ministry in such a place? Ah! where indeed! But I had known of several situations called forlorn hopes, and worked hard in them, and felt the thrilling joy which had come in the hour of victory. Was there here another terrible battlefield, and another victory to win? Then again, had I not walked through a near woodland, and heard the musical flow of water-brooks in its dells, and been reminded of him who found a calm retreat, "Where Kedron's moonlit waters strayed"? Had I not also seen bathed in sunlit and moonlit splendour Rivington Mountain Range, which in stress and storm of conflict I might ascend to gain strength and inspiration after the manner of Him of whom it is said:—

> "Cold mountains and the midnight air
> Witnessed the fervour of His prayer."

CHAPTER XXVII

SETTLEMENT AT HINDLEY

SURVEYING, at the outset, the forces at my command at Hindley, I found some twenty scholars in uncertain attendance at the Sunday School. In the chapel were the same scholars, with ten or twelve elderly persons. By the end of the first year, after much house-to-house visiting, the attendance at both School and Chapel was about doubled. At special services and entertainments, hundreds of persons were sometimes in attendance.

During the next few years, great things were projected, and to the surprise of many, were accomplished. The School House was a dark, damp dungeon, and must of necessity be replaced by a new building. The cost would be £600 or £700, which everybody said could not be raised. After much cogitation, five individuals engaged to subscribe £20 each. The subscribers were James Platt, a collier; William Hotchkiss, a collier; John Jones, a colliery clerk; Abram Hurst, a farmer; and Adam Rushton, the minister. The other members of the congregation were thus stimulated to raise another £100, and further prompted to prepare articles for a bazaar which produced a further £100.

In a begging expedition at Bolton, Manchester, and elsewhere, I met with fair success. Very soon a lofty, light, and commodious School was built and paid for. To match the new School, it was decided that there must be a new Chapel, which was soon built. In this case, the burden on the congregation was much lighter than in the case of the School. The greater part of the cost of the building came from mine rents which were just then beginning to increase in amount.

In the new School were soon found more scholars, and in the new Chapel more attendants. There was now a fair field of operation, and if progress was not so rapid as desired, it was sound and sure.

Amid arduous and crowding duties some hours of joyous and uplifting studies were secured each passing day. Amongst the saints and sages influencing and helping me at this time, as before-time, were Carlyle, setting forth his grimly-humorous " Philosophy of Clothes," presenting the most grotesque figures of human beings, dressed and undressed, and furnishing God Himself with suitable robes; propounding at the same time his philosophy of " Yea and Nay," not, however, so widely applicable as he seems to think, seeing that the great majority of men say " Yea" to superstition to the end of their days. —Emerson, uniting the Transcendant to the Practical, making labour ornamental as well as useful, lifting studious and imaginative men to the Empyrean of noblest ideals, there to solve the Riddle of Creation and descant on the Flux of the Universe.—Martineau, climbing from crag to crag on philosophic heights in search of the truest ideal of the Seat of Authority in Religion: and from thence declaring that a Transcendental Presbyterian Church or a Transformed Episcopal Church might form an ecclestical seat of authority of a kind, and if well watched and restrained: but as to the real and ultimate seat of authority as to right and wrong, time and eternity, heaven and hell, that was found only in each purified, enlightened, individual human soul.*—Theodore Parker, plunging into the deep abyss of the Absolute Religion, or forging thunderbolts more dire than Jove's and hurling them forth in the presence of crowds with extraordinary effect: yet not so deeply sunk in the unfathomed spiritual depths but that he could rise on occasion and rush to the underground passage and help to set free the negro slaves.—Matthew Arnold, displaying in

*Inquirer, May 10th, 1890.

abundance his " Sweetness and Light," but with none to spare for Dissenting Philistines: describing with eloquence the Power outside ourselves that makes for righteousness, but without recognition of that other power that makes for unrighteousness, and which often seems the greater power of the two.—Goethe, entertained in royal palaces, honoured and entitled by great Universities, with a life-story of an intensely interesting kind, and yet, which contains revelations which jar on one's nerves like the Confessions of Rosseau: with his masterpiece, Faust, a splendidly-gifted mortal, like himself eagerly forcing his way through all realms of knowledge, and yet, not able to master himself and lead a moral life, but must needs bring poor Margaret to shame and then go straight to the devil himself.—George Eliot, displaying indiscreet courage in uniting herself to Mr. Lewis; shewing a wiser courage in translating and publishing the " Leben Jesu " of Straus, a work ever potent with Biblical students with open minds; and in producing her splendid and potent novels, with their portraiture of Adam Bede, Dinah Morris, Silas Marner, Felix Holt, and other worthies which the world will not soon let die.—Tennyson, blending with marvellous subtlety belief and unbelief, irony and sincerity, imagination and reason: presenting in his " In Memoriam " a sublime and undying requiem for departed friends: setting forth his gorgeous drama of Arthur and the Knights of the Round Table, who, in romantic and picturesque scenes, have again their being, and live and move before our eyes; as does the strikingly realistic figure of " The Northern Farmer," whose churchgoing experience so exactly represents the religious experience of great numbers of church and chapel goers of the present day.—Henry Ward Beecher, presenting his panoramic discourses, in the study of which we seem to hear the musical murmur of water-brooks, the solemn swell of ocean waves, the æolean chantings of the wind in majestic trees, and seem to see the brilliant sunshine flashing over the whole scene described.—And Darwin, startling the world with his revelations; arousing wild hosts of clerical Dame Partingtons, who are rushing and splashing around with their futile besoms to keep back the mighty tide of evolution which is swamping their antiquated and dying creeds, and threatening to sweep all dead and decaying theological rubbish out of the world.

My joy and inspiration from these studies were often interrupted by influences of a very different kind. Gospel I had to leave, and go to law. On the death of an old trustee who had formerly been Secretary, Treasurer, and Committee, a request was made for a statement of chapel accounts. In reply, it was stated that account books were unintelligible, and that only a small amount of money was due to the chapel. After a long and weary correspondence, I proposed a compromise, which was accepted and the matter closed.

Sad to say, my peace was of short duration, as more legal troubles came soon to hand. A coal seam belonging to the Chapel Trust, it was found, had been invaded by a mine-owner near. Much affirmation and negation ensued, and hundreds of letters were written. And, horror of horrors! the letters from our solicitor were addressed to me, with requests for immediate reply. He was well paid for every letter he wrote, while I was not paid for one. Indeed, I would gladly have paid a sum down to have been delivered from everlasting replies.

The case appeared in court, and eminent councillors engaged. Appeals were made from one court to another, and the matter became appalling. I felt as if I were in the coil of an anaconda, from which there was no escape. Great, however, was my mental relief occasionally when I was called to preach on the Sunday at neighbouring chapels.

My first visit to Rivington was a memorable event. The sanctuary, I found, was a quaint, snug, ancient, and beautifully-situated building. In the congregation, several persons specially arrested my attention, one of whom, happily, invited me to dine with him. He was a venerable, mild-looking, well-mannered gentleman, and well stricken in years. He was a bachelor, or widower, and his household was small. He had long since retired from business at Bolton, where he had filled many civic offices, and rendered good service to the town. His conversation was literary and religious. He had for many years been a Spiritualist, and expatiated delightfully on the pursuits of a future life. Not for many years had I held such sweet counsel, except with my brother, on spiritual things. In a sort of enchantment I walked through the fields to the station on that memorable Sunday night.

On a subsequent Sunday, I was entertained by Mr. J. Crompton, generally designated the Squire of Rivington. He took me through some of his gardens, farmlands, and outbuildings some distance from the Hall in which he lived. Very interesting it was to hear him describe the cattle, trees, and general produce of the farm. He was evidently an advanced scientific agriculturalist, as also a well-read, scholarly gentleman. Mrs. Crompton was a fine-looking, genial lady, often absorbed in books and music, sometimes in domestic arrangements, but absorbed most of all in attentions to her fine baby boy. In this sylvan retreat, in this another Sabine farm—

"Far from the madding crowd's ignoble strife,"

this happy family

"Led the even tenor of their way."

Rivington Hall had, indeed, its inspirations, which I had the privilege of experiencing from time to time.

Very different was my experience in the Borsdane woodland valleys nearer home. True, there was music in the running brooks and in the wind whistling through the trees; but there were nearly always the loud and discordant voices of rough and roving bands of men and lads. Passing at all times were black-faced pitmen, who would always have some amusement at the expense of passers by. "Na', pason, con't tell us what's up this tree?" "That is nothing to what is up this tree," I would reply. "Na', pason, con't preach us a sarmon?" "Yes, this is is—'The way of transgressors is hard. The path of the just is as the shining light which shineth brighter and brighter unto the perfect day'." "Ah! ah!" and laughter. "But na', pason, con't tell us out abait the sarpent that tauked in the garden?" "Yes, there are a lot hereabout." "What are th' loike?" "Just like fellows with black faces and sharp tongues." "Guffau! guffau! Hoora! hoora!"

Going through a small inclosed field behind the chapel, I once saw a crowd of colliers, and heard the sound of heavy bumping in the midst of them, and stood a moment looking on. "Na' then," shouted some one, "here's pason; let him see"; and there two men each on his hands and knees I could see butting their heads together. There was no biting, nor scratching, nor kicking going on, but simply a banging of the two heads together. "Na', pason, wil't have a go?" said one. "Nou," said another, "his yead's too soft." "Ah!" cried several, "au parsons' yeads are soft." "Ah! made a squash," said others. Amid loud guffaws I departed thence. This, I was informed, was a common way of settling disputes. Another strange diversion, I was told, was formerly very common, which was a sort of night orgie. A treat would be given to as many men and women as could be crowded into the largest room in the largest public house. For some hours they would sit freely drinking ale and spirits until late in the night, when suddenly the door would be locked, the lights put out, and a general scrimmage begin. When, in some half-hour, the candles were lighted, the scene was astounding. All chairs and tables were overturned and broken, all faces daubed black or red or yellow, all clothing torn and stuck over with old ribbons, rags and tatters, and everyone's hair dishevelled, so that it was impossible to tell who was who. I do not think these night orgies took place in the township while I was in it, although very curious and very objectionable things were done then.

Personally, I never received harm from these original and primitive people, but often received acts of kindness. Frequently a collier would come to the Parsonage with a huge fossil stone on his shoulder, saying, "Here's a big cob which you may have and welcome." When, as happened sometimes, one met with rough speech, it could be easily and effectively parried by a little quiet wit. Unfortunately, this testimony of immunity from injury could not be made by my poor wife, who received an injury which caused her long and intense suffering, and maimed her for life. Going down Ladies' Lane carrying some garments to the house of a young man who had been seriously hurt in a coal-pit, she was overtaken by a crowd of colliers, who rushed against her with such force that she was knocked down, and lay unconscious in the road for some minutes. At length some passer-by lifted her up, placed her in a conveyance, and brought her home. Besides other injuries, the doctor found a thigh-bone disjointed. She was boarded and strapped, and placed in bed in a certain position in which she remained six months. A specialist was engaged, who examined the fracture, and said she would never be able to walk again: and she never did, except on crutches and in great pain. A great longing came over her to get home to Macclesfield, which communicated itself to me.

Under the influence of depression, and borne down with hard and anxious work, my gaze would sometimes fix on the distant hills, now darkened with solemn-looking clouds, and now again bathed in sunlight glory. Although they seemed to invite me to ascend to their summits and there find temporary rest and peace, it was very seldom I could obey this behest. Happily, however, once a year, in company with my brother Samuel, the ascent was joyously made. Memorable occasions were these, every one of them. Much was said, but much more was felt which could not be expressed. Reminiscences crowded on our minds. Incidents of our pilgrimages over the Derbyshire and Cheshire hills were recalled with the greatest delight. The trials, the struggles, the conquests, the defeats we had met with; the friends we had made, the enemies we could not escape; the books we had read, the duties we had done or left undone, came up for searching review. Then followed the formation of life-plans for the future, quickening our aspirations and awakening new and cheering hopes. The last of these indescribably interesting occasions came in the Easter week of the year 1880.

My health had long been breaking down, and so from incessant overwork, had his. We felt and said we must have more rest of body and mind, or we should soon have the rest of the grave. On his return he would at once rearrange matters at home. Then as soon as possible I must leave Hindley, and return to our native scenes. Together, then, we could become familiar with the loved haunts of other days. We could climb the hills, walk along the field paths in the valleys, traverse the hidden and sheltered roads, with all of which we had been so sweetly familiar in the long past years. How glowing and comforting were these anticipations! How awfully terrible the disappointment which suddenly came!

In the succeeding month of May I was hastily summoned to the side of his bed, on which he was visibly dying. Only with choking sobs could I utter parting words. I stammered out the passage, " Though I walk through the valley of the shadow of death, I will fear no evil; for Thou art with me," which he caught up and repeated with a brightening countenance, and evidently with an uplifting heart and mind. Happily, he was more calm and resigned than I was myself. Shortly, amid awful pains, but with bright hopes, he passed hence away.

I managed, somehow, to get to the side of his grave, where I felt as if transfixed, and with only the wish to be laid beside him there, and that my spirit should pass away with his into the heavenly realm. At times, for several days, my heart almost ceased to beat, and my life seemed ebbing away.

At Hindley I could, now, find no repose. No more would he come to visit and cheer me. I must away and seek peace in scenes common to us both. I at once gave notice to resign my ministerial charge. Very soon the time of departure was at hand. The farewell party was held in the School, when Mr. Paul Partington, Clerk of Pemberton Local Board, took the chair, and spoke of my influence over him and a band of men and women who came all the way from Westhoughton to the Sunday services in the Hindley Chapel. Rev. Henry Banks, Congregationalist, gave a graphic account of the battles for reform we had fought together in the Public Hall and elsewhere. Revs. C. C. Coe and Herbert Mills of Bolton made bright and sympathetic speeches. Revs. George Fox and George Ride said kindly farewell words. Mr. John Jones, Trustee, told of large success in the Chapel and School during the last twelve years. Mr. Abram Hurst, representing the oldest family connected with the Chapel, presented a purse of gold. The purse was not very heavy, but contained a fair sum, considering the position of the givers. Mr. James Platt and Mr. Unsworth spoke in kindly words of the good work done in Hindley by Mrs. Rushton and myself. And then this touching, trying, farewell meeting closed.

A last look was given to the Chapel and School, so much improved in appearance within the last twelve years, and doing so much better work than before. A farewell was also taken of Borsdane Wood and river, and of Rivington Pike, bright with the sunshine beaming over it, and of the genial and noble-souled friends living on its slopes. We were only a few minutes at the station, and then glided away from the region of smoke, cinder heaps, slagg, and sulphur, toward the Hills of Beulah situated between the old town of Macclesfield and Buxton beyond.

On a dark, sad, and dreary day in November, 1880, we reached our house in the old town to rest a little time until the end should come. That time was not likely to be long in coming either to my wife or to myself. Only with the help of crutches could she move a little about the house. I was in a sick, weak, wan, and spasmodic condition. With the ability to work gone, what would life be to either of us now? But for our ever-faithful helper Gertrude, we should have been in a helpless condition. There was at least rest and quiet, which until now we had never known. But rest, if continued long, becomes more tiresome than toil. Favourite books, however, were at hand, which had often proved the best and most helpful friends. But if the noble thoughts of such friends be not transmuted by the reader into noble deeds, what then? In such a case, does not inspiration cease, and the soul become dull and inert? Is it, then, possible for a confirmed invalid on the verge of the grave to speak or write some true and touching word before passing hence? And might not such message reach some open and sensitive soul, and prompt it to noble impulses and worthy deeds? Certainly, while life is continued some useful work can and must be done. And thus " Hope springs eternal in the human breast." Athwart our darkest days flash Hope's golden rays. The dream divine will not leave us long if we only court its stay. By and by, these dreary winter days will have passed, and spring-time be here again.

In the garden, on the sunny side of the house, I may possibly be able to do some little work and gain increased health. Then a Sunday School may be visited, or a Chapel attended. And so, happily, after a time, these things came to pass. The first meeting I attended was in a Conventicle built on land belonging to Mr. Roe, who forbade in all his trust deeds any Dissenting worship being held on his estates. Mr. Edward Hammond, who built the chapel without recognizing this proscription, received orders to stop the services or quit the place. Mr. Hammond quitted the premises, and quitted the country at the same time. He and his brother John, with their families, emigrated to America, intending to secure land on which they could work and worship in the way they thought best. The religious expulsions undergone by the Hammonds up to this time were numerous and curious, and showed the penalties incurred by fidelity to truth.

From the Fence Sunday School, for pointing out defects in the Bible, they had to depart. From the Unitarian Sunday School, for the defence of advanced religious thinkers, they, with nearly all the teachers, were ordered to retire. From Parsonage Street Chapel, for being smirched with Spiritualism, they were shunted aside. From the new chapel in Great King Street by a persecuting trust deed, they and their friends were ignominiously cast out. Then out of a persecuting country they cast themselves, and sought a free home in a free land.

At the farewell meeting I wished the two families a safe voyage to America, and success in the new life on their own land, with no more expulsions or orders to quit. Edward Hammond settled on land sloping down to the Pacific Ocean. From his home in California he could look down on the gleaming waves of the mighty sea. Ah, indeed! I too, had once glorious dreams of a free home in that great western world. But now I have to be, and am, content with this cottage and garden, from which I have sight of Ecton Woods, the Parnassus of my early days. Here I ought to rest as calmly and contentedly with the trees, and flowers, and birds around me as I could in the boundless prairies or endless forests of the great Transatlantic World.

CHAPTER XXVIII

RESUMED MINISTRY

My health having improved a little, I visited Parsonage Street Chapel and School. But alas! all the old friends and workers had departed thence, and the new race of rulers knew me not. I was cautioned against the Spiritualists, who had been compelled to leave the Chapel and School. But what good can there be in a religious society without spiritualism of some kind? It is simply a society on its way to decay and death. I sometimes preached in the Chapel and lectured in the School. But going through these services was like sleepily gliding on Lethe's waters, when all the faculties of body and mind become gradually benumbed and inert.

When efforts were made to create new life in the Chapel and School, many objections were raised. The old, easy, drowsy, droning ways were preferred to anything new. Under such circumstances my labour was in vain, and I sorrowfully departed thence. But there was the old chapel in King Edward Street. Should I be able to worship there in rest and peace of mind?

The history of this ancient sanctuary was of a most interesting kind. The glamour of antiquity was over it. Next to St. Michael's Church, it was the oldest place of worship in the town. The descendants of Cromwellian soldiers might have attended and given vigorous help at its earliest services. Sharp theological conflicts had taken place within its walls. The wit, wisdom, and eloquence of its able ministers had been flowing from that carved oaken pulpit during two hundred years. Led by curiosity, I had entered its portal in my early days, with fear and trembling as to results. Later on, I was irresistibly drawn to the place by the thought-compelling discourses of Vance Smith, the plain, practical preaching of John Wright, the fine deliverances of Coulston, of Dean Row, the surpassing eloquence of William Gaskell, and the poetic utterances of T. E. Poynting, who glowingly descanted on "The Heaven that Lies Around Us," and made these words the title of a fine work which he wrote and published.

With all these crowding associations about the ancient sanctuary there ought to be uplifting inspirations in all its services. In feebleness of body, I might here, surely, find strengthening of soul. In this venerable earthly temple I might get vivid glimpses of the temple not made with hands, eternal in the heavens. Having no longer the anxieties of a settled minister, I might on the day of rest lay myself open to such continual streams of divine influence as flow into the undistracted soul after a long, active, and not useless life.

Such were my hopes, desires, and intentions: alas! only fulfilled to a very limited extent. I attended the services regularly for a time, and sometimes preached, but with little fervour of spirit. An antipathetic influence seemed to pervade the place. Instead of divine fire warming each soul, a chilling insensitiveness prevailed and ruled over all. Was it a guardian angel that whispered the words, "Arise ye, and depart; for this is not your rest"? If it were so, the messenger omitted to say where rest might be found.

But just at this juncture I was approached by certain friends who said, "Come thou with us, and we will do thee good." "When and where?" I asked. "To-day, and to an upper room in Derby Street," was the reply. Upper room indeed! How suggestive are those words! And what an illustrious history they have! They remind us of the brave and noble heretics of all the ages of time. Upper rooms rank with dens and caves, with forest depths and mountain clefts, as the holiest places on earth. The meeting of the disciples in the upper room at Jerusalem was only one of the innumerable heretical meetings, each as holy as itself. One such upper room was that in Lower Hurdsfield, where a band of pilgrims and strangers, outcasts from the popular synagogues, joined in free and happy worship and work which I conducted so long ago.

And here in Derby Street, it seems, is another upper room exactly of the same kind. Hidden away from the tumultuous world, forcibly separated from the great popular churches, I found a band of twenty-five brave, thoughtful, and devout men and women. Here were the Rogers family, originally Methodists, and now Spiritualists and Unitarians, and as earnest and devout as in their Methodist days.

The Hammond family was represented by Widow Pimblott and her two daughters, all with a tendency to heretical inquiry like their kindred now gone over the sea. The Proctor sisters, both mediumistic, took part in the service which ensued. Hayes, Gunn, Burgess, Woolam, and Lovett were the names of parties present.

Proceedings opened with a familiar hymn and tune, which seemed to produce a sweet repose of mind. Then a brief prayer lifted us nearer heaven. A scripture reading, with comments, awakened within myself the old love of Bible instruction and inspiration. My address was attended, as the Methodists say, with holy unction from above. Every one present seemed in a gracious and happy mood of mind. Such experiences I had often known both in my early days and later days, all of which had left blessed influences in their train. But then came revelations I had never known. A medium became controlled by invisible beings, it was said. Certainly the descriptions given were of a marvellous kind. The tones, looks, and attitudes of my mother—whom no one present, but myself, had ever seen— were displayed exactly to the life. Brother Samuel, shy, retiring, aspiring, was said to be present, as I was sure he would be if he found it possible to come. Edward Davenport, bound by contract to meet me at death, had come, it seemed, in great serenity of mind to visit me sooner than either of us had thought.

The ecstasy of that evening did not soon pass away. Thenceforth that upper room became a Bethel indeed. A ladder reaching heaven was certainly there. Not imaginary angels, but real spiritual beings, as it seemed, descended and ascended that heavenly pathway, leaving thrilling messages behind. An elevating influence was ever experienced at each stated meeting. Life for myself had new hopes and new interests. With improving health, I devoted some hours each day to gardening work. Interest in trees, flowers, and birds became as fresh as in my early years. Late despondency was left behind, and I felt again the great joy of being alive.

In June, 1881, a deputation came to me to say that a large room in Paradise Street had been leased for seven years to the Society, and that I had been unanimously elected as minister. "But," I said, "you are Spiritualists, and I am a Unitarian minister." "True," they replied, "but in face of those facts you are elected minister of our Society, and we cannot take a refusal." "But," I said, "I can only serve in a Free Church." "Be it so," they replied, and placed the title "Free Church" on the front of the building. At the same time, it was understood I should not be required to speak on every Sunday in the year. As a matter of fact, I was present at nearly all services, both on Sundays and week-evenings.

Nearly seven years this connection continued, and a glorious time it was. If dark clouds sometimes rolled over our sky, they seemed only there to reveal the wealth and splendour of the silver and golden glory with which they were lined.

From the first I determined to have a Sunday School, and soon over thirty scholars were enrolled. The elder part of them were formed into a class of my own, and every Sunday afternoon I had the great joy of meeting these young men and women. Included in this interesting class were Samuel Hayes, Charles Challinor, William Challinor, William Pimblott, George Gunn, Hannah Pimblott, Harriet Pimblott, Ada Lovett, Alice Dickens and Lilly Rogers. All these have done well in life. Some of them became the leaders and most active and useful members of the congregation and School in Cumberland Street. My own benefit was great indeed. Health of body and mind considerably increased. Thus it came to pass that the two ends of my life were completely harmonized and united together.

The memory of my connection with the old Sunday School in Hurdsfield, in my early days, had always been unspeakably enchanting; and now I was plunged into the last enchantment, which was just as rich and sweet as the first.

The class-books used in the Sunday School were numerous, and all of them excellent for the purposes in view. The Bible was read and freely discussed, but with due reverence and respect. Scientific readings, with questions and answers, familiarised us, to some extent, with the wonders of the universe. Botanic readings were made interesting by flowers and shrubs presented for illustration. English literary history placed our minds in close contact with the works of great men, from Caedmon through Chaucer, Milton and Shakespeare, to Tennyson in our own time.

"The Story of Religion in England," by Brooke Herford, was read over again and again, and created a strong zest for a still wider study of historic lore. Not the least interesting of our studies was that of Philology. The ground-work of these studies we had in "Butler's Spelling Book." Given a Greek root, what English words had been derived from that? Given a Latin root, what words had grown from it? The answers often showed much ingenuity and good judgment. Indeed, after a time, the process became easy and pleasant. Hence, the exact history and meaning of many hundreds of important English words became quite familiar to most of the learners. In some a strong desire was created for more knowledge of the same kind, and thus a foundation was laid for a clear and exact use of our noble English language.

A Singing Class was successfully carried on, and greatly aided the services in both Chapel and School. A Phonography Class, also, was established, which proved to be of much benefit to several of the learners in after years. Thus our weeks, months, and years glided on harmoniously and usefully at our sanctuary in Paradise Street.

But, although our proceedings went on quietly and without ostentation, we did not escape attacks from without. Mr. S.

—— who was a patron of the Dams Mission Room, did not like us, and often spoke against us. One day he said to me that a woman from the Mission had ventured to attend one of our meetings, and had been greatly terrified at the spirits there. "Did she see or hear any spirits?" I inquired. That he could not say, but was sure she was much afraid. "Do you never mention the subject of spirits at the Mission?" I asked. "But our spirits," he replied, "are not like yours." "What, exactly, are your spirits like?" I asked. The question puzzled him. He could not say what their spirits were like, nor what they said, nor what they did. Running away from the subject, he exclaimed, "You do not believe that Jesus Christ is God?" "How is Jesus Christ God?" I asked. "Look at Christ's own words, 'I and the Father are one,'" said Mr. S.——. "And look again," I said, "at Christ's words when He prays that His disciples 'may be *one* in us,' which, according to your argument, imply the existence of more Gods than either I or you desire."

Mr. S. —— was the patron of Richard Weaver, the revivalist who made a strong personal attack on me in the large Sunday School in Roe Street. In my reply, before a crowded audience in our Chapel, I pointed out Weaver's mistakes, exposed his misrepresentations, and related some of the amusing incidents which happened at my interview with him and his interlined Greek Testament. In a succeeding chapter will be found a full account of the grotesque scenes witnessed on this extraordinary occasion.

Another attack on our Society was made by the Rev. Mr. Ashcroft during several meetings he held in the large School. His discourses were made up of ludicrous caricatures, and, of course, drew crowded audiences. Application was made for the use of the School in which to reply. A peremptory refusal was given, which led to a sharp controversy in the local newspapers. In the end, the managers of the School came to the decision that the School should not again be let to Mr. Ashcroft nor any other party for religious partizan controversy.

Another and more trying opposition came from a certain party, in a certain congregation, who continuously urged the editor of the Unitarian Almanac to erase the name of our Society from the congregational list. A long and painful correspondence was carried on in a local paper, and in the "Unitarian Herald." As long, however, as Mr. Phillips remained connected with the Almanac, the name of the Society remained on the list. But on his death it was at once expunged. Still, even yet, the Society was unwilling to be separated from the Unitarian Churches, and so made application for admission into the Provincial Assembly of Lancashire and Cheshire. This time the reply was courteous, but there could be no admission. Inasmuch as the Chapel was held on lease and not on ownership trust, admission to the Provincial Assembly could not be obtained. In this isolated state the Society must bravely pursue its independent course, and vigorously plough its religious and educational furrows alone. In seeking union, the Society did not seek for monetary or ministerial help, but simply sought to unite with a brotherhood to which it was so nearly akin. Indeed, personally, I had never separated from it.

But another important change, both for myself and the congregation, was at hand. For some years past, I had been induced to undertake certain public duties which I had not strength to perform. Having in public contended that every man ought to be a politician, I was taken at my word, and pressed into political service. Having commended co-operative societies, I was placed on the committee of the local co-operative society, and kept busy in educational affairs.

Taking interest in the reconstruction of the Useful Knowledge Society, I was appointed Secretary of the new Society, which required considerable thought and labour.

But all these duties came suddenly to a close. Long failing health ended in complete nervous collapse. At a congregational farewell meeting I received many valuable presents and more valuable benedictions, and thus my ministerial career came to a final close in the sixty-eighth year of my age.

CHAPTER XXIX

THE MACCLESFIELD AMATEUR PARLIAMENT

IN the years 1880 and 1881 came the great boom of Local Parliaments. Never before had such an extensive confusion of tongues in this country been known. Carlyle tried to limit the exercise of other men's tongues by a liberal use of his own. And just then, in most considerable towns, crowds of young men were meeting in debating societies, each party trying to show that the language of the other party had neither ornament, nor use, nor worth.

Having become Speaker of the Macclesfield Local Parliament, I had to make the best of a babel of tongues. Previous experience in debate for many years in many places had prepared me for the position. And, besides, I had a strong conviction that public debate, if rightly conducted, was an excellent means of finding and defending truth. The meetings were held in the Townley Street Schools, and were arranged in the following manner: On one side of a long table sat the leaders of the Liberal Party, with their supporters massed behind. On the other side of the table were massed the leaders and supporters of the Conservative Party. On the cross benches at the foot of the table were seated the Free lances, ready to hurl a javelin at either of the other parties, just as they saw fit. At the head of the table, on a raised platform sat the Speaker, duly arrayed.

When the Liberals were in office, the Prime Minister was Mr. — McGloon, a rather tall, good-looking young man, with a fair command of language, a distinct utterance, forcible emphasis, and the gift of eloquent peroration. When the Conservatives were in office, the Premier was Mr. T. Savage, a slim-built, rather low-set young man, with a bright, intelligent face, alertness of speech, and evident tenacity of purpose. One of the ablest members of the Liberal Cabinet was Mr. Andrew Cross, an active, although burly, young Scotchman. The strong northern burr in his speech seemed to give force to the wit and wisdom, not to say overflowing fun, of his words. In his frequent interruptions and interjections, he was an exact set-off to the Tory Premier, Mr. Savage, who could always throw in a word or phrase during a pause in an opponent's speech. A faithful colleague of Mr. Cross was Mr. Adam Cooper, a young man of middle height, stout build, and with a voice clear, distinct, and musical. His language was coherent and grammatical, and would have become very effective if he had made speeches oftener. His ancestors for two or three generations had been Methodists. How he had escaped becoming a local and then an itinerant preacher, I never learned. It could not have been heresy that barred the way to the ministry, as in my case. Still, he held broad and liberal and independent views on many things, and thus became disqualified from becoming an obedient minister, in the judgment of official superiors.

Another gifted member of the Liberal Cabinet was Mr. J. W. White, a tall, fair-complexioned, pleasant-looking young man. His diction was good, and his voice clear, if not very strong. But his speech would have become more effective if he had spoken more frequently. His want of readiness to speak on request was a disappointment to his party. In this respect he was the very opposite of his able and oratorical father, who was always ready at a moment's notice to rush in and storm the enemy's camp.

Mr. Mobey was a middle sized, firmly built, fair complexioned, clear skinned, pleasant faced young man. He was a staunch and consistent Liberal member of the Cabinet, who however, preferred throwing interjections into opponents' speeches to making speeches of his own to be subject to similar interjections.

Mr. George Gunn was rather low set, but well built, with a

strong head and face, with keen eyes and broad, large, firm nose. Moreover, he had a fine, clear, strong voice, fully displayed in frequent recitations and dramatic representations, but only in the briefest remarks in the parliament house.

As members of the same cabinet, the brothers Newton, tall, well-made men, did good service with a small amount of public speech. In this respect they followed the example of their father, who, for a great number of years, was a hard worker as Councilman and Alderman, but hardly ever spoke in public. These silent workers, however, have a noble function in making up the deficiences of such as speak much but work little.

Mr. Henry Rushton was of middle height, slim in form, and quick of walk. He was skilful, honourable, and successful in business; but as a member of the Liberal cabinet he shrank from public speaking, although fluent enough in business circles.

Mr. Samuel Hayes was a sprightly-looking young man of medium height and slender form, and of quick movements. As an official of the Liberal cabinet, he had to make speeches, but they were short, and few and far between. Nevertheless, he was preparing for good public service elsewhere, including the long presidency of an advanced and successful religious society in the town.

The Liberal government having been overthrown and a Conservative government set up in its place, we proceed to notice the several members of which the new cabinet was formed. Its Premier—Mr. T. Savage—we have already described, and pass on to notice his chief lieutenant, Mr. Fountain, a middle-sized, stout, energetic, and decisive young man. His voice was fairly good, and his little hesitancies of speech he struggled perseveringly against, and nearly, if not entirely, overcame. He has acknowledged the aid received in these exercises in preparing him for his future career, which has proved to be one of incessant and useful activity. Besides conducting very successfully a business of his own, he has, for a great number of years, rendered valuable service to the town as Councillor, Alderman, and Mayor.

In the same cabinet was Mr. H. Mitchell, of middle height and sprightly manners, who was always present at the meetings and attentive to his duties. His attitude in speaking caused considerable amusement. Rising to speak, he placed one foot on a chair, while on the uplifted knee he placed his paper of notes, which he held firmly with one hand while holding a pencil in the other hand, and seemed as if he were going to take notes and make a speech at the same time. On one or two occasions he tried to stand straight while speaking, but the speech would not go on; but lifting the foot on to the chair, the speech went freely enough.

The attitudes of speakers are of wonderful variety and very interesting to notice, but the observer should never let a speaker become aware of such observation. A popular Manchester preacher was so strongly affected by a printed description of his attitudes in the pulpit, that for some time he could not speak at all without great embarrassment. The different attitudes gone through by Mr. Gladstone in a single speech amounted to some forty to fifty, but the numbers were greatly exceeded during a speech by Lord Churchill. I do not suppose that either of these statesmen would have their equanimity disturbed by any enumeration of their gymnastic feats during their harangues.

A notable member of the Tory cabinet was a young man of middle height, slight build, and vigorous action. His speeches were earnest and vociferous, and his gesticulations so far-reaching as to endanger the heads of his colleagues. He aimed at great oratorical effect, and might have attained his object with wise and persevering restraint of voice and limbs. He was engaged in a law office at Churchside, where he stayed late at nights to practice elocution and recite his speeches for parliament. These exercises were heard and reported, accompanied with the statement that the very dead in the graveyard were stirred in their coffins, and sent their ghosts to protest against being disturbed by the loud tearing of his oratorical rags to tatters. This annoyed him, and made his diction more scathing than before. He should have met derision like Disraeli, and quietly said, "The time will come when you will hear me."

A very different individual was his colleague, Mr. Cave, a middle-aged, broad-set, grave, and thoughtful-looking man. His speeches were calm, sensible, and impressive, and secured attention. Inquiring about Mr. Cave, I found that by self-education he had stored up much useful knowledge. He had become well read in popular science, natural history, and general literature. As a Sunday School teacher and occasional lecturer he had brought forth his treasures new and old for the edification of all attentive learners in his classes and meetings. He appeared to have been altogether a very worthy man.

The cross benches were occupied by Independents, Individualists, cranks, and nondescripts. From this part of the house a fluent Irishman delivered perfervid orations on the wrongs of Ireland, and on its claims of justice from England. Unfortunately, these appeals met with indifference instead of sympathy.

A Mr. Mason moved the house considerably by ultra-Radical and Socialistic harangues. On one occasion he caused much excitement by speaking of Ingersoll's "Mistakes of Moses." An uproar was prevented by ruling the subject out of order. The incident led to much outside discussion. The majority of the assembly had never before heard of the book or its author, but judged from its title that the book was wicked and blasphemous, and that the author was an infidel. A few of the orthodox had heard the book condemned, and so, without reading it themselves, joined in its condemnation. A fewer number of real truth-seekers had read the book, and although not agreeing with all its statements, were much impressed by its contents. My own opinion was that the logic of the book was cogent, its language eloquent, and its facts indisputable. As to Ingersoll himself, I could enter into and fully adopt the favourable description of him by the Rev. Henry Ward Beecher, who declared him to be one of the greatest orators that America had ever produced. The best answer to the excited Bible worshippers was, I contended, "that they did not know everything down in Judee."

Personal criticism of the speakers was trenchant and continuous, both in the house and in the public press of the town. Some of the members replied in kind, and with interest, and grew bold and daring. Others shrunk from the ordeal, and were silent or fled. These personal attacks had considerable educational value, as a few illustrations may show. In continuance of an incessant practice, a certain member said, "I rise to a point of order," pronouncing the word "point" as "pint." "Make it a quart," exclaimed someone. "Yes, a quart! a quart!" exclaimed others, amid roars of laughter. The original culprit apologized by saying he was trying to prevent the murder of a diphthong. And sure it was—such murders became fewer and farther between. In a debate on the army and navy, a member spoke emphatically about "the harmy and 'orses," and became much shocked and disconcerted by the laughter that ensued. But both he and others were led to pay more respect to the letter "h" than they had previously done.

Many of the speakers made free use of the interjections "Eh!" "Hem!" "Haw!" to fill up stops at the end of sentences. With many aristocratic speakers, it is said, these gap-stoppers are inevitable, and form the most notable points of their discourses. In the Free Trade Hall, Manchester, I once listened to a speaker of this kind, who, during one of his pauses was much upset by a man shouting, "Leave out the burrs and stops, and get on." For a while the burrs and stops increased, but the speech soon ended, to the relief of everyone but the speaker himself.

Any public man inclined to these excrescences of speech should strive with his utmost power to get clear of them. Certain stock phrases, much used as props in speaking, were constantly in evidence in the house, such as "I beg to say," "As I said before," and "As it were." I once heard this last phrase used over twenty times in a discourse of fifteen minutes by a student training for the ministry. When he told the tutor he did not know he had used the words once, the amusement was great. But the correction did the student good, who somehow managed to speak without using this special prop quite so often as before. The trick of extending a word now and then in a speech might be sometimes heard in the house. A most striking exhibition of this peculiar trick was given in the speeches of a clergyman of this town. The word "command" would be sounded "command-d-d-d-d." The word "overmuch" would be sounded "overmuch-ch-ch-ch." The word "walking" would be extended into "walking-ng-ng-ng-ng." Two or three times in a speech these extensions would come out, which some of his hearers listened for and greatly enjoyed.

That curious but involuntary manœuvre by which the initial letters of adjoining words become transposed was occasionally displayed by one or two members of the house. This ludicrous proceeding may be illustrated by the case of the curate, who, when repeating the passage, "Do men gather grapes of thorns or figs of thistles?" said, "Do men gather thrapes of gorns or thigs of fistles—I mean, fistles of thigs?" Of course, a speaker's trick of that kind must at once be mended or his public speaking ended.

Letters having reference to the proceedings in parliament, which appeared in the local newspapers, were sometimes witty, humorous, funny, and sarcastic, but never ill-natured. Some of these letters were instructive, inspiring, and soothing. The following extracts are from a letter in "The Macclesfield Chronicle" dated December 23rd, 1881, and signed "A Voice from the Ladies' Gallery":—

> "Place me on Sunium's marbled steep,
> Where nothing save the waves and I
> May hear our mutual murmurs sweep."

"Not many of us will climb as Byron did that marbled steep, nor hear the waves of the blue Egean Sea dashing at its foot beneath. But hardly less interesting is it from our own position here to listen to the waves of human emotion and passion as they rise and fall below. But now, on the eve of Christmas, laying aside all strife and contention, and forgiving and forgetting all enmities and offences, let us enter into the true spirit of the season, and feel that we are all brethren and sisters of that same Jesus Christ whose advent was heralded by angel voices singing, 'Glory to God in the highest, and on earth peace and goodwill to men.'"

A certain member delivered in a loud tone a rapid flow of words with the fewest and faintest ideas. A letter in one of the papers applied to him the following words of Dean Swift, "It is with narrow-souled people as it is with narrow-necked bottles, the less they have in them the more noise they make in pouring it out." Rather severe, certainly, but still useful if only it prompted the speaker to secure ideas as well as words.

Another letter advised a member to keep to the reading of his notes, and not to attempt extempore speech, as the instant he opened his mouth he put his foot into it. The advice was good, although roughly put. The best thing, no doubt, for a new speaker would be to read his notes until he could read them well, and then proceed to speak extempore until he could do that well.

Under the signature of "Clara Sherwood," several letters appeared in the papers full of humorous descriptions of the names and trades of the members of the house. In reference to the elder of the Newton brothers—a silk dyer—she says, "He is so tall, and thin, and stiff that he might pass for a giant's walking-stick if he were pushed into a corner. But no one could push him nor sit on him without being hurt in a tender place. His address was a fair one, although towards the end he seemed shaky as if going to die. But Agnes Copperfield whispered to me that he was not going to die, but to dye, seeing he dyes to live and lives to dye."

The same writer, in reference to Adam Cooper, says, "He dresses well and not gaily, and is gentlemanly in his manner. If there should be another Garden of Eden, Adam would, of course, be there, and if there were a vinery he would be the Cooper to make casks for the wine, and then I would be his Eve."

In reference to a member who was in the drink trade, Agnes Copperfield says, "There is always an exasperating smile on his phiz, whether owing to the strong spirits he keeps I cannot say. Clara, who has some knowledge of British and Foreign, as well as that dealt in at the Spiritualist Chapel in Paradise Street in the Dams, will be best able to judge. By the way, how strange it is to find Paradise in the Dam(n)s!" Such wit or witticism as this may not be of a high order, but the exercise of it in this way might lead to the expression of a higher order of humour in later times. As to the parties assailed by these harmless jokes, they should thereby be the better prepared for the far harder rubs and scrubs they would get as they jostled their way through life amongst their fellow-men.

As Speaker, a considerable amount of animadversion, favourable and the reverse, fell to my lot. Agnes declared that "the ladies in the gallery much admired the Speaker sitting so majestically on his throne and presiding with so much dignity and authority over the house, but I hope his wife will not be jealous."

Clara wrote saying that "although the Speaker was a Reverend Gentleman, there was nothing gloomy about him. The remarkable twinkles in his eyes seemed to indicate that there was a good deal of mischief lurking within him." Again wrote Clara, "I would fain tell of my feelings as I gazed on the scene in the house below. At one moment as calm as a May day at the coast when you climb the hill side, and look down on the still and placid waters below; when you feel as if the great thoughts of an Infinite Being crept upon your soul: but there comes a sudden rush, and the gloom gathers and the lightnings flash, and the thunders peal. I have gazed on these scenes with strongly-excited feelings, and if there was one thing that charmed me beyond another, it was that when the storm was over the Speaker invariably sent forth a dove with an olive branch, and all was peace again."

"The meetings of the House," continues Clara, "have been a source of instruction and amusement to many. 'It's as good as a pantomine,' said one to me. 'I learned more than I do from Rev. Block,' said another." In that case the House must have supplied the place of both the theatre and the church.

After my confinement by illness for some weeks, I found the Local Parliament had closed. This sudden closing of an important educational institution caused much regret, both by members and outsiders, in which I fully shared. Its great use had just begun to be clearly seen, and if it had continued its educational influence would have been great.

Several debates had thrown considerable light on local public affairs. One very earnest and able debate was on "Fair Trade versus Free Trade," which bore directly on the interests of the silk trade of the town. For some time there had been a strong reaction against Free Trade, and it was quite expected that at the end of the debate there would be a majority for Fair Trade. When, however, the vote was taken, there was a large majority for Free Trade. Loudly triumphant were the Free Traders, while the Fair Traders as loudly exclaimed that they had laid the foundation of victory at a future time.

The most harmonious discussion that took place in the House was on the motion for an appeal to the Imperial Government for the immediate release from prison of Messrs. Mair and May, who had been penalized by the Commissioners for all the sins committed at the last Parliamentary Election in the town. After a most interesting debate, there was a unanimous vote in favour of the motion, and an all-round triumph of the House.

Previous to the formation of Local Parliaments, a large number of Debating Societies were vigorously at work in many parts of the country aiding the many efforts at reform in Church and State then being made. With the formation of Local Parliaments, the old Debating Societies became mostly extinct, and then, in a few years, the Local Parliaments died out also. This double destruction was followed by disastrous results.

In the mental stagnation which ensued, the minds of masses of young men seemed only capable of one-sided views of men and things. This was a grand opportunity for the application of the schemes of the landed aristocracy, trading millionaires, brewers of strong drink, chief priests and scribes of the Yellow Press. Through these agencies, the bulk of the people were allured on to the down-grade line towards militarism, sport, and mental blindness, along which they rushed with headlong speed. It is true there remained, in connection with churches and chapels, numerous Mutual Improvement Classes, but their mental exercises moved, for the most part, only along narrow and one-sided ways. The main features of these class exercises seem to be the sounding of the praises of the Old Theology and kicking against the pricks of the New Theology, and raising financial bulwarks to the large or little Bethels to which the classes belong.

Clearly, any educational effect of such institutions as these, is utterly inadequate to train young persons to become intelligent, tolerant, and good citizens of the world. There are, again, the great and fashionable Young Men's Christian Associations, which claim, to be sure, to be comprehensive in their aims and operations. But is not each member required to bear the hall-mark of orthodox theology? Would a Unitarian, Spiritualist, or heretic be permitted to partake of the great trade, educational, and social benefits afforded by these rich, numerous, prosperous, and very respectable associations?

And if not, where does the charity, tolerance, and fairness of these associations come in? And why have not these numerous and flourishing institutions had more influence in checking the military, mercenary, and gambling spirit of the age? At the Bristol Peace Congress of 1905, the Bishop of Hereford said it was shocking that England was spending 71 millions sterling a year on its army and navy, and at the same time be priding itself on its Christian progress. He might have said—and especially priding itself on its great and flourishing Young Men's and Young Women's Christian Associations.

CHAPTER XXX

CONTROVERSY ON SPIRITUALISM

B.—Spiritualism, strange to say, holds on its course with wonderful tenacity, and evidently with considerable success. Seeing its societies contain so many cranks, frauds, fanatics, hypocrites, and fools, one wonders its adherents hold together at all.

A.—But then rogues, beggars, hypocrites, cants, fools, and moonstruck mortals have ever swarmed through Christian communities, and found their happiest hunting-grounds in Christian Churches. The proportion of these distinguished parties, it may be safely said, is not larger in Spiritualist Societies than in other Christian congregations.

It may, however, be admitted that in Spiritualist meetings may be found a number of wonder-seeking skinflints who, having placed one halfpenny in the collection box, think themselves entitled to an unlimited amount of flattering and profitable advice from the invisible world.

Stinginess of this kind, it is evident, is a prevailing infirmity in Christian Churches. We have read of a clergyman who gave notice from the pulpit that he had sufficient buttons from the collection boxes to serve all family needs of that kind for years to come. He then sharply remarked that the collection boxes went through the church, not for buttons and thread, but for current coins of the realm. Another clergyman, to stimulate the niggards in his congregation, gave out the following lines to be sung at each collection time:—

> "Were the whole realm of nature mine,
> That were a present far too small.
> Love so amazing, so divine,
> Demands my soul, my life, my all."

But even that device did not hit the mark nor draw forth the cash. So absorbed and inspired became the parties aimed at by these noble lines, and so firmly fixed were their eyes upward and heavenward, that they could not see the collection box, even when held up to their noses.

In "Good Words" of February, 1906, were several striking pictorial sketches bearing on this same point. One lady with uplifted head, open mouth, and eyes fixed on the ceiling, is singing so earnestly "Salvation is free," that she cannot possibly see the money box in front of her, even when nudged by the collector. A gentleman fairly swings round in musical ecstasy, and presents his back to the collector. Another gentleman is represented as singing unctuously "My silver and gold I dedicate to Thee," while at the same instant he is slyly slipping a penny into the collection box.

C.—You have borne so heavily on niggards in the churches that I am moved to expose niggards outside the churches. When Darwin, on one occasion, was on travel (says G. J. Holyoake), he called at a solitary wayside inn, where he found a dog comfortably reposing near a good fire. On asking the landlady what he could have for dinner, she mentioned eggs, when the dog looked pleased. When she suggested bacon, the dog seemed more pleased. But when she said chicken, the dog bolted through the open window. In explanation, the landlady said that when chickens were roasted, the dog had to turn the spit, but shirked the duty when it could.

"And so," said Holyoake, "when we speak of the noble principles of Co-operation, the members of the society are pleased. When we speak of the great material benefits of Co-operation, they are more pleased. But when we plead for twopence a year from each member to aid the Co-operative Union, they suddenly skedaddle like Pompey the dog, and leave the committee in the lurch." But now let me say in concluding this story that I shall utterly repudiate any suggestion that these skedaddling co-operators learnt their niggardly tricks at church or chapel, as that would be a stigma which—without proof—churchgoers ought not to bear.

D.—But is it a fair assumption that every person in a congregation is under an obligation to give money to a collection? I think not. An individual may distrust the collector, or disapprove of the object of the collection, or doubt the honest application of the money, and so prudently refuse a contribution. As an illustration, I may give the case of the coloured preacher who was so exasperated at certain parties in his congregation, who refused to give to the collection, that he proceeded to make personal attacks. Addressing a non-contributing brother, he said, " Don't yo' know, Brudder Slowfoot, dat yo' am due and elected to lend to de Lawd? Don't yo'?" "I knows all dat, and mo', too!" replied Slowfoot. "I knows dat, all right enough, and I stands ready and willin' to lend to de Lawd. When de Lawd comes atter de money, I's gwine to fork it ober; but I aint gwine to hand it out to nobody else."

B.—But this Spiritualism you speak of seems to be founded on weird ghost stories and fantastic fairy tales.

A.—And so with every religion the world has known. In the ghost stories of the birth, death, resurrection, and ascension of Jesus Christ, Christianity had its birth. On the ghostly stories and fairy tales concerning the Virgin Mary and the Catholic saints floated the mediæval Church for a thousand years, grasping the dominions of the world, absorbing its wealth and forging and firing thunderbolts for the destruction of all noble, independent, and free-thinking men. And when and where would have come the great Reformation but for Martin Luther's haunting devilish ghost? And how could have come the great revival sweeping like a fierce simoon over the mountains and valleys of Wales, but for the ghostly angels which smiled in the face of Evan Roberts, and the ghostly devils which grinned in his teeth?

B.—But modern science is sweeping down upon all ghostly rubbish of this kind, and will ultimately sweep it out of the world.

A.—Modern science would do better by sweeping its own rubbish out of the world. Certain leading scientists, in trying to sweep out Spiritualism, swept themselves into it, and stuck fast in it, and stood up in its defence. Professor Hare invented the Pneumatiscope to test and disprove the facts of Spiritualism. But that very instrument made him a true and earnest Spiritualist himself. Dr. Hodgson, an eminent scientist and inveterate sceptic, earnestly and carefully investigated the facts of Spiritualism for years; and then declared he could no longer resist the conclusion that departed spirits could and did communicate with living men and women on earth.

The Rev. Dr. Minot J. Savage—who was closely intimate with Dr. Hodgson—said he was one of the most careful scientific investigators he had ever known; and that only by the overwhelming force of facts had he been driven to the certain conclusion of communication between the living and the dead. Here, then, we have the striking cases of two eminent scientists who, while attempting to sweep out ghostly rubbish, found flashing gems of truth, and discovered the impregnable facts on which Spiritualism rests.

Nor less striking are the investigations of Sir William Crooks, who was President of the British Science Association in the year 1898. Great was the curiosity of the many Savants present as to whether in his address he would refer to his work in explanation and defence of Spiritualism, and as to whether he would adhere to the facts stated in that book. To the great joy of all Spiritualists, he did refer to his book, and he did adhere to the facts it contained. If he had to republish the work, he might alter a few technical terms, but nothing more.

More important still is the testimony of Professor Alfred Russell Wallace, the joint discoverer with Darwin of the great principle of Evolution, which is fast revolutionizing all philosophy, all theology, and all the higher literature of the world. After long and close investigation he was forced to the conclusion that Spiritual beings can and do communicate with living human beings on earth; and that for good or evil greatly influence the course of human affairs. Even Sir Oliver Lodge, the idol of theologians, is impelled to the conclusion that ghostly forces rule the world. When the redoubtable Hæckel and his brilliant henchman, McCabe, in tracing the evolution of the earth from a nebula through its various inorganic changes, marched boldly up to the line of life, they were suddenly scotched. *" Stand back," cried Sir Oliver Lodge, "At this dividing line comes in a mighty spiritual force and creates organic life. Thence evolution goes on through insect, beast, man, archangel, and God Himself. And may not the Cosmos itself be the 'brain of some transcendent mind?'"

B.—But what need of ghostly force can there be in the case? The radium rays applied by Burke will create as lively a dance among—so called—lifeless atoms, as can be created among atoms said to be vitalized by ghostly force. Science can better explain the Riddle of the Universe and more beneficially rule the world than any imported spiritual force.

C.—The Lord God Omnipotent reigneth! Hallelujah!

D.—" Divided empire with Heaven's King I hold," said Milton's Devil, and kept his word, and proved himself the more potent ruler of the world.

C.—These mysterious things are fully explained in Holy Writ, where we learn that Satan, who is the prince of the powers of the air and has principalities at his command, will be bound in chains and cast into the bottomless pit.

D.—But, as Milton shows, Satan was cast into the pit when hurled from heaven, but escaped to the earth, where he has been working havoc ever since. By this time he will be too wary to be caught, chained, and cast again into the pit. But even if he were again secured, he might again escape, and in his rage work worse ruin than before.

A.—Again we are revelling in ghostly lore from which neither science, nor religion, nor philosophy will ever be set free.

Nevertheless, if modern Spiritualism can present something like a rational, sensible, evidential, and practical form of this omnipresent and inevitable theme, let it not be despised and rejected of men.

*Literary Guide, 1906, p. 1.

E.—But opposition to Spiritualism comes more from clericals, I think, than from scientists.

A.—Yes, that is so. A local Vicar carried on a tirade against the Spiritualists in a Church publication during several months. At length the Spiritualists published a reply which was widely circulated, and produced a strong effect when the opposition closed.

E.—As no copies of that reply can be obtained, could you favour the present company with some account of its contents?

A.—To meet the general desire, the following quotations may be made:—" The Vicar states that during his mission in Liverpool, he was told by the Roman Catholics that his Church was not the true Church. That just served him right. While he was unchurching the Spiritualists, the Roman Catholics unchurched him. Actually, then, our poor Vicar is our brother in tribulation, condemnation, and exclusion from heaven! 'Where was your Church,' asked the Romanists, 'before the Reformation?' And echo answered 'Where?' He, the Vicar himself, seemed dumb with surprise. Was he brooding over the coming fate of his own Church, when it might be stripped of its ill-gotten gains obtained from the older Church? With such awful things looming before him, why cannot he let the Spiritualists alone?

" But—says the Vicar—the Spiritualists lower the Bible. But they do just the contrary. They elevate the Bible. They place it on the throne of reason. They treat it with respect and reverence, so far as it respects righteousness and truth. But how is the Bible treated by the vicar himself? Placing aside the Revised Version, he holds to the Authorized Version, in which, he says, 'errors and slips have been made, but they are insignificant.' That is an astounding statement to be made by an educated man!

" Referring to the seventh verse of the fifth chapter of the first Epistle of John, we find these words: 'For there are three that bear record in heaven, the Father, the Word, and the Holy Ghost; and these Three are One.' Those words are a pious fraud, and so are left out of the Revised Version. But with that spurious verse cut out, the foundation of the Athanasian Trinity is gone. What, after that, will become of the superstructure, it is easy to see. And yet, says the vicar, such errors and slips are insignificant!! The Spiritualists—affirms the vicar—also lower Christ. But they do nothing of the kind. Of more than thirty alleged Godmen who have appeared in the world, they gave Christ the highest place. Most of these singular personages have been born of virgin mothers, and some of them are said to have been crucified like Christ Himself. And now, how does the vicar treat Christ? By means of his Prayer Book creeds he simply makes Him an impossible being. The Son (Christ), he affirms, is of the Father alone, and from the Father and the Son proceeds God the Holy Ghost. And yet not one of the three is afore or after the other."

Then comes a contradictory climax affirming that there are not three Gods but only one God. And then follows an awfully savage denunciation in these words: "Which faith, except every one do keep whole and undefiled: without doubt he shall perish everlastingly." Although this creed with its horrible jumble of words, its flat contradiction of terms, its hurly-burly of Gods, and damnatory clauses may be dear and sweet to our Vicar, yet to some of the best clergymen in the Church, it has proved an awful rock of offence. The Rev. David Simpson, formerly minister of Christ Church, Macclesfield, gives his judgment in these words: "To be sure it (the creed) ascended from the bottomless pit to disgrace the subscribing clergy, and to damn the souls of those who for the sake of filthy lucre set their hands to what they do not honestly believe."

Might not the Vicar, therefore, be better employed in mending his own creeds than in condemning ours? He might begin with the first of the Thirty-nine Articles, wherein it is affirmed that "God is without body, parts, or passions." With all these qualities gone, will the Vicar tell us what is left? Can anything be imagined as remaining? Is not God altogether gone? Anyway, that creed ought to go, and the vicar would be better employed in hastening its despatch than in meddling with us.

Might not some of these ancient, imaginary, and contradictory definitions of God and man be superseded by the clearer and more rational definitions of modern times? For instance, Pope says, "An honest man's the noblest work of God," and Ingersoll says, "An honest God is the noblest work of man." Might not these statements serve for a beginning in the new departure? Anyway, they are better and clearer than anything on the subject in the creeds of the Church.

But, again—says the Vicar—Spiritualism does not promote spiritual holiness; which is just what it does promote. Good deeds, it contends, are better than all the creeds. With Jesus Christ, it affirms that on the love of God and man hang all the law and the prophets. But does the Church of England promote spiritual holiness? Its devotees, as we know, incessantly confess that they have left undone those things they ought to have done; and done those things they ought not to have done; and that they are "miserable offenders." If those declarations are true—and we do not dispute them—then it is quite certain that the Spiritualists cannot possibly be on a lower plane or scale of holiness than the devotees of the Established Church.

E.—Another persistent antagonist of Spiritualism in general, and of yourself in particular, was a notorious revivalist who, many years ago, made a great sensation in the town. Any information about this peculiar individual would, I am sure, be interesting to all present.

A.—The particulars of my first and only interview with this gentleman I wrote down at the time, and from these notes I give the following account:—

On the occasion of a visit to a farmhouse in Fallibroome, the farmer pointed out a man crossing a field, and said "That is my neighbour, Richard Weaver, the Revivalist." "Ah! Indeed!" I said; "and so he lives near?" "Yes," said my host, "he lives in that large, fine house a little further on the Alderley Road. With his family he seems to lead a happy and merry life."

"But," I said, "seeing he was working in a coal-pit a few years ago, how can he afford to live in such high style now?"

"Oh, easily," said my host. "For several weeks at a time he goes on mission journeys. On these occasions he tells the people that the Lord has called him out of the pit to preach the Gospel and save souls; and that the Lord takes care that he and his family shall not want. Then, after each journey, he comes home and leads an easy, pleasant life, receiving almost every day letters by post containing cheques and Bank of England notes as offerings from parties who have been benefited by his services, or who think he is doing a good work. When he is in London he is patronized and supported by Lord Shaftesbury and other men of high rank."

Later in the day, as fortune would have it, the Revivalist called at the house, and was introduced, when the following colloquy ensued:—

Weaver.—And so you are a preacher?

A.—Yes, you and I are of the same calling.

W.—I suppose you preach for a salary?

A.—I get a salary, I am happy to say. But I hope you don't think the salary my main object in preaching.

W.—Oh, you should do as I do: preach the Gospel without money and without price.

A.—Still, you get a price in one shape or other, or else how do you live?

W.—The Lord does and will provide.

A.—No doubt. The Lord provides for you in one way, and for me in another. It comes to much the same thing in the end. Only, perhaps, in a pecuniary sense, yours is much the best arrangement of the two.

W.—But you don't preach the true Gospel.

A.—That is a most unjust assumption.

W.—But you are a Unitarian, and don't believe in the

Trinity, and you don't believe in the Divinity of Jesus Christ, and the Bible is full of them, especially in the Greek.

A.—Oh! in the Greek! Is the Greek, then, a favourite study of yours?

W.—Certainly I read the Greek. And if I had only my Greek Testament here, I could upset all your doctrines.

A.—As to the upsetting of doctrines, that might possibly be the other way. But I should like to see your Greek Testament.

At once a servant was sent to Mr. Weaver's house for the Greek Testament, but he returned without it, saying Mrs. Weaver could not make out what book it was. Evidently she was not up to Greek. Shortly, however, the book was produced, and filled me with delightful amazement. In the first place it was as large as a family Bible. It the second place, it contained a remarkably large and finely cut Greek text. And in the third place it had a large, clear English text underlining the Greek text throughout.

"A fine book, truly," I said, "but which lines do you read: the Greek or the English?"

With much sharpness he said, "Of course I read the Greek."

At my request he then read a few lines, but with such a pronunciation and with such accent as would have given Professor Gaskell of Manchester a nervous attack, and made him stern and severe with his students for many a day. But the Revivalist's greatest difficulty was in trying to fit the English words to the Greek words. This exercise made him angry and he gave up the effort, exclaiming, "Let us pray"; and then prayed a fast and furious prayer. And so ended my first and last interview with Richard Weaver, the distinguished Revivalist.

At various times subsequent to this encounter in the farmhouse, Mr. Weaver mentioned my name disparagingly in public meetings. In his garbled account of the event, he invariably boasted that he had vanquished both me and my doctrine with his Greek Testament. At the urgent request of many friends, I replied to Mr. Weaver's mis-statements in the Paradise Street Meeting Room, on Sunday, May 1st, 1887. There was a large congregation, and all seemed pleased with my account of the lively meeting in the farmhouse.

F.—Before the symposium closes, please tell us what you saw and heard at a séance in which a Church curate and a lady medium had a serious encounter.

A.—By special invitation I attended a meeting at which Mrs. Groom, the distinguished Birmingham medium was present. On arriving at the house, I was surprised to find a lady present whom I knew to be a zealous devotee of the Established Church. I was still more surprised when a curate entered the room making singular motions with his hands. Fixing his eyes on the medium, who was speaking under control, he began to make crosses in the air with his fingers. Then, taking his stand in front of the speaker, he exclaimed in awfully sepulchral tones, "In the name of God the Father, God the Son, and God the Holy Ghost, I command thee, Satan, come out of this woman." Then a storm of words broke forth from both parties, and raged furiously for some time. In the awful uproar I caught up the words of the medium, uttered with terrific force, "Stand back, thou taunting priest, thou false prophet, thou thing of evil! Avaunt! Begone!" At length the face of the curate paled, his body quailed, and then in half a dozen big strides he stalked out of the room. Certain it is that before the curate arrived, there was no sign of a devil in the house, nor after he had gone. The inference is clear. Either the curate brought the devil to the meeting, or the devil brought the curate. Together came these two chums to the meeting house, and together they departed thence.

CHAPTER XXXI

PREACHING THE GOSPEL — CRITICISMS — REV. R. J. CAMPBELL

B.—Happily for our nation, King Edward VII. is a much abler, wiser, nobler man than Constantine the Great. By bribery, intrigue, fire, and sword, Constantine welded the Church to the state, and aided the Christian priests to crush out of existence all parties who objected to their ceremonials and creeds. Our King pursues a more just and peaceable course. Adhering to the State Church himself, he conciliates Dissenters from that Church. By special invitation, General Booth has had an interview with the King, when mutual benedictions were pronounced. Taking their cue from the King, the aristocracy follow suit, and hob nob with Bramwell Booth and other Salvation Captains, who tell their wonderful stories of the Army's success.

Indeed, that high-sounding word " success " is the dominant note in all the Army's meetings, whether large or small. As we know, an enthusiastic crowd once shouted for the space of two hours, " Great is Diana of the Ephesians." But General Booth and 20,000 Salvationists in the Crystal Palace can shout hallelujahs in the Highest, to the Highest, and to themselves, for several days together at a stretch. But a few steps down from the sublime, and the ridiculous is reached. Having travelled many years in many lands, and made many careful observations, the General has to confess that while the people generally are making progress in earthly things, they are not making progress in heavenly things. The people everywhere—

he continues—are getting more of the good things of this life, but they are not getting nearer to God. And besides, they are everywhere falling away from Churches and creeds.

C.—The same dismal lamentations are being made by many of the leading men of the day. The Rev. A. Brown of the London Tabernacle says "the world is not getting better, but is hastening on to its final apostacy."* The Bishop of Carlisle declares that although "it has made many beautiful lives, Christianity has been a dismal failure."† A fearful admission is that, surely, for the high official of a great, wealthy, and powerful Church to make. But more fearful still is the statement of Rev. J. E. Rattenbury, who says that of the hundreds of millions of worlds created, our world is "God's failure." He then asks, "Why should He (God) not fling this one to the scrap heap?"‡ In that case, how many of the fifteen hundred millions of human beings on the face of the earth would, according to the Methodist creeds, be sent to eternal torment in hell? Dr. Beet, as we know, tried to quench somewhat the fires of perdition, but the pastors and masters would not have it so, and he had to quit the Professor's Chair. It is to be assumed, we suppose, that the fires of hell still burn as fiercely as ever before. But what an awful holocaust when the scrap heap is reached!

Not a whit less scathing on this subject are the strictures of eminent literary women and men. "If Christ were to come again," says Marie Corelli, "He would most probably destroy all the Churches, saying, 'I never knew you; depart from me ye that work iniquity'."§ But would He be able to do it? We know when He was formerly here on earth, He overturned the tables of the money-changers within the temple and drove the traders out. But if He were now to do anything like that with the clerical tithe receivers, He would be at once run into jail by the police, and kept in durance vile. Marie Corelli's

*Christian World, March 19th, 1908.
†Literary Guide, February, 1905.
‡Literary Guide, 1906, p. 167.
§Literary Guide, 1903, p. 26.

probability is an impossibility. Neither man nor God, nor the devil are likely ever to be able to destroy the Churches of Christendom, for they are founded on rocks of gold. "When speaking about Christianity," says Mr. T. Stead, "to the rulers and great men of Europe, they shrug their shoulders and say that the Christian Church has been allowed to go to the devil."† What the devil is doing to the Churches, or what the Churches are doing to the devil, Mr. Stead does not say. No doubt he could give long and startling disclosures if so required.

C.—And so from religious experts themselves we learn that Christianity, starting from the Cross—inspired at the Pentecost —patronized by great emperors—aided by powerful kings— served by endless processions of zealous priests—proclaimed by innumerable preachers—animated by the grandest music ever sounding in magnificent cathedrals, lowly meeting houses, and under the broad and glorious canopy of heaven—and having finally pierced the skies with bang of drum, clash of cymbals, boom of trombones, and ceaseless prayers at street corners and elsewhere—has, generally, made the world no better than it was before this long and expensive Christian paraphernalia was begun.

A.—But now, is it Christianity, or its counterfeit that is being so sharply condemned? Superstition has grasped and ruled Christianity from the first. Had Jesus, Paul, James, Marcion, Arius, Pelagius, Abelard, Bruno, Servetus, Erasmus, Priestley, Swedenborg, Channing, and Emerson, with their disciples had the shaping and guiding of Christianity, it would have been a grandly-moving, ethical, rational, and spiritual, reforming force in the world. But most of these great religious leaders were frustrated, repressed, banished, hunted, imprisoned, one crucified, and several burnt, their writings sharing the same fate. I submit, therefore, that it is not Christianity *per se* that we condemn, but that charlatan thing which has stolen its name, usurped its throne, and reigned in its stead.

D.—But why, in these more tolerant days, does not rational

† *Freethinker*, 1907, p. 260.

Christianity go more quickly ahead? Unitarianism, for instance, with a reasonable religion, intelligent adherents, and a most learned ministry, makes but little advance. There is a complaint in the Unitarian Churches, says a leading writer in the "Inquirer,"† that with all their learning, many of their ministers do not know how to preach with effect. Exactly the same complaint has been made of the ministers of the Congregational Churches, which has led to an inquiry as to whether the grinding out of Hebrew roots by theological students is a fit preparation for an effective preaching of the Gospel. My own opinion is that Sanscrit roots, Hebrew roots, and other dead things, are not worth poking into at all, except by dry experts who are root diggers by nature. The great Jesuit preacher, Loyola, decided he could do better without such dry things than with them, for he found that "going to Latin was going from God."

Peter Mackenzie knew no language but English, and that defectively, but many correct rhetoricians might have envied him his marvellous power of speech. Gipsy Smith with but little study of English and none of any other language, speaks with amazing power. Ringing the changes on two or three orthodox lines in a hymn, he enchanted 2,000 persons in the Drill Hall, seventy of whom rushed into the penitent rooms to confess their sins, and obtain forgiveness for the same. Apart from other effects, such preachers awaken strong emotion in the minds of a certain class of people, who afterwards delight in expressing their feelings in class meetings and love feasts. Sometimes these parties will break out into loud ejaculations during preaching services. Rev. Dr. Leech mentions the case of a man who never could hear a sermon without making loud ejaculations. On one occasion, a lady promised to give him a pair of boots—which he much needed—if he would keep silent during a certain discourse. He tried his very best to be silent. But during a pointed appeal, he bursted out the exclamation, "Boots or no boots, here goes, Glory be to God! Amen!"

†*Inquirer*, 1904, p. 28.

Dr. Leech also tells the story of a woman who got into one of her usual ecstasies and exclaimed that if God would but give her another feather to her wings of faith, she believed she could fly away to heaven. Thereupon the minister closed the meeting by praying that God would give their dear sister the additional feather to her wings of faith, and let her be gone.

I have not the least doubt about these stories, as I have heard in meetings statements quite as humorous and crude. And I may say further that such interjections add greatly to the interest of the meetings, and give effect to the preacher's words.

F.—But besides appealing to the emotions and experiences of men, the preacher should be able to appeal, with clearness and force, to their mental powers. What course of study, then, should a student for the ministry pursue?

E.—First, he should secure a thorough mastery of the English Grammar. Second, he should steep his mind in the best literature of the world, ancient and modern. Third, he should pursue a rational and thorough study of the English Bible. Fourth, he should acquire an extensive knowledge of Christian history. He will then be fairly equipped, mentally, for preaching the Gospel with success. Hardly less necessary than the mental is the physical outfit of the student. By daily work in the garden or farm, by daily exercise in singing and reciting, and by constant attention to diet and the bath, the student should secure firm muscles, strong nerves, expanded lungs, and a clear, penetrating, soft, sweet, and melodious voice.

A.—On learning that the Unitarian Home Missionary College had acquired an estate with extensive recreation grounds, I wrote to an official the following letter:—" What a happy thing it would be if the exercises proposed should include gardening. Students might then qualify themselves for joining in the efforts which are being widely made to secure colonies, settlements, and garden plots in connection with religious societies. John Ruskin induced a number of his students at Oxford to work like navvies on the land at stated times, by which means they secured exercise in its best form, and also qualified themselves for taking part in the best forward movements of the time. Emerson and Thoreau delved and cultivated the soil together, talking philosophy and religion all the time; which is just what all students should do. When John Wright was minister here in Macclesfield, he secured a large tract of land and had it laid out in garden plots, which were cultivated by teachers, scholars, and members of King Edward Street Chapel. Those were the best and most successful days the Chapel had known within the century. Outsiders first drawn to the gardens were afterwards drawn to School and Chapel. Why should not every minister be prepared for movements of this kind by a union of physical, mental, and moral training in his student days?"

Perhaps the most powerful, moving, and successful preacher of all time was Peter the Hermit. His natural gift of speech was greatly strengthened by a good mental training at school, and by a thorough physical training when a soldier in the army. Hence, it is said, he spoke to the multitudes in thunders. His sentences were short, bold, graphic, and full of figures. His discourse was heart speaking to heart, and soul speaking to soul. If any speaker desires a model preacher as a guide in effective speech, he may study the words and methods of Peter the Hermit, leader and inspirer of the great and awful crusades. We would not, however, have him imitate the Hermit in preaching unrighteous war, but rather imitate Jesus Christ in preaching blessed and universal peace.

F.—The great and popular preacher of to-day is the Rev. R. J. Campbell, M.A., of the City Temple, London. A fair estimate of this great Nonconformist minister might be interesting and instructive.

A.—For a considerable time I have read weekly, with much interest, Campbell's sermons as reported in the "Examiner" and other periodicals. These discourses are critical, ethical, illustrative, illuminating, sometimes bewildering, but always eloquent. The Bible he treats in a free and easy and quite unpopular fashion. Luther said that in his day the Bible was made into a nose of wax, and pinched into any shape the operator required. That was how Luther himself treated the book, and nearly all theologians have done the same. But in this matter Campbell beats them all. If need were, he could dispense with the Bible altogether. "The early disciples," he says, "were Christians without the New Testament, and we can be Christians without either the Old or New Testament." "You may even burn the Bible," he says, "and we shall be Christians still."

To the question as to whether the narrative in the Book of Daniel concerning the three Hebrews in the fiery furnace is an actual and literal truth, Campbell makes this reply: "Personally, I may say frankly, I am inclined to believe that it is not, but it has been true many a time for all that, and is in essence true to-day." That reply, at first sight, seems to be a contradiction or evasion. But on consideration, it may be seen to be the figurative expression of an important truth.

"The Song of Solomon," says Campbell, "is simply a love song, and it treats of human love pure and simple." "In 'The Flower of Love Lies Bleeding,' or 'Mary in Heaven,'" he continues, "we catch something of the spirit in which this still greater love song, the Song of Solomon, was written." But we are not left to that secular view alone, but are further informed that the "Song of Solomon has become a song concerning love divine." We have now two strings to our bow, one human and one divine, the latter of which he would have us use. This latter, however, we set aside as artificial and crude, and choose the former as being natural and true. He, as his method is, holds on to both strings of the bow.

The same dual method is applied by Campbell to the story of Abraham's attempt to slay his son. "Biblical scholars," he tells us, "teach that Abraham was a myth and the story a legend." "Well, frankly," he says, "it matters not to me if it were so, because the offering of Isaac is repeated and consummated by some servant of God every day. But for all that, I think the story historically true." Evidently either legend or history will suit his purpose, only he is somewhat perplexed between the two. Ah! how happy could he be with either if only the other dear charmer were away. In a gush of passion, he clutches them both, and hugs them in a warm embrace.

Evidently Campbell's preaching is interesting, exciting, and perplexing. In one of his sermons he says, "Good old Christians listening to me to-night are trembling for what I shall say next." That may well be true, for he deals much in surprise. I read his discourses weekly in wonder at each new caprice which he springs upon his people. Most interesting it must be to hear his curious comments on the bundles of books he takes into his pulpit. From a copy of Jane Eyre, on one occasion, he read these words, "I cannot believe in everlasting punishment. I hold another creed, which makes eternity a rest, a mighty home, not a terror and an abyss." This passage induces Campbell to say, "We do not believe, however stern the consequences of wrong-doing may be, that they ought to continue from everlasting to everlasting." This is the only one clearly-stated heresy we have detected in his printed discourses. Other heresies, indeed, glimmer and flicker through almost every sermon, but we are unable to define them. We see them through a glass darkly, and not face to face.

On the same occasion, he read from Ruskin's "Crown of Wild Olives" thus—"A youth thoughtless! When the career of all his days depends upon the opportunity of a moment! A youth thoughtless! When his every act is as a torch to the laid train of future conduct, and every imagination a fountain of life and death." Inspired by these solemn words, the preacher's discourse must have made a profound impression on all present. Stranger still, George Eliot's "Middle March" got into the pulpit, when the preacher fiercely seized on its chief character, Bulstrode, the hypocrite, stripped him of his disguises, and presented the real and repulsive man to view. He had committed a great wrong, traded on it, and gained great success thereby. At length, however, he is wrecked in fortune, broken in health, and sunk in wretchedness and despair, with not a friend in the world but his wife, whom he has so badly used. In his dire distress, he is approached by his wife. Few were the words said, but intense was the emotion felt by both. Describing the scene, the authoress says, "She did not say, 'Repent,' and he did not say, 'I have sinned,' but in that moment of intensity one soul became a saint through atoning tears, and the other was born again." What! Born again? Without a priest to absolve? Without an orthodox dogma to guide, or delude? Without being washed in the blood of the Lamb? Yes! certainly! A poor soul was born again through a noble woman's atoning tears, and by the saving power of her mighty love.

But more remarkable still, Campbell reads in the pulpit private letters containing confessions of sin. Roman Catholic priests are familiar enough with private confessions, but they never reveal them. Protestant priests, also, have to deal with private confessions of sin, but, for the interest of the Churches, they are careful to hush them up. But here is a minister who reads in the pulpit this confession from four young men: "We are four Christian friends, and help each other in Christian work. But lately, in a moment of confidence, we have confessed to each other our chief besetment, and to put it frankly, it is sensual sin." If the audience of 2,000 persons were shocked by this startling confession, they would become still more shocked by the minister's following words: "So prevalent is this sin," said he, "that it is tolerably certain there were considerable numbers of young men and some young women in that audience guilty of the same sin." Such, then, is the character of a section of a great, respectable, intelligent, Christian, London congregation. If all Christian ministers were as penetrating into the condition of their congregations, and as faithful and daring in their utterances about them as Campbell, what an awful revelation there would be of the internal condition of the Christian Churches.

"It is a loathsome subject," the minister continued, "but the manhood of the nation is imperilled by this sin. The vast empire of Rome fell, not from the attacks of fierce, untutored, *clean-living* barbarians, but from the vices of its own manhood and womanhood within itself. And to-day England is endangered by this particular kind of sin." But if Christianity, the professed guardian of the State, be thus rotten at the core, what is to be done?

From another letter the minister read, it appeared that certain parties had come to the conclusion that such a demoralized Christianity should be set aside, and something better put in its place. On behalf of himself and others, a young man writes to the minister the following message:—" We have been reading the life of Marcus Aurelius, and we feel that this man's life was a higher and nobler one than that of most Christians. Would it not be better for some of us to live as well as Marcus Aurelius without professing Christianity at all?" Such a proposition as that the minister could not, of course, entertain. They had much better, he said, put aside Aurelius and follow Christ and Paul instead. But the Churches have both these worthies already, and with them a flood of corruption which they cannot restrain. Quoting from Lecky, the preacher points out " that some of the early developments of Christianity were intolerance, fierceness of spirit, and almost brutality of living." Of what good, then, we may ask, were Christ and Paul to them? For a thousand years—truly called the dark ages—Christians were in fierce conflict with each other, freely shedding each others' blood. Of what use were Christ and Paul to them? How little good these great saints have done throughout the Christian ages is clearly manifest from the error and corruption that have ever prevailed in the Christian Churches, and that still prevail. Could Marcus Aurelius have done less? Might he not have done even more good, if he had been fairly tried?

In all Mr. Campbell's sermons there is a great wealth of illustration. His vivid restatement of historic facts must forcibly impress the minds of all his hearers. Even as we read the printed pages, we seem carried along with the preacher from one sacred spot of earth to another. With him we stand in front of Balliol College, Oxford, where the noble martyrs, Latimer and Ridley triumphantly died. With him we are on the wild moorlands of Scotland, where John Brown, the Covenanter was shot dead while at prayer by Claverhouse, the commander of the ruthless dragoons. With him, too, we are beside the Solway shore, where Margaret Wilson was fastened down upon the sands and slowly drowned by the inflowing tide, and who refused to the last to save her life by recanting her faith. With the preacher, also, we feel the greatest admiration for these great martyr souls. But while he is exalting these Christian martyrs, I am also thinking of their Christian persecutors. If Christianity must be credited with the heroism of the martyrs, then, surely, Christianity must also be credited with the murderous tyranny of those who took the martyrs' lives.

I must not go on to notice the biographic sketches, poetic lines, and literary gems which brighten and enliven the preacher's discourses. But I will in conclusion quote a passage full of sound, sensible, ethical, and pointed advice to a young man: "Look here, young fellow. I am not asking you for dogma; very little will do of that. I am asking you to believe this: that it is better to be true than to be false; it is better to be clean than to be dirty; it is better to help than to injure; it is better to suffer wrong than to inflict it; it is better for you to take account of God than to be worldly wise, and cynical, and bitter of heart. Can you fight these devils in your Valley of Humiliation? Well, then, I may tell you that you are not fighting your battle alone, but it is vastly important how you fight it, for

> 'The tissues of the life to be
> We weave with colours all our own;
> And in the field of destiny
> We reap as we have sown.'"

Low murmurs against the preacher have at length swelled into a loud and stormy chorus. A whole pack of heresy-hunters are now on his track in full cry. He is denounced as a Tolstoyan, a Buddhist, a Pantheist, and a Unitarian. Dr. Forsyth compares his discourses to bad photographs: and someone, in retort, compares Forsyth's discourses to fireworks in a fog. Principal Fairbairn denounces Campbell's theology as being "a farrago of nonsense." Campbell replies that the "older theologies are all a wretched failure." Confront Campbell with the Trust Deeds of the City Temple, say some, and oust him from its pulpit. That is found to be a dangerous process which might lead to the ousting of large numbers of preachers from other pulpits. Already—says Campbell—many of his adherents are scuttling away from him like rabbits to their holes. In "The Christian World," June 6th, 1907, we read that Canon Mackintosh has earned the Pontifical blessing by pronounced Mr. Campbell to be a "silly blasphemer." In "The Christian World," October 17th, 1907, Mr. Campbell says it is not Jesus, but the Pharisee that has won in the history of official Christianity. "It is the Pharisee that has drafted our creeds, liturgies, and public confessions. I could lay my hand on one Pharisaic rascal who is a pillar of orthodoxy, but who is not too particular as to the ways in which he makes money, or the lives he crushes in the process. And these people claim to speak in the name of Jesus, who, if He were in the flesh, would say in return, 'Woe unto you, Scribes and Pharisees, hypocrites!'" Such is the conflict going on in the Churches which is shaking the Old Theology out of the minds of some, and the New Theology into other minds; while, at the same time, in a vast number of more open minds it is sweeping out both theologies never to return.

CHAPTER XXXII

UPTON TOWNSHIP—VISITORS' CONVERSATION

First Visitor.—As you have no poor people in the township of Upton, why are your poor rates so largely increasing?

Host.—Since the County Council has come into operation, all rates here and everywhere have increased by leaps and bounds. The educational rates are becoming alarming. This was best explained by the girl who said she wished to be trained for a day school teacher, because she should have then short work days, long holidays, and a big wage. Thus we are having a great inrush of teachers, and a great uprush of rates.

Second Visitor.—What classes of people have you in Upton, and what are their callings in life?

Host.—We have lawyers, surveyors, ironfounders, brewers, manufacturers, shopkeepers, farmers, a banker, a Colonel, an engineer, and several independent ladies and gentlemen. All live in nice houses in the midst of gardens, with trees and flowers blooming around them. Evidently they are doing well in business, and are fast laying up treasures to be enjoyed in coming years of Edenic repose.

Third Visitor.—I have not been able to discover any public buildings in Upton. Have you none?

Host.—No. We have no churches, chapels, taverns, nor prisons.

Third Visitor.—So then you have no taverns to ruin you, no prisons to punish you, nor any churches to save you. Seeing, however, that these incongruous institutions are nearly always grouped together, you are fortunate in being clear of the whole lot.

Fourth Visitor.—Going from Mount Pleasant along Prestbury Road, one observes two smart, new villas—one having fine mountain views, and the other situated amid sweet sylvan glades. Just beyond are three somewhat ancient mansions, concerning which, no doubt, interesting stories could be told.

Host.—That first house near the road is the Grange, where I beheld a picturesque scene on a fine, summer day some years ago. When passing the house, I saw a carriage containing two ladies stop at the entrance gate, just as two gentlemen on horseback came out into the road, when a series of elaborate and amusing courtesies took place. The prancing and capering of the horses, the nods and becks, and smiles of the ladies and gentlemen, with a profuse badinage of pleasant words made up an entertainment quite delightful to an observer like myself. Going along, it suddenly struck me I had seen the description of just such a scene in one of Trollope's novels—perhaps "Framley Parsonage"—which I had read more than forty-five years before.

On another occasion in mid-winter, when the snow was lying thick on the road, I observed a noticeable girl of twelve or fourteen years of age cleverly guiding a sledge down the incline in front of the Grange. As she rose up from the vehicle, I noticed that she was tall, slender, and lithe in form, had prominent and expressive features, and had a mass of red-brown hair. Just the figure, I thought, for Burne-Jones to paint on a pane or panel for some sacred fane. Whether she was a member of the family at the Grange, or only a visitor there, I never knew. Certainly the girl had a saintly form, and I hope, had, and would ever retain, a saintly soul. It is only in such quiet country places as this that there is leisure and composure enough to notice and appreciate striking personages, scenes, and events.

Visitor.—To the north of the Grange, there seems to be two ranges of buildings joined together.

Host.—One of the ranges is Upton Hall Farm, and the other is the Hall itself. A notable occupant of the farm was Mr.

Warren, who was an orator as well as a farmer. At Township meetings he was a match for the subtle-minded and lawyer-like Mr. Carr. He did good service in vigorously urging the keeping down of the rates by the economic use of public money. We called him our "Village Hampden," and we were sorry to lose him when he went to a distant farm.

The present occupant of the farm is notable for managing to keep so large a stock of cattle upon the ground. The great number of lambs at their happy gambols each returning spring-time presents a scene wonderful and delightful to behold. Whether the farmer has some secret method of securing a large birth of lambs, we cannot tell. We know of the amazing method of Jacob the Jew in securing large flocks of sheep. We hardly think our farmer practises the same method. Still, he knows best.

At the Hall, when I knew him, lived Mr. Croston, whose tall form, firm and quick footstep, and strenuous-looking face made him notable wherever he went. Although he proceeded daily to business at Manchester, he evidently took more pleasure in literature than he did in managing trade accounts. His topographical writings are of a superior class. For the lords and ladies, the squires and dames of Cheshire, he had almost worshipful respect. Their family records he loved to rewrite, and took great delight in describing their halls and mansions, and the picturesque landscapes around them. By these and other writings, Mr. Croston has become one of the literary worthies of Upton Township.

At a later period might be seen, at times, proceeding from the Hall a nice carriage, containing two comely-looking maiden ladies, drawn by two of the most beautiful horses to be seen on the road. It was a joy to observe the fine forms, graceful motions, and remarkable colours of these noble animals as they bore along the carriage with its worthy occupants on benevolent deeds intent.

But alas! on a certain day there proceeded from the Hall a quite other kind of carriage bearing away the dead form of one of the ladies to its last resting-place on earth. There, by the grave side, the priest pronounced the solemn words, " Earth to earth, ashes to ashes," and then prophecied the resurrection of the body to eternal life. How much more fitting, comforting, and true, would have been the pronouncement that the soul was already risen to eternal life, and would need the decaying atoms of the old body no more.

Visitor.—Leading southward from the Grange to the third mansion is a picturesque road with some fine trees near the entrance gate.

Host.—Those trees, I think, must be amongst the finest in Cheshire. It is an unspeakable charm to observe the beauty, grace, and ever-varying aspects of these noble forms. Nor are they without associations of an interesting kind. I have seen groups of happy children at play under these ancient shades, and tried to calculate the great number of generations which have had their merry groups of children playing there. I have seen lovers softly pacing the road under these venerable trees, repeating the everlasting tales of love, and thought there could not be a more delightful spot for billing and cooing to go on, and only wished they might be wisely done. For alas! here, as elsewhere, vows may have been plighted and then broken, and tender hearts broken at the same time. Or happily, noble vows may here have been made and nobly kept, and human souls have been lifted heavenward thereby.

Along this favourite walk I have seen two clergymen pass, engaged in deep discourse. No doubt they were discussing the spiritual interests of their flocks, but could hardly have avoided the great question of the poverty of the clergy, which is as rampant as ever to-day. In heart-rending tones, the new Bishop of Manchester cites the cases of some poor parsons who have only £200 a year. But he does not cite the case of Goldsmith's man of Ross—

> "To all the country dear,
> And passing rich with forty pounds a year."

Nor does he cite the case of his Lord and Saviour, who had not where to lay His head. Nor, again, does he promise a handsome subscription towards relieving the awful clerical distress. Nor, still again, can the public be induced to subscribe as they should because—says the Bishop—they are incredible as to the tales of clerical distress that are told. That is the unkindest cut of all.

Passing along this same road I have seen a solitary Roman Catholic priest. The nervous expression on his face seemed to indicate that he was under the influence of both fear and hope. His thoughts might have found expression, perhaps, in the following words: "This is holy ground. Saintly men have walked and devoutly meditated here. Near by was a noble sanctuary where everlasting prayers ascended to heaven for blessings on the living and deliverance for the dead. Now I find here no sacred fane, nor any successors of the true saints of old. How long, O Lord, before the Restoration comes? When will all England return to the true fold of Christ? O! certainly the time will come. It may be near. The saints of the sister isle have long been coming over to aid us in overcoming the opponents of this great and glorious return. And now France is sending her saintly legions to join in this holy war." But why are the High Churchmen such laggards in the fight? What is the use of their singing—

> "Onward, Christian soldiers,
> Marching as to war,"

when they are standing still all the time? Why not bravely break down the State Establishment and be free. Why should they not make a bold and decisive dash for Rome, where every returning prodigal of them would be received with open arms and feasted with fatted calves, dances, and songs?

Hither also comes along on occasion a dreamer and maker of verse, when one may observe that—

> "The poet's eye, in a fine frenzy rolling,
> Doth glance from heaven to earth, from earth to heaven.'

What rich and varying music—he possibly exclaims—may be heard amongst these lofty branches as the seasons come and go. Like sweetest angel voices sound the springtime breezes in these glorious trees. Like the shrieks and sobs of despairing souls sound the wailing autumn winds. While in the tearing and wrecking storm winds of winter rushing through these trees may be heard the howlings as of pandemonium itself when its wild orgies are on, and full steam is let off, and the devils' dance has begun.

Visitor.—May I ask if this notable pathway along which so many cranks perambulate, is a road on sufferance?

Host.—Yes, but Colonel Beck is a tolerant man, and will stop no passers-by except damage was being done. The Priory —to which the road leads—is a plain but pleasant building containing ample space, plenty of window lights, many comfortable rooms, and numerous snug nooks. Near by is a mysterious-looking little chapel which long excited my imagination. Often I longed to look into it, but I was quite unknown to the Colonel, and would not ask favours. Evidently it was a memorial fane, and might contain valuable and interesting relics. An ancient altar stone might be there, or a notable cross or crucifix before which eminent saints and sinners had often bowed in worship. Or there might be a strong, old, oaken chair in which a venerable prior had sat, wearing his scapulary, reading his breviary, or counting his beads, or inditing his dull and drowsy thoughts, until he finally snored.

Long the mystery remained, and long we had serious thoughts on passing by. At length, and unhappily, the revelation came. On a certain day a fête was being held in the ground; the gates were open, and free ingress allowed. I hastened to the chapel, peered into its recesses; made a careful search, and looked again and again. But O! what a blank was there! Not one relic, not one single sacred object could I behold. Slowly I walked away, sadly thinking that another of my pleasing illusions was gone. And yet—as I again thought— that little chapel itself was a relic of a most interesting kind.

Seeing that worthy men had lived there and worthy deeds done there, this memorial fane was worthy of veneration and deep respect.

Visitor.—Your intercourse with such worthy people as the dwellers in Upton seem to be, must be pleasant and extensive.

Host.—Pleasant, certainly, but not extensive. With a few individuals I exchange friendly greetings, but the larger portion of the people, I take it, are unaware of my existence. My intercourse is mostly with elderly gentlemen retired from business, who walk along our quiet roads on fine days for the benefit of their health.

J—— B—— was one of these, and a fine, tall, portly, and good-looking old gentleman he was. Living just outside the township, he often walked to the bottom of Westminster Road, where he stood and took great delight in watching the passing railway trains. One day he gratified my curiosity by saying he had formerly bought a number of railway shares at a low price, and that now the price had risen and the dividend was higher. And so—I thought—where the treasure is, there will the heart be also. As if divining my thoughts, he said, "I do not love to watch those trains only because of their benefit to me personally, but also because of their great benefit to the town at large." And I did not doubt his word. He had all his life been a steady, hard-working, careful, saving man, and so had secured a comfortable independence for his old age. Later on, his visits to the much-loved spot became few, and then altogether ceased. By an invisible train he had passed to the invisible world. After a well-spent life, one thinks, he would not fear any judgment day he might have to face there.

R—— S—— also crossed Upton boundary to walk along these roads and to breathe our life-giving air. He was a low-set, broad-built, rucibund, genial-faced man. He had long been on the Board of Guardians as well as in the Council of the town. "I always aimed at two things," he said to me: "efficient public service and economic expenditure of public money. In doing this I met with determined opposition. One gentleman constituted himself my special opponent. On one occasion he got so furious as to propose pistols and coffee for supper. Seeing I was right in these contentions, my colleagues ought to have supported me, but they seldom did. Whenever I and my opponent got rather hot, they simply laughed and said, 'Now then, pistols and coffee for supper.' Such was the treatment I got in doing my best for the good of the town." Although he was a very decided Tory and Churchman, we never had an unpleasant disputative jar. Recognizing each other's sincerity, we avoided personal condemnation, and did not try to argue each other down. Sometimes our attention was directed to the striking and ever-varying aspects of the Cheshire and Derbyshire Hills. Both of us, it came out, had ancestral memories in connection with the mountain sanctuary called Jenkyn Chapel. Talking of the sleepers in that moorland graveyard near the ancient chapel, we could not avoid thinking and saying that our own poor bodies would soon be lying at rest somewhere in the same way. His turn came first. To the eternal hills he was summoned hence. There the honest and well-meaning man expected to find a better world than he had found on earth, and we hope he has.

J—— H—— was tall, well-built, had a placid face, and snow-white hair, and walked with footsteps measured and slow. The hard and grinding wants and scants of life he never knew. When living on his own farm in Clarke Lane, he held some office at the Church Mission at Bollington Cross, and sometimes read the service lessons. He was half a Churchman and half a Methodist, and loved both Church and Chapel. Religious doctrines he neither questioned nor disturbed. Dogmas were settled for all time, and he would not erase a jot or tittle from the creeds. On my pointing to any defect in the Catechisms of Methodism or the Church, he would gently lift his eyebrows, smile a pleasant smile, and say "A-hem!" That was his unanswerable reply, his theological fullstop, from which he would not budge an hairsbreadth. He was the quietest man

I ever knew, and it would be difficult to imagine that he had ever quarrelled with any person during his life.

During many years he spent much of the summer-time with his excellent wife at some watering-place on the sea coast. In his old age he was more at home in Upton, and loved to take his daily walks in the rural pathways near. There I met with him until he was no longer there to meet. He had passed on full of years and full of faith—a faith that would lead him to select a quiet spot, if permitted, beside the Apocalyptic crystal river flowing from the Throne of God.

W—— C—— was, in nature and character, a complete contrast to J. H. He had a tall and lithe form, a defiantly fixed head, a prominent nose, flexible mouth, and voluble tongue. By sheer force of character he became Councilman, Alderman, Mayor, and Poor Law Guardian. He was, generally, remarkably polite in word and gesture, but could be quite otherwise if in any way provoked. More than once he has described to me incidents in his life career in these words, "In my early days I sowed freely my wild oats, and reaped very bad harvests as the result. By an overruling Providence, I was happily led to change my whole course of life. I assure you since I gave up my wild companions and abstained from the deadly drink, I have saved the purchase money of the house in which I live." In religion he was a Wesleyan, but at one time attended Gawsworth Church. In doctrine, he said, Church and Chapel were alike, and the creeds of either Communion would save the soul. On one occasion I pointed him to a case in the newspapers bearing on his doctrinal views, which gave him serious pause. A brutal monster of a man who had murdered a woman had been coached by a chaplain into saving faith, by which he was switched from the gallows triumphantly to glory in heaven: while his poor victim—who had no time to be coached in the faith—had gone to the torments of hell. "Where," I asked, "is justice in this case?" "In the Bible," he replied, "we learn that man is justified by faith alone. In arguing against that doctrine, you discredit

God's Word and dethrone God Himself." "Whether," I said, " I dethrone God or you enthrone Him is of no consequence to anyone. The sun would continue to rise and set and the stars pursue their courses as before. But it is of infinite importance that justice be administered in heaven, earth, and hell."

Although he was not deep in theology, he was profound in law, and often gave sound legal advice to parties unable to pay lawyers' fee. In our higher literature he was fairly well read, but his favourite study was our English historic lore. My own historic authorities such as Hume, Macaulay, Froude, and Cassell, he considered quite antiquated. To bring me up to date, he insisted I should take the historic works of Green and Bishop Stubbs from his own library and read them at home. This I did, and much pleasant intercourse ensued. It was with much regret I found our intercourse had come to an end. He, too, had joined the endless procession of pilgrims to the eternal bourne, where he was fairly sure of finding heaven. His proceedings there we can only faintly divine. He would be sure to want to put somebody or something right. If there were any jars amongst the archangels, he would rush into the fray. Milton's Satan said defiantly, " Divided empire with Heaven's King I hold." W. C. would not do anything like that, but he might order Gabriel to stand down from his elevated seat, give an account of his stewardship, and try conclusions as to whether or not he should retain his exalted post. But these things—as he would say—are mysterious, and best let alone.

J. B. was a piecer in the silk mill when a child, and afterwards an handloom weaver. He attended night-classes at the Useful Knowledge Society when I was a teacher there. He was a diligent learner, and made rapid progress in various studies. He thus qualified himself for an important business situation which he obtained and retained until he reached an advanced age, and is now an independent man. Very pleasant is a passing word with this worthy self-made man as he walks along our Upton roads.

B. H—— is an aged and venerable pilgrim I often meet on the way. I first knew him when he was a smart young man and visited the Useful Knowledge Society. Since those early days he has built up a large business and established his two clever sons in the successful concern. But just as he was seeking rest by a partial retirement from business concerns, one of his sons suddenly died. Meeting sometime afterwards, we seriously moralized on life, death, and eternity, and of the uncertainty of earthly affairs. Patience, we concluded, must have its perfect work before man can attain to anything like solid peace on earth.

R. H—— is another worthy man who, after an industrious, steady, and quietly useful life, has retired from commercial pursuits. Often I meet him and his wife in our Upton lanes, when vivid memories arise of long past times and long departed friends. On the 18th April, 1908, I entered their house and beheld the dead form of the mother of Mrs. H. As a fine, tall, blooming, beautiful maiden, I knew her sixty years ago. Visions arose of the time when she was married to my dear brother Samuel, and of many happy meetings in their home.

By request I read a short Bible message, said a brief prayer, and uttered a few broken words in reminiscence of past events.

In the cemetery I saw the coffin lowered into the grave on the side of which I stood nearly twenty-eight years ago, when with a breaking heart I saw my brother's body placed in the same grave.

Strange it is that while all my elder kindred and friends have departed hence, I linger here. And stranger still is the fact that I am not yet eager to go.

Mr. W. is our foremost teacher of youth. On meeting him in Westminster Road we get a whiff of wisdom from ancient or modern tomes, or a breeze of inspiration from "Athens, the eye of Greece," or from the seven-hilled city of Rome, or from our ancient Universities at home. And how our mentor loves the Established Church, and how eager he is to throw wide open its gates so that all may freely enter in and find enlightenment, rest, and peace.

Just such a passion had our noble Dean Stanley, who longed to see the day when creedal bars would be broken down and all people should be able to pass freely into the fold of the Church. He died without the sight. Will our learned mentor be more fortunate than the Dean? Or will he share the same fate?

Visitor.—Even in the sylvan abodes of Upton, it seems, the visits of Death are not few nor far between.

Host.—In nearly half of these abodes there has been a death during the last fifteen years. Here, as elsewhere, a successful man founds a beautiful home and furnishes it with all possible needs, and says to himself, "Soul, thou hast much goods laid up for many years; take thine ease, eat, drink, and be merry": when suddenly comes the summons, "This night shall thy soul be required of thee." Then vivid flashes of memory gleam over the past and the present, and there is an intensely eager clinging to life.

> "For who, to dumb forgetfulness a prey,
>   This pleasing, anxious being e'er resigned,
> Left the warm precincts of the cheerful day,
>   Nor cast one longing, ling'ring look behind."

Then come tender hand-clasps, fond embraces, and flowing tears, for

> "On some fond breast the parting soul relies,
> Some pious drops the closing eye requires."

Then doctors come and go; undertakers follow in their track; the solemn hearse comes on apace; ashes are laid to ashes; excitement subsides; memory fades, except with a dear few, and, finally, oblivion envelopes all.

Visitor.—But what about the survival of the soul?

Host.—Ah! the soul! In one case so small, so thin, so poor, so worn out with abuse that there is next to nothing to survive, nor good for anything if it did survive. But from that dismal thing we turn to the case of a departing soul after a noble life—when radiant hopes make partings blessed, when the shroud becomes a glorious robe, the funeral march a joyous harvest home, and the last hymn in the sacred fane a pæan for the soul passing into the splendours of celestial climes.

Then—

> "Build thee more stately mansions, O my soul,
> As the swift seasons roll;
> Leave thy low-vaulted past:
> Let each new temple, nobler than the last,
> Shut thee from heaven with a dome more vast,
> Till thou at length art free,
> Leaving thine outgrown shell by life's unresting sea."

CONTENTS

OF THE SECOND VOLUME OF "MY LIFE."

To be published shortly. **Not published.**

CHAPTER XXXIII.—BRIBERY COMMISSION — CO-OPERATION — USEFUL KNOWLEDGE SOCIETY.

> The Judgment Day—Judge on the Throne—Culprits at the Bar—Sheep—Goats—Sale of Votes—Voters Bottled—Unbottled—4,000 Voters Bribed—Two Victims—Disfranchised—Refranchised—On the Co-operative Committee—Address at Buxton—Mr. Acland, M.P.—Derby Congress—Controversy—Home Secretary—Labourer's Wages—Mr. Craig—Useful Knowledge Society—Syndicate—Public Meetings—Messrs. W. B. Brocklehurst, J. O. Nicholson, John May, William Barnett, John Willott—Success—Placed under the School Board—Regret—Teaching by Cram—Herbarts' Method.

CHAPTER XXXIV.—GREAT FREETHINKERS—DR. HORTON.

> Voltaire—Jesuitry—In the Bastile—In England—"Henriade"—The Queen—In Paris—The Divine Emilie—In Berlin—Frederick the Great—Voltaire at Ferney—Torture of Calas and La Barre—Indignation at the Priests—Deathbed of Voltaire—Repulse of Priests—Their Revenge—Voltaire's Tranquil Death at 84 Years of Age—His 50 Volumes on the Index of the Inquisition.

CHAPTER XXXV.—THOMAS PAINE.

> Unjust Treatment—Conway's Vindication—Paine's Expulsion from the Excise—In America—Attack on Slavery—"Commonsense"—Collects Money for Washington's Army—In England—"Rights of Man"—"Age of Reason"—The Bonnevilles—Dr. Torrey's Slanders Exposed—Illness—Repulses Priests—Cobbett's Vindication—Serene Death—Funeral Scene.

CHAPTER XXXVI.—G. J. HOLYOAKE.

> Secularism—The Trinity—Combe's Constitution of Man—Robert Owen—Lord Brougham—Co-operation—"The Oracle of Reason"—Holyoake's Trial—Nine Hours' Speech—In Prison—Clerical Visitors—Paley's Natural Theology—"The Reasoner"—Visit to Rev. Brooke Herford—Debate with Brewin Grant—Rev. H. P. Hughes and G. W. Foote—Leigh Hunt—G. H. Lewis—Margaret Fuller—Buckle—Froude—Carlyle—Dr. Johnson—Maurice—John Bright.

CONTENTS OF VOL. II.

CHAPTER XXXVII.—CHARLES BRADLAUGH—GEORGE WILLIAM FOOTE.

The Rationale of Unbelief—Bradlaugh and the Bible—Expelled from Sunday School—In the Army—Prosecution—Ejection from Parliament House—Carried the Affirmation Bill—Death—George William Foote—His Religious Conversion—Study of Shakespeare—Possible Rival of H. P. Hughes—Freethinker—Prosecution for Blasphemy—Noble Defence—Twelve Months in Prison—Books Burnt—The National Secular Society.

CHAPTER XXXVIII.—ROBERT GREEN INGERSOLL.

Escaped Rivalry with Moody and Talmage—Historic Christianity—*North American Review*—Debate with Dr. Field—The Design Argument—Debate with Gladstone—Reverence for Jehovah—Elijah and Baal—Heavenly Treasure in the Church—Which Church?—The Church and the Scaffold—A Dead Horse—Henry Ward Beecher—Walt Whitman—Dr. Aked—Ingersoll's Personality—Happy Home Life—Funeral Orations—Saladin's Lines.

CHAPTER XXXIX.—CONDITION OF MACCLESFIELD.

Essay at Brunswick Chapel—Ex-Inspector Steele—Trade Not Improving—Manners Not Improving—Commercial Honour Not Improving—Drunkenness Increasing—Improvement in the Local Press—The Workhouse—The Cancer of the Town in Chestergate—Remedies—Religion Progressing!—Nominal Religion—Easy Theology—Ruskin—Horsfall—The Clergy—Laymen—Colenso on the Bible.

CHAPTER XL.—REV. G. W. CADMAN—WELCOME MEETING.

Addresses by Colonel Brocklehurst, Chairman—Mr. Hill, Mayor—Revs. Dowson, Gordon, Constable, Reynolds, and Rushton—Rev. Barkell (Wesleyan) on "Our Wicked Town"—Herbert Spencer on Rebarbarization—Dean Gregory on School Boards—Cardinal Newman—British Fleet—Costly Workhouse Women.

CHAPTER XLI.—REMEDIAL AGENCIES.

Churches—Chapels—Schools—Missions—Wesleyans—Primitives—United Free Methodists—Baptists—Congregationalists—Unitarians—Spiritualists—Mill Street Mission—Salvation Army—Large Sunday School—The Established Church—Its Great Wealth—Fascinating Prestige—Great Rewards—Stampede from Chapel to Church—The Families of Broome of Hurdsfield—Thorp of Rainow—Birchenough, Wright, and Brocklehurst of Macclesfield—The Roman Catholic Church—Father Matthew.

CHAPTER XLII.—EDUCATION BILLS.

Balfour—Foundation of Belief—Clergy—Lord Carrington—Dr. Clifford—Horse—Feed—Ride—Bishop of Hereford—Church Grab—Lord Halifax—Lord James—Bishops' Trick—Lloyd George—Chamberlain—Creation—Pro-Boer—Colonel Slaney—Tom Jones—Tory Performance—Macnamara—Schoolmasters—Bishop Moorhouse—Blunder in Figures—Church and Chapel Ministers in Manchester—C. Rowley, J.P.—Archdeacon Taylor Defends School Boards—Statistics of Schools and Prisons—Education in Germany—T. C. Horsfall—Churches and Schools in America—Catechisms—Mafeking Madness—Graham Wallas—Bishop of London—A Colenso Teacher Needed—Education Bill (1906) Dead—Bishop Knox and River Thames—Hugh Cecil—Cross Roads—Lord Cross Alarmed—Prison Statistics—The Round Table.

CONTENTS OF VOL. II.

CHAPTER XLIII.—CYCLE JOURNEY TO GAWSWORTH.

Johnson's Grave—Battle of the Two Tombstones—Abraham's Breast!—More Stones Suggested—Cremation—Cato—Plato—Emerson—The Peripatetics—Aristotle—The Church—Images—The Fitton Family—Mary Fitton—Shakespeare—Rector Newcome—Puritan Soldiers—The Rector at Manchester—Ejected—Conventicle Preacher—At Cross Street Chapel—Buried inside the Chapel—Cross in the Village—Dialogue.

CHAPTER XLIV.—ALDERLEY CYCLE JOURNEY.

Monk's Heath—Monasteries—Farms—Population—Abbot Samson—Stone Images—Eagle and Child—Battle of Bosworth Field—Richard III. Slain—Henry VII. Crowned by Lord Stanley—Shakespeare's Lines—Viscount Amberley Married Lord Stanley's Daughter—A Welsh Rector—Clerical Wealth and Result—Lord Stanley's Death—The New Peer—Rector Stanley—Prelate of the Pope—His Dreams—Mission Statistics—The Church—Rector Stanley and the Queen—Dean Stanley—Canon Bell's Invitation—Thunderstorm—Fearful Journey Home.

CHAPTER XLV.—CYCLE JOURNEY TO CAPESTHORNE.

Dairy Farm — Shippons — Horses — Docking — Servants — Stewards — Votes — Parsons — Sermons — The Hall — Sculpture — Roped Heads — Robin Hood — Stolen Heiress — Reeds Mere — Walden Lake — Thoreau—Emerson—Froude—Foote—Conway—Sea of Galilee—Fishers of Men — Crowds — A Test — Gadarene Swine — Jesus — Gladstone — Huxley — Brantwood Lake — Ruskin — Providence — Music — Conversion — Budd Taylor — Gallows to Heaven — Ruskin MSS.—Walter Scott MSS.—University Grinding—Wind and Souls—Wesley and Souls—Home, Sweet Home.

CHAPTER XLVI.—DEATH OF THE POPE.

Hammer Scene—Church Exclusions—Mammon's Clutch—Gab and Grab—Scriptures—Dr. Mivart—God's Winks—Pope's Winks—Campbell's Winks—Encyclopædia Biblica—Schmiedel—Gospel Books—Sibylline Books—Kaiser—Babel and Bible—Code of Hammurabi—Jawbone of an Ass—Dr. Beet—Science—Truth—Light—Life.

CHAPTER XLVII.—CYCLE JOURNEY TO LANGLEY.

Love Feast—Means of Conversion—Passing Bell—Funeral March—Picturesque Village—Chapel—Institute—Paradise to be Regained—Gardening *versus* Football Play—Tegs Nose Declivity—"Excelsior" Poem Localised—Eddisbury Hill—Chartist Drill Ground—The Hall—Builder—John Thompson—Trouble and Death—Shakespeare's Lines.

CHAPTER XLVIII.—PARNASSUS.

Locality—Description—Recreation—Ghosts—Recitations—Cowper and Newton—Calvinism—Spanish Armada—Storm and Battle—Burns *versus* Cowper—God wills it—Russian Murder—Eugenie—Boer War—David Clayton and Norval—John Lea as Hamlet—St. George's Church—Judgment Day—Young's Night Thoughts—Torments of Hell—Paley—Plato—Vedic Hymns—Immortal Life.

CHAPTER XLIX.—DELPHI.

Predestination—Bible Texts—Athanasius—Arminius—God—Good and Evil—Earthquakes—Leslie Stephen—Eden—Satan—Martineau—Free Will—Determinism—Libertarianism—Popularityism.

CONTENTS OF VOL. II.

CHAPTER L.—THE DELPHIC SHRINE.

Sceptics—Paley's Natural Theology—Lord Brougham—Design: Good or Bad—God—He, Him, She, It—Dr. Horton—A Personal Devil—"No Dogma, No Dean."

CHAPTER LI.—DELPHIC DEBATES.

Methodist Student—Butler's Analogy—Revelation—Nature—Historic Tests—Hypatia—Inquisition—Latimer—Servetus—Earthly Paradise—Its Inhabitants—Idealism and Berkeley—Rashdall—Lotze—Hoadley and George III.—Martineau—Professor Upton—Moore—Such Stuff as Dreams.

CHAPTER LII.—SWISS COTTAGE—CONVERSATION.

Death of Wife—Death of Brother Enoch—Milton's Eve—Birds—Insects—Fruits—Wheat Experiment—Strawberries—Mother Nature—Flowers—Sentimental—Symbolic.

CHAPTER LIII.—SECOND CONVERSATION.

Carlyle-Froude Controversy—Craigenputtock—Emerson's Visit—Mrs. Carlyle—Drudgery—"Sartor Resartus"—Compositor's Flight—Cromwell Defended—Literary Abuse—Irving—Lady Ashburton—Froude—Newman—St. Patrick—Alexander Carlyle—Sir J. C. Browne.

CHAPTER LIV.—DARK IN CHRISTENDOM—LIGHT IN HEATHENDOM—LIGHT IN JUDEA.

Romance—Bishop of London—Council of Constance—Constantine—Fiery cross—Hypatia—Diet of Worms—Petrarch—Paris—Fraud—Russia—Chaldea—Light in Egypt—Pyramids—Osiris—Christ—Light in Greece—Sibyl—Plato—Light in Rome—Cornelia—Vestals—Light in Judea—Christ—Bethany—Samaria—Paul *versus* Christ.

CHAPTER LV.—CHRISTIAN ECCENTRICITIES.

Evan Roberts—Mary Jones—Devils—Angels—Lights—A Church Theatre—Whistling Lady—Religious Picnics—Thomas à Kempis—Dr. Mivart—Clerical hunting—Dr. Beet—Seal of authority—Greenwood—The three R's—Campbell—Note of conviction—The brewer's fire-escape.

CHAPTER LVI.—MORAL PERPLEXITIES.

You Ought—You Ought Not—Serpent in Eden—God—Hell—Thugs—Dr. Richter—The Trial—Thief in Paradise—Criminal Statistics—Parliament—Boys Essay on Missions—Canon Robinson—Missions and Lawsuits—Mutual Missions—Hindoo Trinity—Battle of Bibles—Darwin—Chunder Bose—Plant Response—Khayyam—Japan—Buddhism—Shintoism—Mohammedanism—Mutual Councils—Yellow Peril—White Peril—Japanese Life.

CHAPTER LVII.—ETHICAL UNION OF ALL RELIGIONS.

Missionary Methods—Rev. H. Rees—Chinese—Negroes—Zulus and Colenso—Red Indian—Penn—Hiawatha—Minnehaha—Laughing Water—Bishop and Chief—Heine—Kant—Heathen Morals—Ancient Greece—Milton and Plato—Martineau and Socrates—Theo. Parker and The Phædrus—Lilly—Stoics—Olympus—Sinai—Siloa—Ilyssus—Sages Hague Conference—Wordsworth on Pagans—Elijah—Apollo—Venus—Father Loisy—Stanleyites—Campbell—Unitarian Vans—Spiritualists—Vegetarians—The Simple Life—Rationalist Saints and Sages—The Choir Invisible.

Milton Keynes UK
Ingram Content Group UK Ltd.
UKHW022237180624
444315UK00013B/746